Teacher's Book

the Pre-Intermediate

CHOICE

Sue Mohamed and Richard Acklam

Longman

Longman Group UK Ltd,
Longman House, Burnt Mill, Harlow,
Essex CM20 2JE, England
and Associated Companies throughout the World.

First published 1993
Set in Adobe ITC Garamond and Frutiger
Printed in Italy
by G. Canale & C.S.p.A – Turin

British Library Cataloguing in Publication Data
Mohamed, Sue and Acklam, R
   The Pre-Intermediate Choice.
   Teacher's Book.
   I. Title
   428.24
ISBN 0582 070988

Acknowledgements

We are grateful to the following for permission to reproduce
copyright material;

Hit & Run Music (Publishing) Ltd for the lyrics of the song 'This
Must Be Love' by Phil Collins, © 1980 Philip Collins Ltd/Hit & Run
Music (Publishing) Ltd. International Copyright Secured. All Rights
Reserved; International Music Publications for the lyrics of the song
'If you were the only girl in the world', © 1916 B Feldman & Co Ltd/
International Music Publications.

Contents

Unit		Structures	Vocabulary	English in Action
0	**What do you know?**	• Revision of positive and negative forms of: *be/can/have got/do/like*	Revision of lexical sets: food, clothes, colours, rooms, family, weather, places, body, transport, jobs	
1	**Person to person** (Focus on the Present)	• Question forms: inversion and auxiliary *do* • Likes and dislikes (1): *like/love/enjoy/ prefer/don't like/hate* + *-ing* form • Present Simple (routine) • *Could you . . .?* (requests)	• The alphabet • Work and free time activities (1) • Jobs (1) • Question words: *What/Where/ When/How/How many?* • Greetings and health	Making a class magazine
2	**Lookalikes** (Focus on the Past)	• Comparatives + (*not*) *as . . . as; the same as; different from* • Past Simple (irregular verbs) • *Be like* vs *look like* • *Used to*	• Clothes and accessories • Describing people (1 + 2) • Face and body	Conducting a survey about relationships
3	**Traveller's check** (Focus on the Future)	• *Going to* vs *will* • *Really/quite* + verb • Likes and dislikes (2): *can't stand* + *-ing* form • Superlatives • *Instead of* + noun	• Travel objects • Transport + *get on/off/into/out of* • Holiday activities	Writing for a travel brochure
4	**Necessary business** (Focus on Modals)	• Degrees of obligation (1): *should/have to/don't have to* • Advice (1): *should/shouldn't* • Possessive pronouns: *mine/yours/hers, his/ours/theirs* • Suggestions (1): *Let's/Why don't we . . .?*	• Work and free time activities (2) • Jobs (2) • Personal qualities	Planning a new business
5	**Consolidation** • Across cultures: lifestyles • Thinking about learning: strategies • Language in context: eating out			
6	**Obsessions** (Focus on the Present)	• Present Simple vs Present Continuous (now vs habits) • Adverbs of frequency (word order): *always/often/sometimes/ occasionally/ never* • Likes and dislikes (3): *don't mind* + *-ing* form	• Everyday actions • Sports (football) • Hobbies	Talking about a hobby
7	**Spotlight** (Focus on the Past)	• Present Perfect (experience) vs Past Simple • Past participles (1 + 2) • Present Perfect (recent past) +/– *just* • Subject/object pronouns and possessive adjectives • Suggestions (2): *How/What about . . .?* + *-ing* form	• Adjectives ending in *-ed/-ing* • Types of films	Planning an evening at the cinema
	Movie time	Making movies		

Pronunciation

Skills

Pronunciation	Skills
Sounds: the alphabet: /ə/, /ən/ for *a/an* and *er/or* endings (jobs) **Stress:** Sentence stress on questions; word stress on jobs **Intonation:** Imitation of questions forms, polite requests and telephone numbers	**Listening:** Three conversations (greetings) **Speaking:** Asking personal information questions; asking for and giving names, addresses and telephone numbers; greeting people and saying how you are feeling; discussing which questions are polite in different countries **Reading:** Magazine article about people from different countries **Writing:** Dictation of names, addresses and telephone numbers; writing personal information about another student
Sounds: /ə/ in unstressed *than/as/from* **Stress:** On comparatives and ways of comparing **Intonation:** Imitation: *used to* in sentences	**Listening:** Conversation about Cher's cosmetic surgery **Speaking:** Comparing people and places; retelling a story from the newspaper; describing resemblances to family members; discussing cosmetic surgery; talking about past personal life; conducting a survey of people's similarities to their friends or partners **Reading:** Newspaper article about identical twins **Writing:** A comparison of two people; a questionnaire
Sounds: The letter 'a' pronounced /eɪ/, /ɑː/, /ɔː/, /æ/ and /ə/ **Stress:** On compound words **Intonation:** In lists	**Listening:** Conversation about preparations for a business trip **Speaking:** Information gap activity: describing pictures; talking about leisure plans and transport; talking about and booking a holiday; describing home-country tourist attractions **Reading:** Tourist information about different places **Writing:** An article for a tourist brochure using conjunctions *and/but/or/because*
Sounds: Pronunciation of /dʒʊ/ vs /duː/ **Stress:** Stressed and unstressed *do*, uncontracted *have to*; stress on possessive pronouns **Intonation:** Imitation: expressing advice and obligation	**Listening:** Two discussions between a boss and an employee **Speaking:** Discussing conventions of politeness when visiting friends for dinner; discussing tipping; deciding on qualities needed for different jobs; discussing good time management; describing things you enjoy doing and things you have to do; planning a new business **Reading:** Text about tipping in Britain; ideas for good time management **Writing:** Completing a diary and an official form
	Across cultures: lifestyles: Reading about lifestyles in different European countries **Thinking about learning: strategies:** Ways of finding out unknown vocabulary **Language in context: eating out:** Listening to people ordering food in restaurants, reading about and deciding which restaurant to go to
Sounds: /n/ vs /ŋ/ **Stress:** Contrastive stress **Intonation:** Imitation: using contrastive stress to express irritation	**Listening:** Song 'Tom's Diner' (Suzanne Vega); someone talking about their hobby **Speaking:** Describing previous and past habits; 'How often' questionnaire; information-gap pictures; describing how you feel about doing different activities; giving a talk about a hobby **Reading:** Article about a football fanatic **Writing:** Writing sentences using adverbs of frequency
Sounds: Weak forms of *have* /əv/ and *been* /bɪn/; /æ/ vs /ʌ/ in Past Simple forms and past participles **Stress:** Stress and unstress in Present Perfect forms; word stress on adjectives and types of films **Intonation:** Imitation: expressing feelings; questions to find out about cinema programmes	**Listening:** People commenting on films they have just seen **Speaking:** Asking about people's experiences; describing films seen recently; deciding which film to go and see **Reading:** Film review of *Scandal* **Writing:** Writing a review using pronouns and possessive adjectives

Unit	Structures	Vocabulary	English in Action
8 **Consequences** (Focus on the Future)	• *So* vs *because* • *If/when* + future time • *If* + present + *will* (first conditional) • *Definitely/probably* + *will* (word order)	• Education • Examinations	Finding out about English exams
9 **Face value** (Focus on Modals)	• Logical deduction: *must be/might be/ can't be* • *Look* vs *look like* • *Really/very/quite* + adjective • Present Perfect (indefinite time) +/– *yet/already*	• Describing people (3) • Music and concerts	Talking about and buying records
10 **Consolidation**	• Across cultures: money	• Language in context: shopping	• Thinking about learning: approaches
Images	A visual imagination activity		
11 **Changes** (Focus on the Present)	• Present Perfect (unfinished past) • *For* vs *since* • *Been* vs *gone* • *Give* + two objects	• Life changes • Expressions of time	Emigrating and writing character references
12 **Memory** (Focus on the Past)	• Past Continuous (interrupted action) • Sequencers: *first/then/next/after that/ finally* • *Some/any* + countable/uncountable nouns • Infinitive of purpose	• Everyday objects • Products and shops	Improving your memory
13 **Time for politics** (Focus on the Future)	• Subject/object questions • *Will/won't* (promises) • *As soon as* + present + *will* • Present Continuous (future arrangements)	• Political leaders, systems and issues	Forming a political party
14 **Generation gap** (Focus on Modals)	• Degrees of obligation (2): *should/must* and *shouldn't/mustn't/don't have to* • *Too/enough* + adjective • *Although/but/however*	• Ways of expressing movement and change	Reading and writing poems
15 **Consolidation**	• Across cultures: children	• Language in context: corporal punishment	• Thinking about learning: improving your memory

Pronunciation

Skills

Sounds: Catenation in future questions *What_will ...?* and *Where_will...?*
Stress: On adjectives ending in *-ic*
Intonation: In first conditional sentences

Listening: Student talking about school and exams in Britain; dictation of address
Speaking: *What will you do if/when...* conversations; deciding what to put in a time capsule; discussing schools and exams in different countries
Reading: 'Time capsule' newspaper articles
Writing: Game 'Consequences'; sentences with *so* and *because*; formal letter requesting exam information

Sounds: Elision: omission of final */t/* in *must/might/can't* before *be*
Stress: Word stress on adjectives describing people
Intonation: Imitation: making requests

Listening: Descriptions of people in the class; song 'It must be love' (Phil Collins); interview with Phil Collins
Speaking: Making a story from picture prompts; solving lateral thinking problem; discussing people's characters; discussing nationality stereotypes; talking about a singer; record shop dialogue
Reading: Magazine descriptions of different people's characters
Writing: Descriptions of own character

Across cultures: money: Discussing attitudes to money, reading a cartoon, discussing present-giving
Language in context: shopping: Speculating and reading about people's recent purchases; discussing own shopping behaviour
Thinking about learning: approaches: Speaking, listening and reading about different ways of learning languages

Sounds: Unstressed *for* +/– final */r/* sound
Stress: Unstressed *for* and *since*
Intonation: Imitation: questions beginning *How long have you...?*

Listening: Song 'Where have all the flowers gone?'; three people describing treasured possessions
Speaking: Finding out about important changes in other students' lives; talking about possessions; role play emigrating to Australia
Reading: Magazine article about changes in lives of two couples
Writing: A character reference

Sounds: Weak forms of *was* /wəz/, and *were* /wə/; consonant clusters + final *s* (shops and products)
Stress: Stress and unstress in Past Continuous and Past Simple sentences
Intonation: Of Past Continuous (interrupted) sentences

Listening: People remembering what they were doing at important historical times
Speaking: Talking about what you remember and forget; asking about shopping lists
Reading: Article on memory; extract from the novel *Memory Board*; extract from *The Sunday Times Magazine* on the 'LOCI' method
Writing: Sentences using the Past Continuous (interrupted); a paragraph using sequencers

Sounds: /θ/ vs /t/ vs /f/; /ɒ/ vs /ɔː/ vs /əʊ/
Stress: Word stress on political leaders, systems and issues
Intonation: Imitation: making promises

Listening: Interview with a British Member of Parliament
Speaking: Describing political systems; discussing political issues; information gap activity: making an arrangement; forming a new political party and preparing for an election
Reading: Text about government in different English-speaking countries; election leaflets from political parties; a description of a fictitious country
Writing: A notice to advertise a political meeting

Sounds: Weak forms of *should* /ʃəd/ and *must* /məst/; unpronounced */t/* at the end of *shouldn't/mustn't* + consonant
Stress: On selected expressions; unstressed auxiliary verbs
Intonation: Imitation: giving advice vs giving orders; saying a poem

Listening: Song 'Father and Son' (Cat Stevens); conversation about age laws in the USA; two poems about old age
Speaking: Discussing how to stay young; discussing age laws in different countries
Reading: Magazine article about 'secrets of youth'
Writing: A paragraph about age laws using linking words; a poem about a particular time of life

Across cultures: attitudes to children: Discussing what children have to/don't have to do in different countries; listening to children describing their family lives; writing a paragraph about bringing up children
Language in context: corporal punishment: Article about smacking children; discussion about punishing children
Thinking about learning: improving your memory: A variety of games and activities

Pronunciation	Skills
Sounds: Word linking and weak *a* /ə/ and *of* /əv/ **Stress:** Word stress on adjectives describing people/animals; stress/unstress on food and packaging **Intonation:** Imitation: questions beginning *How much...?/How many...?*	**Listening:** Song 'I know an old lady who swallowed a fly'; British people discussing packages and products; a chocoholic talking about her addiction; conversation in a bank **Speaking:** Telling the story of 'The Fox and The Crow'; describing interesting people you know; discussing packages and products; asking other students *How much/How many* questions; talking about chocolate; conversation in a bank **Reading:** Text about chocoholism **Writing:** Writing the story of 'The Fox and The Crow' using time expressions; completing a cheque
Sounds: /s/ vs /z/ vs /ʃ/; weak *was/were* in Past Simple passive **Stress:** stress/unstress in passive forms; stressed *so/such* for emphasis **Intonation:** Imitation: emphasising ideas using *so/such*	**Listening:** People talking about their favourite people in history **Speaking:** Predicting the story behind a newspaper article; describing how different historical figures died; talking about famous people you admire; planning to get information about local history **Reading:** Two newspaper articles on the same story; text about punctuation in English; text about Rasputin **Writing:** Punctuating a text; making a poster about local history
Sounds: Consonant clusters *wouldn't/ couldn't* + verb; adjective *-ed* endings pronounced /t/, /d/ or /ɪd/ **Stress:** Word stress on household equipment **Intonation:** Imitation: Expressing agreement/disagreement; in second conditional sentences	**Listening:** Radio interview with Anthony Hopkins **Speaking:** Discussing what electrical equipment you would be prepared to give up; discussing views on television; interviewing students about what things they would take to their 'desert island'; talking about music preferences; dialogue with music agent about where to go on musical tour **Reading:** Articles about things two people have given up and the effect on their lives; two jumbled letters **Writing:** A letter to get information in response to an advertisement in a newspaper
Sounds: Intrusive /w/ when giving advice using *If I were you* /w/ *I'd...;* **Stress:** Unstressed *were* in *If I* /wə/ *were you...;* sentence stress in questions **Intonation:** Imitation: direct vs reported speech; saying large numbers; of questions with two clauses linked by *when*	**Listening:** Radio phone-in programme **Speaking:** 'Choices' questionnaire; finding out how much money people spend; giving advice to a person with a problem; discussing consumer rights; shopping situation dialogues **Reading:** A newspaper article; a text about how to complain successfully **Writing:** Rewriting a newspaper article and adding extra information
	Across cultures: marriage: Article about marriage in Britain; talking about wedding customs **Language in context: love:** Discussing what makes a perfect relationship; song 'If I were the only boy in the world' **Thinking about learning: outside the classroom:** Radio Magazine including ideas on making penfriend cassettes, listening to the radio in English, watching TV and films in English and reading graded readers

Introduction

The *Pre-Intermediate Choice* is the second level of a multisyllabus course which takes adults up to intermediate level. It is designed for students who have completed a beginners course, such as *The Beginners' Choice*, and provides material for 90–120 hours of teaching. It is suitable for use with both monolingual and multilingual classes. Each level consists of a Students' Book, a Workbook, a Teacher's Book, a set of Class Cassettes and a Workbook Cassette.

As with *The Beginners' Choice*, the material has been extensively piloted.

GUIDING PRINCIPLES

The following points have guided the writing of *The Pre-Intermediate Choice*:

Classes consist of students of mixed ability.

All students have different strengths and weaknesses and make progress at varying rates. In *The Pre-Intermediate Choice*, students are encouraged to share what they know about a target language area in order to bring the whole class to a similar level of understanding before moving on to new language areas.

The practice activities can be attempted successfully by students who have only the language taught in a particular unit but, at the same time, provide an opportunity for other students to bring in language they may have acquired in other contexts

Low level adult students need to be treated as *adults*.

Topics have been carefully selected to be of interest to adult students. There is a clearly adult approach to these topics and to the presentation of grammar. Students are encouraged to speculate on recurrent patterns, requiring them to use their cognitive skills to formulate various 'rules' of language for themselves.

It is very important that adult students have a clear sense of what they are learning and how they are learning it. To assist both you and your students in this respect there is a detailed map of the contents at the beginning of the book, a grammar index at the back and what is being taught at each stage is clearly signposted throughout.

Authentic materials are an important source of motivation and real language for students.

It is motivating for students to cope with English from real-life situations. Therefore, a wide variety of authentic materials is used (from articles to extracts from novels to poems to songs) and students are asked to do tasks that they may be required to perform in the real world (such as writing cheques, completing diaries and buying compact discs in a music shop). Care has been taken to grade such tasks and to select materials which are accessible to students at the pre-intermediate level.

Students need to express themselves in a range of situations with a minimum of language.

Adults, particularly those studying in an English-speaking country, need immediate access to language which allows them to communicate on a variety of subjects and across the complete time range. To provide students with maximum mileage from limited language, we have:
- organised units around topics, with vocabulary introduced in lexical sets to help students learn and recall target language efficiently.
- treated past, present, future and modal forms cyclically to continually reinforce and extend students' ability to express themselves in these areas.

English is a language of *international* communication.

English is increasingly used in a wide variety of international contexts. To reflect this, many of the texts and activities focus on situations in different parts of the world. The Class Cassette has a range of different but accessible accents to accustom students to the variety of ways English is spoken.

COMPONENTS

The Students' Book

The Students' Book consists of twenty units plus an introductory unit. Every fifth unit is a Consolidation Unit. Each unit is broadly linked by theme and presents a range of structures, vocabulary and pronunciation points. The language areas are integrated within the skills work of each unit and thorough practice is given in listening, speaking, reading and writing.

The map of the contents at the beginning of the Students' Book provides a breakdown of the key focus of each unit by topic, structures, vocabulary areas and English in Action sections.

Each unit begins with a Preparation section and then contains a variety of sections dealing primarily with Vocabulary, Grammar, Pronunciation, Listening, Speaking, Reading and Writing. Each of the fifteen main units is six pages long and the final page of each of these units is a Language Review containing grammar summaries and practice exercises.

Consolidation Units revise the main language areas of the previous four units in new contexts. They expose students to different language learning strategies, aspects of cross-cultural awareness and additional authentic material.

Three extra double-page activities, within the body of the book, provide an exciting change of focus for students and help revise and extend the language they have covered so far.

At the end of the Students' Book there are:
– the second half of the information-gap activities.
– four Check What You Know tests designed for use after each Consolidation Unit.
– all the tapescripts of the main listening texts.
– a mini-dictionary preceded by a phonemic chart.
– a Grammar index.

The Students' Book cassettes contain recordings of all the listenings, songs and pronunciation exercises.

The Workbook

The Workbook provides an opportunity for students to consolidate and extend the language presented in the Students' Book. It can be used for homework, in a self-access centre or for further practice in class.

Grammar in the Students' Book is presented in manageable chunks at the end of each unit. The Grammar Summary section in the Workbook complements this by providing a complete overview of all the grammar presented, organised alphabetically for easy access.

A Vocabulary Building section presents, in lexical sets, the vocabulary introduced in the Students' Book and extended in the Workbook. This section not only provides a record of the language taught but also encourages students to organise other lexis as they learn it.

The Workbook contains extensive listening and pronunciation practice, exercises based on authentic materials and regular 'open' exercises which allow a more personal response from students.

The Workbook Cassette provides a range of authentic listenings, dialogues and drills and the complete tapescript appears at the back of the book.

The Teacher's Book

The Teacher's Book begins with an extended map of the contents of the Students' Book, including details of the pronunciation points and skills work covered.

Each unit includes:
– a two-track system of notes containing
   a) minimal explanation for experienced teachers
   and
   b) detailed suggestions for less experienced teachers.
– a summary of the main language presented in each Students' Book unit.
– the aims of each section in the Students' Book.
– answers to all exercises and keys to the Language Reviews, Check What You Know tests and Workbook exercises.
– tapescripts, at the point they appear.

SPECIAL FEATURES

Cyclical treatment of grammar

Students need to express themselves across the complete time range. In order to provide for this, and to help students recall and extend target language, each quarter of the book focuses on and develops in turn present, past, future and modal forms.

Authenticity

The wide variety of authentic reading and listening material has been chosen to ensure it is accessible to students at the pre-intermediate level. Graded tasks help students decipher new language in the texts and listening passages and are chosen to reflect those which students are likely to encounter in real life. Where possible, students are asked to express personal opinions on what they read and listen to, encouraging a realistic response at each student's own level of English.

Songs

Songs provide an important source of authentic listening material and student motivation. The songs relate to the units they appear in, either lexically or grammatically, and have been chosen as representative of different musical eras.

English in Action

Every unit has an English in Action section where the main focus is content rather than language. Students are encouraged to extend their learning outside the classroom, taking part in mini-projects and expressing themselves to the best of their ability. Unless communication breaks down, it is not intended that they should be interrupted by correction.

Sign posting

Students and teachers need to understand what is being taught, and why, at every stage. They also need to find their way around the book as easily as possible. Therefore, the book opens with a clear and accessible map of contents and finishes with a Mini-Dictionary and Grammar Index to allow quick reference to key words and structures. Each exercise is clearly labelled, and the language covered on each page is highlighted in a box at the top of the page.

NB boxes

These feature small but important language points which provide:
- useful information to answer student queries.
- additional language which students may choose to activate.
- a preview of language to be focused on at a later date.

Each NB box requires a response from the students to show that they have understood the relevant point.

Language Reviews

These come at the end of each unit (except the Consolidation Units). There is a summary of the main structures taught within the unit in the left-hand column. This leads to exercises in the right-hand column designed to give controlled practice in the target structure and also to recycle the target vocabulary of the unit. These exercises can be used for additional controlled practice as you work through the unit or can be set as homework once each unit has been completed.

Consolidation Units

These units revise key language from the previous four units in new contexts which, in themselves, will interest and motivate students. They are divided into three sections:
- *Across cultures:* This section allows students to consider aspects of the culture of various English-speaking countries and to compare them to attitudes and behaviour in their own countries.
- *Thinking about learning:* This section gives students the opportunity to consider their own learning strategies and introduces other approaches to language learning.
- *Language in context:* This section revises other key language from the previous four units in different authentic contexts.

Extra activities

At certain points, there are extra double-page activities which do not follow the general format of the course. These provide a change of focus for students and teachers alike, as well as giving further revision of language presented so far.

Check What You Know tests

These are found at the back of the book and are signposted at the end of each Consolidation Unit. They provide an indication of achievement to both teacher and student. They should also highlight any gaps in students' knowledge which may require additional work.

Each test begins with a lockstep activity, which the whole class need to do at the same time.

Once this is completed, students can work at their own pace to finish the exercises.

The tests include speaking exercises which come at the end of each test so that teachers can decide if/how best to include them. If class numbers are small enough, teachers may be able to work with students individually during the test or as they finish. Alternatively, they could ask students to record their answers in the language laboratory or on personal tape recorders. Students could also test each other in pairs or threes, awarding marks to one another, thus increasing their own sense of critical awareness and autonomy.

Mini-Dictionary

At the end of the book there is a Mini-Dictionary of the most important vocabulary items taught. Certain exercises in the book refer students to the Mini-Dictionary, encouraging them to transfer dictionary skills they may have in their own language and to use an English-English dictionary from the start.

The Mini-Dictionary is preceded by a phonemic chart indicating pronunciation of the various British English sounds. After each word entry, pronunciation is represented in phonemics and main stress is marked. There follows a simple definition and/or example sentence containing the target word. Finally, there is reference to the page on which the word first appears and/or is illustrated.

METHODOLOGY

Vocabulary

From the very beginning of the book, students are made aware of the significant quantity of vocabulary that they already know and are then helped to build on that.

Lexical sets introduced in *The Beginners' Choice* are revised, extended and thoroughly practised. For example, the 'food' lexical set is extended by linking known items of food to the packages they come in; the names of school subjects are revised and examination vocabulary is introduced.

Grammar

Students are exposed to examples of target structures taken from authentic/semi-authentic listening and reading texts. They are then asked to consider the meaning, form and pronunciation of the new structures in order to formulate guidelines for use.

Controlled and freer practice is provided within the unit and new grammar is then integrated into the material of subsequent units.

The Language Review at the end of each unit highlights the grammar focused on and provides further practice exercises to check students' understanding and their ability to manipulate new structures.

The Workbook activities give extra practice and the Grammar Review section provides an overview of the grammar presented in the Students' Book.

Pronunciation

Stress is integral to the learning of vocabulary and structure. Therefore, stress and unstress within words is systematically focused on as new vocabulary is introduced. Main sentence stress is highlighted as new structures appear in sentences. Students are introduced to the use of contrastive stress and sensitised to the effect on rhythm of weak forms, contractions and the linking of consonants and vowels.

The sounds focused on have been chosen as those which, experience shows, cause problems, either receptively or productively, for students of many nationalities eg. /r/, /θ/ and /æ/ vs /ʌ/. The weak form /ə/ is highlighted from the beginning to help students recognise in their oral form words which are familiar in their written form and to help them produce natural sounding English.

Students at this level, especially in classrooms, tend to concentrate on the construction of utterances which often interferes with the more spontaneous expression of feelings. For this reason we think that the development of good intonation habits is best dealt with via exposure to and imitation of contextualised examples, with some reference to mother tongue patterns for transfer or contrast and with plenty of opportunity for practice. This allows students to express themselves more freely thereby encouraging a variety of intonation patterns.

Listening

Throughout the book students are exposed to a range of listening text types and accents. They are given practice in predicting, listening for specific information, listening for gist and inferring.

Students can easily become demotivated if they find themselves swamped by a stream of language which they feel unable to break down and understand. Consequently, early listening texts have been kept short and simple in order to build up student confidence. Later on, controlled situations are introduced where, for example, the wording of the questions in interviews has been determined but where the respondents have been left free to answer in a spontaneous and uncontrolled way. By the end of the book, short extracts from authentic conversations have been included as well as opportunities for longer listening, made accessible by graded tasks.

Reading

Students are presented with a variety of written texts, including a lot of authentic materials. Tasks, where possible, reflect real life and are set in order to check students' general understanding, their ability to identify specific information, to infer intended meaning and/or to deduce the meaning of new words from context.

Speaking

Students are encouraged to communicate orally from the beginning, using the language at their disposal to its full effect.

When new structures are introduced, meaning is established and controlled practice is given to ensure that production of form and pronunciation is as accurate as possible. Gradually, students are encouraged to use new vocabulary and structures more freely and to incorporate them into their general pool of productive language.

Writing

In *The Pre-Intermediate Choice*, the writing skill is developed systematically. At word level, spelling and capitalisation are highlighted, with activities such as form-filling or gap-filling for practice. At simple sentence level, model sentences of grammatical points are written down at the presentation stage. Activities such as unjumbling sentences or writing descriptive examples are used to highlight the importance of word order. At complex sentence level, sentences are linked with conjunctions. The more simple items *and*, *or*, *but* and *because* are extended to include *so*, *although* and *however*.

Basic letter-writing conventions are highlighted and more creative writing is encouraged through story telling and poetry writing.

Students are helped to see writing as a process which aims at communication and not just accuracy. For this reason, students are asked to work together on various writing tasks, to pool ideas before they write and to rewrite in order to provide greater clarity for their reader.

Regular recycling and revision

Systematic recycling and revision is crucial for students at this level. This is provided in *The Pre-Intermediate Choice* in the following ways:

– Every unit begins with a Preparation section which revises important language items and prepares students for the language to be introduced in the current unit.
– When a new language area has been introduced in one unit, further examples and practice are given in subsequent units: For example, *going to* is contrasted with *will* in Unit 3, revised in Unit 4 and the following Consolidation Unit, and then reappears in *Movie Time*.
– The Language Reviews, at the end of every unit, revise all the main grammar points of each unit, and the exercises recycle vocabulary introduced in the unit.
– The Consolidation Units themselves thoroughly revise key language areas from the previous four units in new contexts.

Personalisation

Wherever possible, students are given the opportunity to talk or write about their own personal situation and/or to express their own opinions. As students concentrate on conveying the meaning of their thoughts and feelings, so their language becomes more fluent.

Classroom procedures

This section provides brief explanations of the meaning and application of various terms referred to in the Teacher's Book.

Eliciting

This is a technique whereby the teacher encourages the students to produce the target language rather than supplying it her/himself. This can be done in a variety of ways depending on the type of language you are teaching. For example:

– you can use mime to elicit such things as sports, everyday activities, etc.

– you can draw on the board or use pictures to elicit such things as food, methods of transport, etc.

– you can work backwards from answers to elicit question forms. Write:

_____ ? She's a doctor.

on the board to elicit *What does she do?*

Eliciting is particularly good for keeping students involved in their own learning process and for showing the teacher what the class already knows.

Drilling

Drilling allows students to get their tongues round new words/structures as they are presented and builds their confidence in using the new language. It provides a chance for the teacher to monitor pronunciation and to check students can manipulate new language. A high level of accuracy is required at this stage. As students become more fluent in their use of the new language they may become less accurate. Drills can then be used as a correction technique to draw students' attention back to accuracy but beware of drilling for too long as drills are an artificial device.

There are many different types of drill which include the following:

Repetition drills

As new vocabulary is introduced, students are made aware of word or sentence stress and encouraged to repeat after the teacher or the tape. There are various different types of repetition drill:

• Choral drills

These require the class to repeat the target language in unison after a model from the teacher or tape. This gives everyone the chance to get their tongues round the new language.

• Mumble drills

These work like choral drills. After hearing a model, students practise saying the new item to themselves a number of times, but not in unison. This allows students to get their tongues around the new language while working at their own pace.

• Individual drills

The teacher nominates individual students to repeat the target language. This gives the teacher a chance to check that each student can pronounce and manipulate the new language.

Substitution drills

These are useful for checking that students can manipulate verb forms, agreements and word order. They require the student to change a certain element of a sentence based on a prompt from the teacher. For example:

TEACHER: He goes home at 6 o'clock.
STUDENT: He goes home at 6 o'clock.
TEACHER: I . . .
STUDENT: I go home at 6 o'clock.
TEACHER: 8 o'clock . . .
STUDENT: I go home at 8 o'clock.

Backchaining

Backchaining is a way of drilling which starts with the final word/phrase in a model sentence. The complete sentence is gradually built up by going backwards, adding a little more each time. This technique is particularly successful when main sentence stress falls on the last word in the sentence, since it encourages consistent final stress and falling intonation.

To 'backchain' the sentence: *Have you ever been abroad?* students repeat after the teacher:

TEACHER: abroad?
STUDENTS: abroad?
TEACHER: /bɪn/ abroad?
STUDENTS: /bɪn/ abroad?
TEACHER: ever /bɪn/ abroad?
STUDENTS: ever /bɪn/ abroad?
TEACHER: /jə/ ever /bɪn/ abroad?
STUDENT: /jə/ ever /bɪn/ abroad?
TEACHER: Have /jə/ ever /bɪn/ abroad?
STUDENTS: Have /jə/ ever /bɪn/ abroad?

Communicative drills

These provide meaningful dialogue between students at the same time as repetition of a target structure. For example, in Unit 6 students make a questionnaire and ask their partner how often they do certain activities. In this information-gap activity, real information is exchanged and students need to use the target question *How often do you . . . ?* thereby drilling themselves in this structure.

Jigsaw reading and listening activities

Many of the longer readings (Students' Book pages 7, 20, 68, 80, 85 and 109) and listenings (pages 63, 69 and 90) lend themselves to a 'jigsaw' approach. This technique is useful for the following reasons:
- The amount of reading and listening can be limited without losing content.
- Students have to speak to one another in order to complete the task in their book (an information-gap is created).
- You can allocate easier/more difficult sections appropriately thereby providing for the ability range within your class.

Set the jigsaw reading/listening up as follows:
1 Divide the class into two or three groups: Group A, Group B, (and Group C).
2 Allocate a different section of the reading/ listening to each group.
3 Allow students to read/listen, as often as they wish, in order to complete the task for their section and check their answers within their group. (In the case of jigsaw listening, each group will need their own cassette recorder and cassette to listen to, preferably in different rooms or areas of the classroom.)
4 Regroup students to include one person from each original group, ie, one from Group A, one from Group B (and one from Group C). Each student tells the other/s what they heard or read. As they listen to one another, they complete the task about the texts they did not read or listen to.

Correction

Errors are a necessary and normal part of the language learning process. Constant correction can be demotivating for students. However, some students want to be corrected and all students need to know how they are progressing.

When correcting, indicate to students that there has been an error and where the error is. Also indicate what type of error it is eg. grammar, vocabulary, pronunciation, etc. See if the student who made the error can correct their own mistake and if not, invite other students to help. If no one in the class can identify the problem then the teacher should make the correction. Check the students understand the corrected language and get the original student to say it correctly. We suggest correction takes place on these occasions:

1 As new language is being presented. Drills (see above) often reveal initial problems.

2 At times when an error is interfering with communication. At this point the teacher may want to help the student rephrase what they are trying to say.

3 When students make a slip which is below their level and they can easily self-correct.

4 After freer practice activities in a special 'correction spot'. There are various ways of handling correction of this sort:

- Put a selection of mistakes common to the class on the board and get students in pairs or small groups to correct them. Be ready to explain unresolved problems at feedback.

- Note one or two mistakes made by each student and encourage them to correct their own mistakes at the end. Students work together to help each other if they have problems.

- Write a few student mistakes on the board and an equal number of correct sentences. Students work together to decide which are correct and which are not. Once their decisions have been confirmed, they correct the incorrect sentences, justifying the changes.

Student practice

Open-class

All students listen to the teacher or to the contributions of individual students. This is particularly appropriate to demonstrate what is required of a new activity when the teacher is introducing new topics before pair/group work and also when getting students to report back after closed pairs/group practice (see below).

Open pairs

Two students are chosen by the teacher to ask and answer while the rest of the class listen. This often provides a good model and clarifies instructions before a 'closed pairs' activity.

Closed pairs

All students work with a partner. This allows maximum practice and is particularly appropriate for dialogue work.

Group work

Students work in small groups and report back 'open-class' to share their ideas with the class as a whole. This is best for activities which involve the collection or discussion of ideas.

'Milling around' activities

Students stand up and walk from one student to another, asking and answering as required. This allows constant repetition of a particular question or the collection of the opinions of many students. These activities work well when furniture can be moved out of the way to allow for free movement around the room.

Classroom management

Large classes

If your class is large and milling around is not possible, put students in groups of four or five. They take it in turns to ask the question while the others listen and write the answers, or they ask:

- the student on their right.
- the student on their left.
- the student behind them.
- the student in front of them.

Odd numbers in groups

If you are setting up a pairwork activity and you have an odd number of students in your class, put three students together where possible. This will leave you free to monitor the other students. It may, however, sometimes be more appropriate for you to act as a student's partner, in order to balance the numbers and help that student with particular problems.

Multi/monolingual groups

In multilingual classes, most activities will benefit from mixing nationalities for group work. This encourages discussion in English and means that students will be able to exchange information about aspects of life in different countries. However, it is sometimes better for students to work in groups with other students from the same part of the world in order to collect cultural information they have in common which can then be passed to students from other countries.

In monolingual classes, students need to be encouraged to keep English as the language of communication. In our experience this happens most easily if:

a) the instructions for activities are clear.

b) students have enough English.

c) the teacher expects English to be used.

When the teacher is not the same nationality as the students, there is a useful basis for exchange of information, with the teacher finding out about the students' culture and vice versa.

Use of mother tongue

There is a range of opinion about when, how and how often a teacher should use the mother tongue of her/his students. There are a host of relevant factors to consider, not least of which are:

- your proficiency in the language(s) of your students.
- your students' previous language learning experience and expectations.
- your personal attitude to the use of the students' mother tongue.

Whatever you decide, it can be helpful to explain (or get someone else to explain), in the students' own language, a little about the course they are going to follow. This can be done just before or during the first lesson.

Completion exercises and charts

If you do not want students to write in the Students' Book, allow time for them to copy the exercises and charts into their notebooks before they begin an activity.

How to use this book

This Teacher's Book had been written with an innovative two-track format, to cater for the needs of all teachers, whatever their level experience.

The more experienced teacher, or the one who wants quick access to the teaching notes, can refer solely to the 'fast track' instructions, printed on a grey background. These provide brief procedural guidance, along with answers to the exercises, and the tapescripts.

The less-experienced teacher who requires more detailed teaching notes, or the teacher who would like extra ideas for extension activities, can refer to the extended notes following each 'fast track' instruction.

All the answers to the exercises in the Students' Book and the complete tapescripts appear in the appropriate place in each unit, with the exception of the tapescripts for Images; Unit 16 Exercise 7 Vocabulary: Pronunciation: 4 and Unit 20 Thinking about learning: Radio Programme, which all appear on pages 157–160. These tapescripts can be photocopied and distributed to students.

1–2 Students check their answers to the last exercise against the tape and answer questions focussing on their pronunciation. They then repeat the expressions.

Tapescript

a piece of cheese
a can of soup
a tube of tomato paste
a bar of chocolate
a packet of biscuits
a jar of jam
a box of matches
a bottle of milk

Answers

1
1 Main stress is generally on the package eg. a packet of biscuits.
2 a is pronounced /ə/, of is pronounced /əv/.

'Fast track'

Play the tape for students to check their answers and ask the pronunciation questions open-class.

Write the example expression on the board, showing how the final consonant before of is linked to the /ə/ sound.

Play the tape again and get the students to repeat the expressions, making sure they link the sounds correctly.

Extended notes

0 *What do you know?*

AIMS

- To revise students' assumed beginner level vocabulary.
- To revise positive/negative forms of basic key verbs.

1+2+3 Students put vocabulary into columns by lexical set. They add other words they know, comparing and adding contributions from other students.

Answers

1
food: *egg*
clothes: *scarf*
colours: *black*
rooms: *kitchen*
family: *father*
weather: *windy*
places: *bank*
body: *head*
transport: *taxi*
jobs: *dentist*

After greeting the class and introducing yourself and new students, give them a few minutes to flick through and familiarise themselves with the new book. While they are doing this, write columns on the board headed by the superordinate words (*food, clothes,* etc.) from Exercise 1.

Refer students to Unit 0 and tell them that this is a revision unit which will check some of the vocabulary and structures they should know before they begin the main units of the book. (Alternatively, if you are continuing to work with an established class, you may like to give the book out in the previous lesson, asking them to look at it and complete Unit 0 for homework. In this case, students will only need to compare their answers in class before starting Unit 1.)

Do Exercise 1 open-class, getting students to identify the vocabulary in the photographs. Elicit which column to write each word in on the board.

Students brainstorm related vocabulary, first alone and then with other students, adding as many words as possible to each column. As groups finish, encourage them to add their new words to the columns on the board.

4 Students describe the photographs on the page.

Refer students to the example in Exercise 4, asking which photograph is being described. Put students in small groups to use the vocabulary and other language they know to describe all the photographs in the unit in as much detail as possible.

5+6 Students complete the verb tables and check what information these verbs can be used to provide.

Answers

5

Be

I		*am*		Maria/Antonio.
You/We/They		*are*	(not)	married.
She/He/(It)		*is*		30.

Can

I/You				swim.
She/He/(It)	*can*		(not)	speak English.
We/They				stay out late.

Have got

I/You		*have*				a big family.
We/They			(not)	got		a new car.
She/He/(It)		*has*				a headache.

As they finish, ask them to read another student's sentences and to note any information they find particularly interesting. Finally elicit some of this information open-class, checking students' use of the 3rd person singular form as they report on their partner. (eg. *Maria likes skiing.*)

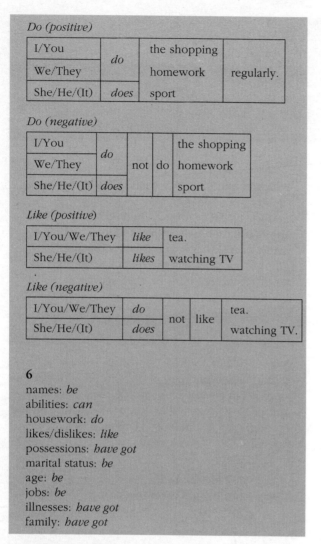

Do (positive)

I/You	do	the shopping	
We/They		homework	regularly.
She/He/(It)	does	sport	

Do (negative)

I/You	do			the shopping
We/They		not	do	homework
She/He/(It)	does			sport

Like (positive)

I/You/We/They	like	tea.
She/He/(It)	likes	watching TV

Like (negative)

I/You/We/They	do			tea.
She/He/(It)	does	not	like	watching TV.

6
names: *be*
abilities: *can*
housework: *do*
likes/dislikes: *like*
possessions: *have got*
marital status: *be*
age: *be*
jobs: *be*
illnesses: *have got*
family: *have got*

Elicit the answers for the first verb table open-class. Get students to use the completed table to produce positive and negative sentences using the verb *be*, eg. *She is not Maria.*

Give them time to complete the tables for the other verbs, checking answers with or asking other students for help as necessary.

Check students understand that *be* can be used to say who they are, eg. *I am Maria.* Put them in pairs to do the rest of Exercise 6, referring to their verb tables.

7 Students use the verbs to write sentences giving personal information.

Use a variety of these verbs to tell students something about yourself first. Then get them to work individually to write ten sentences about themselves.

1 Person to person

1 Preparation

AIMS

- To introduce students to one another.
- To check students can spell in English.

1+2 Students find out each others' names and how to spell them. They then organise the names of students in the class in alphabetical order.

NB Answers

/eɪ/ = A,H,J,K
/iː/ = B,C,D,E,G,P,T,V
/e/ = F,L,M,N,S,X,Z
/aɪ/ = I,Y
/əʊ/ = O
/uː/ = Q,U,W
/ɑː/ = R

Use the dialogue in the book as a model for a similar exchange between you and one student.

Refer students to the NB Box *The alphabet* at the foot of the page and give students a couple of minutes in pairs to check they can say the alphabet correctly. Students who finish quickly could try saying the alphabet backwards! Check answers open-class.

Ask students to make a list of everyone in the class by first name (or surname, if more appropriate). Ask them to stand up and mill around the room, asking as many people as possible their names and how to spell them. If students already know one another well, then go immediately to the next exercise.

Ask students to form a line arranging themselves in alphabetical order. If you want students to consolidate alphabet work in writing, set up a competition with the winner being the first student who can give you a complete and correctly spelt class list in alphabetical order.

2 Speaking

AIMS

- To check/teach and provide practice of a variety of personal questions.
- To highlight the importance of sentence stress.

Students read the information under the photographs in the magazine article to find out which questions each person was asked.

Answers

b) Where do you come from?   g) How old are you?
a) What's your name?   e) What do you do?

Make sure the students only read the captions under the photographs and not the complete texts. Give them time to read the questions and the captions before asking for their answers open-class.

Pronunciation: sentence stress

1 Students listen to the questions on tape and locate main sentence stress.

Tapescript/Answers

a) What's your <u>name</u>?
b) Where do you <u>come</u> from?
c) Are you <u>married</u>?
d) Have you got any <u>children</u>?
e) What do you <u>do</u>?
f) What <u>languages</u> can you speak?
g) How <u>old</u> are you?
h) When did you start learning <u>English</u>?
i) How many English-speaking <u>countries</u> have you been to?

Refer students to the example in the book, saying 'What's your name?' with main sentence stress on *name*.

Ask them to write the questions in their

notebooks. They then listen and underline the word with main stress in each question.

Check their answers, getting a number of students to repeat the questions with appropriate stress and intonation, once a good model has been established.

> **2 Put students in pairs to ask and answer some of the questions.**

Students can choose which questions to ask and need not keep to a particular order. This is a chance for new students to get to know the person sitting next to them.

If students have studied together before then they may not need to ask many questions and the activity will be quite short. This is not a problem as further question practice is given later in the unit. However, weak classes may find this preview useful and you could substitute some of the questions with others using the same grammatical patterns, eg. *What musical instruments can you play?* could replace *What languages can you speak?*

3 Grammar: question forms

AIMS

- To highlight the difference between inverted question forms and those formed with the auxiliary *do*.
- To provide further practice of making and asking questions.

> **1+2 Highlight the difference between the formation of inverted questions and those made with the auxiliary *do*.**

> **Answers**
>
> 1 In a) the question is made by inversion of the verb *be* and the subject. In b) the question is made by the insertion of the auxiliary *do* before the subject.
> 2 Questions formed like a) are c), d), f), g) and i). Questions formed like b) are e) and h).

Refer students to the grammar box in their books or copy it onto the board, eliciting the sentences from the students as you write. Underline the verbs *is* and *come* in the positive sentences.

Now ask the students to tell you how the questions are formed. Encourage students to explain as best they can, without concern for accuracy of the language they are using.

Draw two columns on the board, one headed 'inverted questions' and the other headed '+ auxiliary verb *do*'. Ask students to work in pairs and check the questions a)–i) from Exercise 2 Speaking, deciding which should go in each column.

> **3 Students practise forming questions for given answers**
>
> **Answers**
>
> 1 Can you speak Italian (or another language)?
> 2 Do you like going to the cinema?
> 3 Have you got any brothers and sisters?
> 4 How old are they?
> 5 What do you do in your free time (in the evening/at the weekend)?
> 6 Where do you live?

Do the first question with the class as an example.

Students work alone, writing questions for the rest of the exercise. As they finish, they check their work with another student.

Check their questions open-class. Where more than one question is possible, elicit further examples.

> **4 Students work in pairs to make questions to ask other students or the teacher, using prompts. They then ask their questions.**

Establish who the questions will be answered by. If you/some students are new to the class, use this as an opportunity for the class to find out about you/them.

As students work together, be available to help them with extra vocabulary if necessary. If you see mistakes in their questions as they are working, prompt them to self-correct if possible. Encourage quicker students to write more questions to give slower students time to complete the task.

Group students appropriately to ask their questions or work open-class if they are asking you. Encourage them to listen to one another by getting them to tick off any of their own questions asked by another student. This way, all questions should be new and most students should get a chance to ask something. If you/

students prefer not to answer any questions, respond with something like 'I'd rather not say!'

4 Reading

AIMS

- To provide practice in skimming text for general information, note-taking from continuous text and exchanging information orally.

1+2 Students are divided in three groups, each group reading one part of the article only. They decide which questions were asked in their part of the article and note short answers from the article to these questions.

Answers

- Kadi Secka (number 2) was asked:

A
a) Where do you live?
b) What is school like in your country?
c) What are you going to do when you leave school?
d) What is your daily routine?

- Marc Bloy (number 3) was asked:

B
a) Where do you work?
b) Do you enjoy what you do?
c) What do you think of England?
d) What are your ambitions?

- Lulu Yu (number 1) was asked

C
a) What do you do at work?
b) Have you got a boyfriend?
c) What do you do in your free time?
d) Would you like to live in another country?

Put students in groups of three. They decide who is Student A, B and C. Check this by asking for a show of hands from all As, Bs and then Cs. Tell all Student As to read part 1 of the article, Bs part 2 and Cs part 3.

Refer them to the instructions for the task and the questions in their book. Tell them to read all the questions first. They then read their part of the article to decide which group of questions comes from their article and what order they were asked in.

They check their answers with another student who has read the same part of the article. They then work with this partner and note answers to the questions. As they work, circulate in the class and encourage students to note key words as answers, rather than complete sentences.

3+4 Students talk to one another in their original groups of three. They exchange the information about the three people and finally decide who they would most like to meet.

Each student tells the two others in their group which questions and answers come from their part of the article. As they listen, they note answers to the questions answered by the two people they didn't read about.

They tell each other which person they would most like to meet and why.

Get some class feedback on the last question as this will provide further speaking practice, especially if the students don't all agree.

5 Grammar: *-ing* form

AIMS

- To teach and practise the use of the *-ing* form after verbs which express feelings.

1+2 Students study examples of the *-ing* form from the previous reading text. They then use these forms to express their personal feelings on the subjects listed.

Answers

1
1 *love/enjoy/prefer/like*. They all express feelings, degrees of liking.
2 . . . and I *hate* travelling.
   I *don't enjoy* listening to music or playing with my sister.
   I *don't prefer* living in Paris. I *don't like* just walking around, sitting in cafés, drinking coffee and talking to friends.

Refer students to the grammar box in their book and get them to work in pairs to answer the questions in Exercise 1.

Check their answers as a class.

Listen in as they tell their partner about the things listed in Exercise 2. Correct any mistakes you overhear at the end of the activity.

6 Vocabulary: work and free time

AIMS

- To revise/teach job vocabulary.
- To highlight the frequent relationship between verbs and nouns in this lexical area.
- To provide practice in using the Present Simple to discuss work routines.
- To highlight the frequent er/or (/ə/) endings for jobs.

1-3 Students categorise a variety of job and free time activities. They name these and other jobs ending in er/or, checking pronunciation against the tape.

Answers

1 Jobs: teaching in a secondary school, dancing, writing detective novels, (perhaps going to the theatre if you are a theatre critic!), directing films for TV, driving taxis, reporting stories for TV news, playing football for Real Madrid
Free time activities: dancing, listening to music, going to the theatre, drinking in bars, eating in restaurants with friends, reading novels, going to the cinema

Answers/Tapescript

2+3
teaching in a secondary school - a 'teacher
dancing - a 'dancer
writing detective novels - a 'writer
directing films for TV - a 'film director
driving taxis - a 'taxi driver
reporting stories for TV news - a re'porter
playing football for Real Madrid - a 'football player

er/or at the end of jobs is pronounced /ə/

Refer students to the columns in their book and make sure they realise that some words can go in both categories.

As they finish, they check their lists with another student.

Show them how word stress is marked in dictionaries by referring to the example in their book. Get them to listen and mark the stress on their list of jobs vocabulary.

4 Students brainstorm other jobs vocabulary ending in er or or. They say what these people do at work, using verbs in the Present Simple form.

Answers

Based on Exercise 1:
a teacher teaches, a dancer dances, a writer writes, a film director directs films, a taxi driver drives taxis, a reporter reports stories, a football player plays football

Get students to brainstorm open-class, writing the jobs on the board. Use pictures of different jobs (eg. doctor/waiter/porter/cleaner/train driver, etc.) to elicit vocabulary if the students dry up.

Establish what they need to do by getting them to tell you open-class about the jobs in the chart from the previous exercise.

Students work in pairs to make sentences based on the example in their book. Make sure they use the 3rd person form correctly.

5 Students ask each other about their work and free time activities.

Elicit the question forms: *What do you do? What do you like doing in your free time?*.

Check that students pronounce *do you* in its weakened form /dʒʊ/. Also refer them to the NB box *a/an + jobs* to remind them to use the indefinite article *a* or *an* (/ə/ or /ən/).

Students mill around the class asking as many other students the two questions as possible. If milling is not possible, they can ask students who sit next to/in front of/behind them. (See Classroom Procedures on page 15

7 Writing

AIMS

- To provide practice in recognising and using the alphabet.
- To check/teach the use of *could* for making requests.

1 Dictate your/another name, address and telephone number to the class.

Tell the class the aim of this activity. Elicit how they can ask for repetition/spelling if they need to. Accept all possible ways of doing this and recode some of their examples, using *could*. Finally, drill the speech bubbles in their book.

If you prefer not to disclose your own address and telephone number, dictate the following:

Mr Michael Houghton,
197 Fortescue Crescent,
Elham,
Folkestone,
Kent GE8 9WY

2 Students dictate the information on a business card to one another.

Students work in pairs. Get them to read the instructions in their book and draw a blank business card in their notebook.

When they have both finished, they check their completed card against the one in the book.

3 They dictate their own addresses and telephone numbers.

If students have their own business cards, they can dictate from these. Make sure students know they can invent the information if they prefer not to dictate their real addresses.

8 Listening

AIMS

- To develop skills of listening for general and specific information.
- To sensitise students to the differences in style, depending on the relationship of the speakers.

1 Students describe the photographs to each other.

Get students to describe the first photograph open-class. Encourage use of the Present Continuous form for descriptions of this type

Put students in pairs to describe the other two pictures to each other.

2 + 3 Students listen to the tape and match the photographs and relationships of the people to the conversations. They listen again for further detail.

Tapescript

Conversation 1
WOMAN: Chris! Hi! I don't believe it! When did you get back?
CHRIS: Only last Wednesday. Fancy meeting you. How are you?

WOMAN: Great. What about you?
CHRIS: I'm very well.
WOMAN: Did you have a good time?
CHRIS: Yes, fantastic. Rio was wonderful.

Conversation 2
MAN: You can go in now.
JILL: Thank you.
BOB: Jill! How nice to see you! Come in, come in. Sit down. It's good to have you back in the office.
JILL: Thanks Bob. It's good to be back. How is everything?
BOB: All right, but, well, there have been a few changes while you've been away.
JILL: Oh yes, like what, for example?

Conversation 3
JIM: Hello. You must be Shu's sister.
WOMAN: That's right, and you are...?
JIM: I'm Jim. I'm at college with Shu.
WOMAN: Oh right.
JIM: Look, are you OK? You don't look very well.
WOMAN: I'm not too good. Actually, I feel awful. Could you get me a drink of water?

Answers

2

1 Conversation 1 – top right-hand photograph
   Conversation 2 – bottom right-hand photograph
   Conversation 3 – left-hand photograph
2 Conversation 1 – c)
   Conversation 2 – a)
   Conversation 3 – b)

3
a) - Conversation 3
b) - Conversation 1
c) - Conversation 2

At each stage, refer students to the task in their book before they listen to the tape. Let them confer with another student after listening and play the tape again if they can't agree on their answers.

4 They listen again for how people greet one another and talk about their health.

Answers

1 Conversation 1: Hi! Conversation 2: Jill! How nice to see you! Conversation 3: Hello!
2 very well = great, not bad = all right, not very well = not too good, terrible = awful

Elicit ways of greeting people and write them on the board (eg. *Hello, Hi!*). Refer students to their book for words used to say how people are feeling. Ask students to listen to the tape again and note the exact words used. They may need to listen more than once.

5+6 Students practise saying the phrases with appropriate intonation and add any other words or phrases they know to their list.

Tapescript

very well	not very well
great	not too good
not bad	terrible
all right	awful

Ask students: *How are you?*, to elicit words from their list. Correct flat intonation by repeating their answer and sounding surprised by the incongruity of the words and their meaning. Use grimaces, body language or illustrations to help encourage more appropriate intonation. You could copy the faces below onto the board and point at the face their intonation suggests.

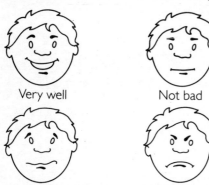

Very well   Not bad

Not very well   Terrible

Finally, brainstorm any other similar vocabulary they know.

Speaking

1+2 Students repeat conversation 1. They then practise it further by changing the names, day and place mentioned and continue it by asking their partner for further information.

Elicit the words of the first conversation. Prompt students to supply the words, line by line, recoding what they say if necessary. As each new line is added, they go back to the beginning and repeat the conversation in their pairs. Finally they practise the complete conversation.

Encourage students to talk about a real holiday they have had, and to continue the conversation as they wish. Some students may enjoy saying their completed, transformed conversation to the class.

English in action

AIMS

- To sensitise students to the appropriacy/ inapppropriacy of direct personal questions.
- To encourage students to start a class magazine.

1+2 Students consider the politeness of certain direct questions in their own culture and the English-speaking cultures they know.

Answers

2

Clearly the 'answer' to this is partly a matter of context and partly a matter of opinion. However, in general, the following questions are acceptable and appropriate in the following situations:

- *What's your name?* To a child, and possibly a person you met for the first time (given appropriate intonation!). However *I'm sorry, I don't know your name* is often used as a less abrupt way of finding out someone's name.
- *How do you do?* To a person you met for the first time (in a formal context).
- *How old are you?* Acceptable to a child, but age can be sensitive to older people.
- *How much do you earn?* To a good friend or person in your family and perhaps to a colleague at work but this is a sensitive area!
- *Are you married?* To a colleague at work and a person you met for the first time but you need to be careful it isn't taken the wrong way!
- *Why haven't you got any children?* It is very difficult to imagine a context where you aren't in danger of sounding quite rude.
- *How much did your watch cost?* To a good friend or person in your family but again you need to be careful as money can be quite a delicate issue.
- *What do you think of the government?* You will probably know the political views of good friends and family, but for people you don't know so well eg. colleagues at work, you need to be careful – politics and religion can both be quite sensitive subjects.

Establish the task of producing a class magazine. If possible, show one made by other students or refer them to the magazine in the photograph in their book. Relate the appropriacy activity to the magazine article, saying that they are going to interview each other and first need to know which questions are acceptable.

Put students in groups of four or five, mixing nationalities in a multilingual class. Refer them to the questions and relationships mentioned in their book. Do the first question open-class, eliciting their ideas about their own country and Britain. Highlight that asking *What's your name?* in Britain is rather abrupt and more likely to be used to children than adults. Elicit ways they think adults might phrase this question. (There is an example: *I'm sorry, I don't know your name.* at the beginning of this unit. You could refer students to this.) Students then work in their groups to discuss the other questions.

In a monolingual class, the discussion about the students' own language will probably be shorter than in a multilingual class. They could therefore discuss what they know about English-speaking cultures at the same time. In a multilingual situation, leave discussion of the English language until the next stage. If students know very little about English-speaking cultures, then get them to ask you.

3 Students work in pairs to interview their partner for the class magazine.

Let students choose their own partner for this activity. If the class know each other well, encourage students to interview a student they know less well. If personal information questions are inappropriate, get students to find out about things that have happened since the class were last together or something particularly interesting that has happened in their partner's life.

Give them time to prepare their questions individually and then to hold the interview. Encourage students to note key words as answers, rather than complete sentences.

4+5 Students write a short article about their partner. The collated articles are made into a magazine for everyone to read.

Students may finish their articles for homework. Refer them to the instructions in their book, reminding them to divide their work into

paragraphs by topic area. Ask them to bring passport-size photographs to the next lesson if possible to stick next to the article about them to help new students identify one another more easily.

Suggest that one pair of students take responsibility for collating all the articles into a magazine format or sticking the pages round the class for others to read. If the students particularly enjoy the activity, they may like to produce further issues of the magazine, on different subjects, with a different pair of students responsible for each new issue. (See this book, pages 34, 66, 79, etc.)

Language review 1

a
She's/he's an 'actor. She/he acts in plays.
She's/he's a di'rector. She/he directs a company.
She's/he's a re'porter. She/he reports for a newspaper.
She's/he's a de'signer. She/he designs clothes.
She's/he's a 'bus driver. She/he drives buses.
She's/he's a 'tennis player. She/he plays tennis.
She's/he's a 'language teacher. She/he teaches languages.

b
1 Odette prefers swimming. Ali prefers skiing. Shelly prefers swimming.
2 Odette likes dancing most. Ali likes skiing most. Shelly likes swimming most.
3 Odette hates skiing. Ali hates dancing. Shelly hates skiing.
4 Odette and Shelly enjoy dancing.
5 Odette and Shelly don't like skiing.

c+d
1 Have you got/Do you have any children? f)
2 Are you a student? a)
3 How many languages do you speak? g)
4 What do you do at the weekends? d)
5 Can you speak English very well? c)
6 When did you start learning English? e)
7 How old are you? b)

e
1 Could you open the window, please?
2 Could you say that again, please?
3 Could you give/tell me your address, please?
4 Could you spell your name, please?
5 Could you help me, please?
6 Could you phone me back, please?

2 Lookalikes

LANGUAGE CONTENT

Productive language
- Comparatives + (not) as . . . as; the same as; different from
- Adjectives for describing people
- A variety of clothes/accessories/body vocabulary

- Past Simple irregular forms
- Be like vs look like (each other)
- Used to

Receptive language
- Selected vocabulary from a newspaper article.

Preparation for this unit

In Exercise 4 Speaking, students will discuss who they look like in their families. Ask them in advance to bring in photographs of their families to show to their partner.

1 Preparation

AIMS

- To revise and extend clothes and colour vocabulary.
- To develop the skill of reading for specific information.
- To introduce the topic of the unit.

1 Students revise clothes and colour vocabulary by describing what one pair of twins in the photographs are wearing. They then describe the clothing of people in the class.

Answers

1 B and E
2 Sunglasses, glasses, T-shirts, blouses and brooches. Pair E are also wearing matching earrings, suits and necklaces.

Check that students understand what *matching* means by showing something that matches in the classroom.

Ask the first two questions open-class. When students have told you which items match, ask them what colour they are.

Extend discussion to clothing worn by the class, pointing to various items and eliciting the necessary vocabulary.

To get further practice of clothes vocabulary, ask students to mill around the class. When you give the signal, get them to stand back to back with the nearest student and try to remember what they are wearing, like this:

A: Are you wearing a black jacket?
B: No.
A: Is it blue then?

2 Students answer the questions by reading the captions under each photograph.

Answers

1 Faye Gallo and Sue Gallo Baugher
2 The Skull Sisters
3 Goss Bros
4 Barbara and Daphne
5 Wesley and Thomas Charnock
6 The Thompson Twins

Give students time to read the questions and ask about any vocabulary they don't understand. Ask them to tell you the difference between *an artist* (someone who draws/paints) and *a pop singer* (someone who sings modern songs).

When they have answered the questions, they check them with another student. Deal with any discrepancies open-class.

2 Grammar: comparatives

AIMS

- To revise and extend the students' use of comparative forms.
- To highlight the weak pronunciation /ə/ in unstressed words used in forming comparatives.

1 Students study comparative sentences to revise how to make basic comparative forms.

Answers

1 left
2 a) You make comparatives of one-syllable adjectives by adding -er. Where the adjectives end in one vowel and one consonant, double the final consonant.

b) You make comparatives of two-syllable adjectives ending in -*y* by replacing the -*y* with -*ier*.

c) You make comparatives of two- and three-syllable adjectives by preceding the adjective with *more*.

Elicit the comparative sentences about the twins Gareth and Nicholas to the board. Involve students in spelling as you write.

Get students to answer the questions in the first exercise with their partner.

As you check their answers open-class, highlight the spelling rules.

2 Students write other comparative sentences to compare the Thompson twins, this time beginning with the second twin.

Answers

Nicholas is smaller than Gareth.
Nicholas is lighter than Gareth.
Nicholas is less independent than Gareth.

Leave students in their pairs to write the example sentences, so they will say as well as write, the new comparatives.

At feedback, write the students' sentences on the board. Some students may use the structures you are about to teach eg. *Nicholas is smaller than Gareth = Nicholas isn't as big as Gareth.* This will serve as a preview for students who are unfamiliar with the *as . . . as* structure. Clean the board before you start the next exercise.

3 Students practise using comparative forms with reference to people they know.

Check that students understand the meaning of the various adjectives before they start the exercise. Go round and check their sentences before they show them to each other.

4+5 They then decide whether pairs of sentences about the Thompson twins, using different ways of comparing, mean the same thing or not. Finally they use the new forms to complete sentences about the other twins.

Answers

4

1	same	3	different
2	same	4	same

5

1 Luke isn't *as tall as* Matt. He is *shorter than* Matt.
2 Bros are *more famous than* The Skull Sisters.
3 He isn't *the same colour as* Thomas.
4 Daphne's hair is *as short as* Barbara's.
5 Daphne's hair isn't *as dark as* Barbara's.

Give students time to consider the sentences in Exercise 4 individually before checking what they think with a partner.

Students work alone or in pairs to complete the sentences about the other twins in Exercise 5. As they finish, they compare their answers with another student then check their answers against the tape.

Pronunciation: /ə/ in unstressed words

1 Students listen again to the answers to the last exercise on the cassette. They mark stress and unstressed /ə/ on the words in their books.

Tapescript

1 Matt is taller than Luke.
  Luke isn't as tall as Matt.
  He is shorter than Matt.

2 The Skull Sisters are less famous than Bros.
  Bros are more famous than the Skull sisters.

3 Wesley is a different colour from Thomas.
  He isn't the same colour as Thomas.

4 Barbara and Daphne have both got short hair.
  Daphne's hair is as short as Barbara's.

5 Barbara's hair is dark brown and Daphne's hair is light brown.
  Daphne's hair isn't as dark as Barbara's.

Answers

/ə/   /ə/
as 'tall as

/ə/ /ə/
'shorter than

/ə/ /ə/
less 'famous than

/ə/ /ə/
more 'famous than

/ə/ /ə/
'different from

/ə/   /ə/
the 'same as

/ə/   /ə/
as 'short as

/ə/   /ə/
(isn't) as 'dark as

Ask students to underline the comparative expression in each sentence in Exercise 5. As they do this, write the expressions on the board.

Refer them to the example in their book then tell them to listen out for the underlined words as they listen to the cassette. Stop the cassette after each sentence to give them time to mark the stress and /ə/ where they hear it.

Check their answers by asking individual students to read the sentences aloud to you, paying attention to the stress. After each sentence, mark the stress and /ə/ on the expression on the board.

2 Students use comparative expressions to decide which pair of twins is the most identical and why the others are not.

Refer students to the lead-in text in the article and ask why the twins are meeting in Twinsburg, Ohio. They then work in pairs to judge the contest, saying why some twins are more identical than others. As they finish, get them to explain their opinion to another pair, trying to persuade them to change their minds if they don't agree. As soon as they agree they try to persuade another pair and so on. Finally, after class feedback, get students to vote on which couple they think should win.

3 Students compare towns and countries they know well.

Students discuss the topics in groups of four or five.

In multilingual classes, put students of different nationalities together. In monolingual groups, find out which countries and towns students know well by naming places and asking students to say on a scale 1-5 how well they know them. Choose some of the better known places and encourage students to form groups in order to find out about places they know little about. In open-class feedback get students to report what they found out, using comparatives.

3 Reading

AIMS

- To preteach vocabulary from the newspaper article.
- To develop the skills of reading for gist and specific information.
- To revise and give practice in some irregular Past Simple forms.

1 Students match words from the newspaper article with definitions.

Answers

1 – h	5 – g
2 – f	6 – c
3 – e	7 – a
4 – b	8 – d

Make sure students know that this vocabulary comes from the text they are going to read.

They work alone or in pairs to match words to definitions.

2+3 Students read the article to find out what is generally surprising about the story. They then read it again to find details of similarities and coincidences in the sisters' lives.

Answers

2 It is surprising because in spite of the long period of separation they have so many things in common.

3 Barbara was standing exactly where Daphne got off the train.
They both work for local councils.
They both met their husbands at dances.
Both their husbands have similar jobs and are quiet, hard-working men.
Barbara and Daphne both have similar gestures and ways of laughing.
Both their halls were painted the same.
They both had the same three-piece suites in their living rooms.
They had both had one miscarriage, followed by two sons and a daughter.
They both drink their coffee black, with no sugar and half cold.
On one occasion they were both going to wear the same dress and jacket.
They tend to cook the same meals for supper.
They sometimes buy exactly the same books on the same day.

Use the photograph to set the scene and establish that these twins are the same twins they read briefly about on page 12. Elicit that these women did not live together as children and make sure the task is clear.

When the fact that, in spite of separation, the twins' lives are/have been so similar has been established, get students to work in pairs to list all the similarities they can find in the text.

Grammar: Past Simple

1+2 After completing the table with Past Simple forms, students use the verbs to retell the story in the article.

Answers

1

Present	Past simple
know	*knew*
be	*was/were*
meet	*met*
come	*came*
forget	*forgot*
can	*could*
put	*put*
find	*found*
have	*had*
go	*went*
say	*said*
buy	*bought*

Elicit that the Past Simple of regular verbs is formed by adding -ed or -d to the base form of the verb eg. look/look*ed*; like/like*d*.

Refer students to the list of irregular verbs and ask them to write the Past Simple forms, checking their answers by finding examples in the article.

Check the answers open-class. Then put students in pairs with their books closed to tell each other the story. One student should start with the other student listening. The second student's job is to correct any incorrect verb forms and to add any details their partner forgets.

If you want your students to have further practice in using the Past Simple, get them to talk about things they did recently. First, ask a student open-class what she did yesterday. Then tell the class to listen to what you did and see if anything is the same. Tell your partner, again

open-class, what you did, making sure that at least one thing is the same.

You could turn this activity into a game by telling students they have a short time to find three things that both they and their partner did last weekend. See who can find three things first.

4 Speaking

AIMS

• To check/teach the use of *look/laugh/talk + like* for describing similarities between people.
• To provide the opportunity for sharing personal information.

1+2 Students find examples of the target structure in the article. They use it and photographs to tell one another about family and friends they resemble.

Answers

1 They talk like each other. They laugh like each other.

NB Answers

1 b)
2 a)

Refer students to the example sentences. Ask them to put the sentences into the Past Simple, thus checking that *look* is the verb, not *like*. Elicit that *each other* refers to both people and that the second sentence can be rephrased as *Barbara looks like Daphne* and *Daphne looks like Barbara.*

When students have found the description of the twins which says they *look, talk and laugh alike,* (at the end of the first paragraph), ask them to rephrase this using *look/talk/laugh + like* eg. *They look like each other.*

Refer students to the NB box *be like* vs *look like* to clarify the difference between *look like* and *be like.* Elicit the answers to the questions.

Use a photograph of someone in your family, if possible, and tell students who you look/act like, etc. Refer students to the questions in their book, checking they understand the task before putting them in groups of three or four to talk about their resemblance to friends and families. Encourage them to use photographs to illustrate what they are saying if possible. This is a chance for freer speaking, so don't inhibit communication by correcting students. You may wish to listen into their conversations and make a note of mistakes to correct later. (For advice on correction, see page 16).

5 Listening

AIMS

- To teach/revise body vocabulary and related adjectives and colours.
- To highlight adjectives which collocate with parts of the body.
- To develop the skills of listening for general and specific information.
- To teach *used to* and give controlled and freer practice.

1 Students match parts of the body to adjectives and colours which collocate with them.

Answers

Hair can be fair/dark, long/short, straight/curly, black/grey/blond.
Eyes can be blue/brown/green/small/medium/large.
Noses can be long/short, small/medium/large and straight but not curly.
Ears can be small/medium/large.
Skin can be fair/dark, black/white.
Figures can slim/thin/fat, small/medium/large.
Legs can be long/short, slim/thin/fat and straight but not curly.

Point to parts of your own body to elicit the body vocabulary.

Check the first pair of adjectives *straight/curly* against each part of the body vocabulary open-class. Make sure they realise that not all adjectives and their opposites collocate in the same way – you can say a *straight* nose but not a *curly* nose! (Reference to 'straight' noses comes up in the next listening exercise.) Feed in that *crooked* is the opposite of *straight* in this situation.

Put students in groups of three to continue working through the adjectives and body vocabulary. Refer them to their mini-dictionary on page 138 to check the meaning of the adjectives, if necessary.

Finally ask students to use the words to describe people they know.

2 Students discuss cosmetic surgery based on two photographs of the actress, Cher.

Answers

1 Before – left-hand photograph
  After – right-hand photograph

Refer students to the photographs of Cher. Elicit that she is a film star and singer. Ask students which of her films they have seen ('The Witches of Eastwick', 'Moonstruck', etc) and what they think of them/her.

Put students in groups of three to discuss the questions. Give them time to read the questions and ask for clarification of vocabulary if necessary.

3+4 Students first listen to the conversation and answer the questions in Exercise 3 to check general understanding. They listen again and answer the more detailed questions in Exercise 4.

Tapescript

A: She looks good, doesn't she?
B: Yeah fantastic. She really doesn't look her age. When I think. . .
A: Here she goes.
B: No honestly, when you think what she used to look like in the sixties, she's completely different now.
A: Yes. But she was always attractive – she used to be a real hippy, flowers in her hair and everything.
B: I know, but she's more beautiful and so much more confident now. She thought she was ugly then.
A: Oh she can't have!
B: Well, why change her nose otherwise? Can't you see it's straighter?
A: Yes. But it's not just her nose. She's changed her whole look. Her hair's curlier now. I also heard she had bits taken out of her legs. They're certainly thinner.
B: Oh no! That must hurt. I couldn't. . .
A: And look at her face. It's still so attractive. She's definitely had a face-lift. And you must admit, she does look better.
B: Yes, but it's not right is it? Do you know how much all that costs?
A: A fortune! It's terrible really.
B: I think it's awful. But. . .
A: What?
B: I do hate my ears. I'd love to do something.
A: Oh no! Not really! You're mad. Your ears are fine.

You look great! Fantastic. Don't be stupid! You don't really mean it.

B No, I don't. I think cosmetic surgery is awful, a disgrace, terrible. . . haven't got enough money anyway.

Answers

3

1 The two women are generally against cosmetic surgery.

2 They think she looks better now.

4

1 nose, hair, legs, face

2 Now - straight nose, curly hair, thin legs, attractive face

Before - more crooked nose, straighter hair, fatter legs, even more attractive face

Students check their answers together after each listening. They listen again if they can't agree on the answers.

Get students to list the body vocabulary and the adjective that goes with each part.

At feedback, ask individual students how they think the parts of the body referred to must have looked before. Where applicable, ask them to note the opposites alongside the adjectives they heard.

6 Grammar: *used to*

1+2 Students deduce the meaning and rules of form for *used to* and use them to complete sentences about Cher.

Answers

1

1 b)

2 Like the Past Simple, you precede it with *didn't* (*She didn't use to have curly hair.*)

3 Like the Past Simple, use the auxiliary *did* (*Did she use to be a hippy?*)

2

1 *used to*

2 *didn't use to*

3 *didn't use to*

4 *didn't use to*

5 *used to*

6 *used to*

Refer students to the model sentence and elicit the answers to the questions open-class.

Highlight the regular Past Simple *-ed* ending on *used to* to help students deduce the rules of form.

Students complete the sentences individually and then check their answers with another student. If there are discrepancies or they are unsure of the answer, replay the tape.

3+4 Students exchange information on how they have changed, and then tell the class what they have found out about their partner.

Give students time to read the areas of possible change listed in their book and to choose one or two to talk about.

Let students talk in naturally formed small groups of two or three. Finally they report back to the class, saying what they have heard of interest.

English in action

1-4 Students make a questionnaire to ask people about similarities between themselves and their friends, to test a psychologist's hypothesis that we make good relationships with people who look like us.

Answers

1 He suggests that we make good relationships with people who look like us.

Ask students to read the extract from the magazine and answer the first question. Then refer them to the accompanying photographs. Ask students if they recognise the people in the photographs and why they are used to illustrate this article. (Andrew Lloyd-Webber and Sarah Brightman, Mick and Bianca Jagger, Ivan and Samantha Lendl.)

Ask students to work in groups of two or four to make a questionnaire based on the one started in their book.

Students then complete their own questionnaire, working in pairs within their group, taking it in turn to ask and answer questions. As they finish, get them to check the questions they asked, ready for asking other people.

If possible, students should carry out the next stage, the survey itself, outside the classroom. If they are in an English-speaking country or a town with concentrated tourist areas where English-speaking people are likely to converge, suggest they conduct their survey in these places. Other possibilities are that they try the questionnaire out on English-speaking family and friends, or on students in other classes. If none of these are possible, then students ask other students in their class.

Ask each group to decide from their results how far the psychologist's hypothesis is correct. Then collate the results from each group. If you have a class noticeboard or wish to continue the class magazine from English in Action in Unit 1, then selected questionnaires could provide interesting class reading.

Language review 2

a
1 D is heavier than F but not as heavy as E.
2 E is richer than D but not as rich as F.
3 F's job is as interesting as E's job, and more interesting than D's job.
4 E works as hard as D but not as hard as F.

b
1 as
2 than
3 as
4 as
5 from
6 than

c
1 He used to do a lot of exercise but now he doesn't.
2 He didn't use to drink very much but now he drinks a lot.
3 He used to have a lot of free time but now he doesn't.
4 He used to enjoy life but now he doesn't.

d
1 Where did you use to live?
2 What type of music did you use to listen to?
3 What did you use to do at the weekend?
4 Did you use to have enough money?
5 Did you often go to the cinema? (or Did you go to the cinema often?)

f
1 look
2 is
3 is
4 looks
5 is

3 Traveller's check

LANGUAGE CONTENT

Productive language
- Selected travel objects
- *Going to* vs *will* (decisions about the future)
- *Get on/off/into/out of* + transport
- *To catch* + transport
- *Really/quite* + verb
- Holiday activities
- *Can't stand* + *-ing* form

- Superlatives
- *Instead of* + noun
- Beginning and ending telephone calls
- *And/but/or/because*

Receptive language
- Vocabulary relating to price/weather/clothes/hotel/transport/times

1 Preparation

AIMS

- To revise/teach vocabulary of travel objects.
- To raise awareness of stress patterns in compound words.

1 Students decide which objects listed can be found in the photograph at the top of the page.

Answers

You can see: sunglasses, an alarm clock, a map, a camera, a passport, traveller's cheques, foreign currency, a walkman and a briefcase.
You can't see: a toothbrush, suntan lotion or an electric shaver.

Put students in pairs to do the exercise. Suggest they look up unknown vocabulary in the mini-dictionary on page 138, if necessary.

At feedback, elicit the names of the objects not illustrated, by showing pictures or the real objects, if you have them.

2+3 Students decide which of the vocabulary is made up of separate words and which are compound words. They check their answers against the tape.

Answers/Tapescript

2 **Two separate words:** alarm clock, traveller's cheques, foreign currency, suntan lotion, electric shaver
Compound words: walkman, passport, briefcase, toothbrush, suntan, sunglasses.
Neither column: map, camera

3 The stress on the compound words is on the first syllable.
a 'walkman	a 'toothbrush
a 'passport	'suntan
a 'briefcase	'sunglasses

Students continue to work in pairs and check their answers with another pair as they finish.

Play the tape or say the compound words yourself so students can check their answers and mark the word stress. Highlight this typical stress pattern in compound words. Ask students what other compound words they know. Then elicit the words made up of two separate words and check pronunciation.

To get further practice of the words, get students to tell their partner which things on the list they usually take/don't take on holiday.

2 Listening

AIMS

- To develop the skill of listening for specific information.
- To highlight the range of ways of pronouncing the letter 'a' and to practise the intonation pattern used when saying lists.

1+2 Students listen to the tape and answer the questions in their book. They listen again and note which things from the photograph at the top of the page Martine is taking with her.

Tapescript

CARL: Martine, you are lucky, you know, going to Paris for the weekend. I wish I was coming with you.
MARTINE: Me too. Trouble is, I've got to work.
CARL: Yeah, but you enjoy your work. Anyway, it's better than going to Philip's for dinner.

35

MARTINE: Oh, I wanted to go.

CARL: Well, I don't. In fact, I don't know why I'm going.

MARTINE: Well, I'll think about you when I'm in my nice, comfortable first-class hotel. . .

CARL: Yeah, you do that. Look, you'd better hurry. You're going to miss the plane if you're not careful. Which of these things on the bed do you need?

MARTINE: I'll take my sunglasses, my walkman and the map.

CARL: What do you need a map for?

MARTINE: To get to the conference hall from the hotel.

CARL: Oh right. Well, what else do you need? What about the camera?

MARTINE: No, I don't think so. No time to take photographs.

CARL: What, no time at all?

MARTINE: No, it's a meeting. I'm not going to be a tourist. Pass me my passport and traveller's cheques, will you? They're over there on the table.

CARL: OK. Here you are.

MARTINE: Now, where's my briefcase? I need those papers for the meeting.

CARL: Here it is. There's the taxi. Come on let's go. Now, are you sure you don't want to take your camera?

Answers

1
1 Martine.
2 She is going to Paris by plane (and taxi).
3 She is going to a business meeting.
4 He is going to have dinner at Philip's.
2 She decides to take her sunglasses, a walkman, a map, her passport, traveller's cheques and her briefcase (not her camera).

Establish that Martine is a woman and Carl a man so they recognise the names when they hear them. Give students time to read the questions and query any unknown vocabulary before they listen.

Let students compare their answers after listening. If there are discrepancies, play the tape again before they go on to the next task.

Pronunciation: letter 'a'; saying lists

Tapescript

I'll pack my sunglasses, my walkman and a map.

Answers

1
/eɪ/ take/shaver/briefcase
/ɑː/ sunglasses/passport/alarm
/ɔː/ walkman
/ə/ a/camera/walkman/alarm
/æ/ map/suntan/traveller's/camera
2
1 *and* appears once.
2 a comma.

Refer students to the model sentence and questions in their book. After listening to the tape, let them work together to find other words with a similar pronunciation of the letter 'a'. Encourage early finishers to add other words to their groups.

Elicit the correct use of commas and 'and' in lists referring to the model sentence. In a monolingual class, get students to translate the model sentence and say it to one another, checking each other's intonation. In multilingual classes, students say the sentence to themselves.

Ask students to compare their own intonation with Martine's words on the tape. They then repeat Martine's words imitating her intonation, rising as new things are listed and falling when the list is complete.

Demonstrate the instructions for this activity. Seat students in one or a number of circles of about nine students each. Sit in one circle and ask the student on your left to say one thing she will take on holiday to elicit *I'll take X*. You then take the part of Student B, in the example in the students' book, by repeating Student A's sentence and adding another object eg. *I'll take X and Y*. Tell Student C, sitting on your right, to continue. Point at Student A while Student C repeats her sentence, at yourself as he adds your addition and at himself as he adds something new eg. *I'll take X, Y and Z.*

Leave the circle and designate someone new as Student A. Each circle begins the game with each student in turn remembering and adding a new object to the list. Encourage students to continue going round the circle for as long as they can.

3 Grammar: *going to* vs *will*

AIM

- To contrast *going to* and *will*.

1+2 Students answer questions about the British Rail advertisement and deduce the use of *will* for spontaneous decisions.

Answers

1 Every 30 minutes
2
1 London
2 Her attraction to the man.
3 *I'll catch the next train.*

Establish that the advertisement is for trains, showing that they run frequently (every 30 minutes). Elicit answers to the rest of the questions open-class.

3–5 Students deduce the different uses of *going to* and *will*, then complete the dialogues with *going to* or *will*, and finally practise the dialogues with two other students.

Answers

3
1 a)   2 b)

NB Answers

It isn't necessary to say *going to go* because it would be repeating the verb *go*. It is necessary to say *catch* because a main verb is needed to give meaning.

4
1 'll (will)
2 's (is) going to
3 're (are) going to
4 'll (will)
5 're (are) going to

Refer students to the sentences in the grammar box. Ask the check questions open-class, and point out that the contraction *'ll* is generally used in natural speech.

Students do Exercise 4 individually, checking with a partner when they have finished. Then put students in groups of three to practise the dialogues. As they finish, get them to change roles and practise the dialogues again.

4 Vocabulary: transport

AIMS

- To revise/extend transport vocabulary.
- To introduce verbs frequently used with transport vocabulary.
- To give further practice of *going to*.

1 Students pool their knowledge of transport vocabulary, discussing what transport you catch at the places listed. They then discuss each form of transport, deciding whether it collocates with *get into/out of* or *get on/off*.

Answers

1
a bus stop: a bus; a station: a train; a coach station: a coach; a taxi rank: a taxi; an airport: a plane; an underground station: an underground (tube) train

2
a) and b) taxis
c) and d) buses, trains, coaches, planes, underground trains

Put students in groups of three or four to answer the questions. To follow up, get students to list as many other forms of transport as they know between them (eg. bicycle, horse, etc.).

At feedback, use pictures to check the names of the different forms of transport.

Mime getting on/off a bicycle and elicit the appropriate words. Then mime getting into/out of a car. Ask students to make a note of the correct verb before each word on their transport list.

2 Students use the transport vocabulary (get on/off, etc.) and the Present Continuous form to describe the two pictures to each other, finding the eight differences between them.

Answers

1 In picture A the businessman is getting out of the taxi, in picture B the businessman is getting in to the taxi.
2 In picture A the young woman is getting on her bike, in picture B the young woman is getting off her bike.
3 In picture A the woman and children are getting on the bus, in picture B the woman and children are getting off the bus.

4 In picture A the two boys are getting off the bus, in picture B they are running to catch the bus.

5 In picture A the middle-aged man with a beard is getting in to a car, in picture B he is getting out of the car.

6 In picture A the woman is walking in to the sweet shop, in picture B she is walking out of the shop.

7 In picture A the old woman is eating an ice cream, in picture B she is eating a banana.

8 In picture A the man is carrying two suitcases, in picture B he is carrying one suitcase.

Students work in pairs and turn to different pages in their book. Make sure they realise that they should find the differences by speaking, not by looking at both pictures. To ensure this, get students to sit facing each other while they do the activity. To demonstrate, take the part of one student. Use the Present Continuous to describe something happening in Student A's picture, eliciting a difference from Student B. Leave them to work in their pairs to find the other seven differences.

3 Students tell one another what they are going to do after class and where they are going/ how they are going to get there.

Students talk in groups of three or four, using the new language to discuss their after-school activities. Listen in and, if you wish to correct some of their mistakes, note them down and have a correction spot at the end of the activity. (For advice on correction, see page 16.)

5 Speaking

AIMS

- To revise -ing form for activities, going to, like + -ing form and holiday vocabulary.
- To extend students' repertoire of verbs expressing feelings + -ing form.
- To provide practice in using quite/really + verbs.

1+2 Students discuss holidays in pairs then work in groups to list how much they enjoy certain holiday activities.

Introduce the topic of holidays by telling students where you intend to go for your next holiday. Ask one or two students about their preferences and then put students in pairs to discuss the questions in Exercise 1. Circulate as the students talk and help with any vocabulary problems as they arise.

As students finish, get them to join another pair to go through the activities again, listing any they all agree on in the three categories: *really enjoy, quite like* and *can't stand*.

At feedback ask different groups what they agreed on and ask students to listen out for anything the whole class seems to agree on. Check that students stress *really, like* and *stand* as they give their information.

6 Reading

AIMS

- To develop the skill of reading for specific information.
- To revise/extend students' use of superlatives.

1 Students read the article and complete the chart in their book.

Answers

	Interesting things to see/do	Things to buy	Best time to go
Sri Lanka	ruins of ancient cities, green tea plantations, golden beaches	precious stones and sapphires	any time
Cairo	gold mask of Tutankhamun, the Sphinx, the Pyramids, bazaars, churches, mosques, restaurants	local crafts. eg. carpets and gold jewellery	September –May (not June to August)
Bangkok	shops, hotels, nightclubs, markets, the Grand Palace, religious temples	silk, jewellery and fake 'Rolex' watches	November to February

Introduce the article by asking if students have been to any of the places mentioned. If they have, elicit their opinions of interesting things to see/do/buy.

38

Students read the article and complete the chart. Make sure they realise that they do not have to understand every word.

As they finish reading, get them to compare their notes with a partner. Finally, elicit answers open-class.

Grammar: superlatives

1-2 Students look at the example sentence and find the irregular superlative of *good*. They then look for other examples of superlatives in the article. They list the adjectives the superlatives come from and deduce the rules of form. Finally students use words from each box in their book to create true sentences using superlatives.

Answers:

1
1 good
2 worst. It is describing the weather.

2
1 **Sri Lanka:** friendliest, most beautiful, best
   Bangkok: hottest, most sophisticated, (worst)
   Cairo: largest, oldest, happiest, friendliest, best
2 a) Regular one-syllable adjectives: Put *the* before the adjective and *-est* at the end of the adjective. eg. old – *the* old*est*
   b) One-syllable adjectives ending in *e*: Put *-st* at the end of the adjective. eg. large – the large*st*
   c) One-syllable adjectives ending in one vowel and one consonant: Double the final consonant, then add *-est*. eg. hot – the hot*test*
   d) Two-syllable adjectives ending in *-y*: Change *y* to *i* before adding *est*. eg. friendly – the friendl*iest*
   e) Two, three or more syllable adjectives: Put *the most* before the adjective. eg. beautiful – *the most* beautiful
   f) Irregular superlative: *good – the best*; *bad – the worst*

3
Bangkok is the hottest place in Thailand.
The Nile is the longest river in Africa.
Paris is the largest city in France.
China is the most populated country in Asia.
Everest is the highest mountain in the world.

Write the model sentence on the board and ask students the questions in Exercise 1 open-class.

Students work individually or in pairs to find other superlatives in the article.

They work together to decide which adjectives

each superlative comes from. Then elicit the rules of form open-class.

You could set up Exercise 3 as a competition, the aim being to finish first, having used each word once only and having created correct sentences.

7 Speaking

AIMS

- To provide opportunities for using *going to/will* for decisions.
- To introduce *instead of* + noun to present alternatives.
- To provide telephone speaking practice.

1-3 Students answer questions and decide which holiday from the article they would prefer to go on. They then make changes to their plans in order to go on holiday with another student.

Ask students to read the article again and to note answers to the three questions.

Check the questions students need to ask to elicit this information open-class. Then get students to mill around asking and answering as many other students as possible. Their task is to listen out for the student whose ideal holiday most resembles theirs.

They then sit with this student and discuss what changes they should make to enable them to go on holiday together. Give an example yourself using *instead of*. If they have found another student who wants exactly the same as they do, then they should go to Exercise 4.

4+5 Students list questions to ask the travel agent and then roleplay the telephone conversation with their partner.

As students prepare their questions, help them by feeding in vocabulary and answering queries. Check a selection of the questions open-class before they go on to the roleplay. Possible questions might include:

- What's the weather like in X in August?
- What clothes should I take with me?
- How will I get there?
- How long does it take to get there?
- How much does it cost to get there?
- What time does the plane/train leave/arrive?
  Refer students to the beginning and end of the

39

telephone call in their books. Demonstrate intonation by incorporating these into short model phone calls with individual students, before they have the complete conversation, sitting back-to-back with their partner.

To finish the activity, ask students what information they were given by the travel agent.

If your class is in Britain, encourage some students to really phone these or other travel agents with their questions. They then report the information they have found out back to the class.

English in action

AIMS

- To provide writing practice using language from the unit.
- To revise the use of the conjunctions *and/but/or/because* in sentences.

1+2 Students make questions from prompts and then discuss them with another student/s from the same town or country.

Answers

1
1 What are the most interesting tourist sights in your country?
2 Who is the most famous singer or entertainer in your country?
3 What is the most typical food in your country?
4 What is the most popular drink in your country?
5 What are the best things to buy in your country?
6 When is the best time to visit your country?

Give students time to make the questions from the prompts individually. Organise them to work together and get them to check their questions and answers.

3+4 Students write answers to their questions in complete sentences. They then organise their sentences into a paragraph, using conjunctions to link the sentences.

NB Answers

a) but   c) or
b) and   d) because

In a monolingual class, get students to speak and later write about the same country/town in pairs/small groups and turn the activity into a competition. The best articles will be chosen by a travel company for inclusion in their brochure.

In a multilingual class, students speak and later write about their own country either individually or in pairs/small groups with students from their own country.

Students work together to write their short article. Refer them to the NB box *and/or/but/because* before they start Exercise 4.

5 Students read each other's articles to decide which place they would most like to visit.

If you have continued the idea of a class magazine, begun in Unit 1, then these articles could form the basis of a new issue. Otherwise, they could be displayed in the classroom or circulated in class.

If the activity has been set up as a competition, get students to read the articles and vote on the best one/s.

Language review 3

a
1 are going to   4 am going to
2 am going to   5 will
3 will
b
1 the most expensive   5 the friendliest
2 the hottest   6 the most comfortable
3 the straightest   7 the cheapest
4 the fastest   8 the longest
c
1 I really hate being late.
2 I quite enjoy watching TV some of the time.
3 I quite like going shopping when it's not too crowded.
4 I really love visiting good restaurants on holiday.
5 I really can't stand Pedro's mother.

4 *Necessary business*

LANGUAGE CONTENT

Productive language
- *Should/have to/don't have to* (obligation)
- Jobs and qualities
- *Should/shouldn't* (advice)
- Everyday activities
- Possessive pronouns: *mine/yours/hers/his/ours/theirs*

- *Let's . . ./Why don't we . . .* + verb (suggestions)

Receptive language
- Words which collocate with *time: pass/waste/manage/spend*
- Business/management vocabulary

1 Preparation

AIMS

- To introduce *should/have to/don't have to* for obligation.
- To provide personalised speaking practice.

1 Students discuss accepted behaviour for visiting friends.

Students look at the chart individually and decide what happens in their country.

In monolingual classes, ask students to check their ideas in a small group to see if there are any differences between the conventions of particular families or groups of friends. In multilingual classes, students work in mixed nationality groups to exchange information.

Since all information of this sort is subjective, encourage disagreement and anecdotal contributions at feedback. Ask students who have been to English-speaking countries to contribute information on these places. If nobody has this knowledge, get them to question you. Suggestions for you to include about Britain are as follows:

People usually dress up a bit to visit friends if there is a formal invitation and/or a special occasion is being celebrated. Otherwise, dress is usually quite casual. You should arrive on time. If you know you are going to be late, ring. A small present is appreciated, usually a bottle of wine. Good friends often help one another with the washing up after the meal and would usually ask before using the phone. Coffee is not a sign that the evening has finished. It is often served immediately after the meal and may be served away from the table while people chat.

2 Grammar: *should/have to/don't have to*

AIMS

- To teach/revise ways of expressing degrees of obligation.

1+2 Students match sentences using *should/have to/don't have to* to their definitions. They then use these forms to write sentences summarising the discussion in the last exercise.

Answers

1
a) have to - necessary
b) don't have to - not necessary
c) should - a good idea

NB Answers

A verb, not *to* comes immediately after *should*.

Write the words *a good idea/necessary/not necessary* on the board and elicit the model sentences from the book. Give students time to copy the sentences matched to the words into their notebooks for future reference.

Refer students to the NB box *should vs have to* and remind them when to/not to use *to* before the main verb. They then write sentences based on the prompts in Exercise 1 Preparation. They check their sentences with another student.

3 Pronunciation: *have to*

AIMS
- To highlight the sound difference between stressed and unstressed *do*.
- To signal that a contracted form is not possible between the subject and the verb *have to*.

Tapescript

1 Do you have to work? Yes, I do.
2 I have to work.
  I don't have to work.

Answers

1
Do is unstressed in the question. *Do* is stressed in the answer.
2
1 *work*
2 You can contract *do not (don't)*. You cannot contract *have to* (*I have to work* **not** *I've to work*).

Get students to repeat the model question and short answer from the tape and answer the first question.

Before they listen to the second part of the tape, remind them what *contractions* are (eg *cannot = can't*).

They listen and write the sentences down as dictation either from you or the tape.

They then answer the questions open-class.

3 Students ask and answer in pairs about things they have to/don't have to do every day.

Demonstrate a possible dialogue. Tell the students something you have to do every day and ask one of them if they have to do the same thing. Elicit and drill the question form *Do you have to X?*

Give students time to think of things they *have to/don't have to* do. Put them in pairs to exchange their information. As a final check on meaning, get them to look at the Snoopy cartoon at the bottom of the page. Ask them *How independent is the bird?* This should prompt them to retell the story, using *have to/don't have to* as it occurs naturally.

4 Speaking

AIMS

- To develop the skill of reading for specific information.
- To encourage freer speaking practice, using *should/have to/don't have to*.

1 Students read the text on tipping and complete the chart in their book.

Answers

Job	How much?
waiter	10%
hairdresser	10%
taxi driver	10%
cinema/theatre usherette	0%
petrol pump attendant	0%
porter	a little per case
milkman dustman postman	possibly a Christmas box

Elicit the word *tip* by asking students what it is called if you give more money than it says on your bill.

Students copy the chart into their notebooks and read the text in order to complete it. They check their answers with another student as they finish, and then with the class as a whole.

2-4 Students discuss tipping conventions in their own country based on the questions in the book.

Put students in groups of four or five to discuss the questions, mixing nationalities in a multilingual class. At feedback, encourage further discussion.

5 Vocabulary: jobs and qualities

AIMS

- To teach/revise jobs vocabulary.
- To teach a lexical set of personal qualities.
- To provide further practice in expressing degrees of obligation.

1 Students pool their knowledge of the listed vocabulary. They look up words they don't know in their mini-dictionary and check word stress.

Put students in groups of three or four. Tell them to check they understand each word. If possible, they explain unknown vocabulary to one another and list any that they all don't know. They divide this vocabulary between them and look it up in the mini-dictionary on page 138, reading the definitions to one another and checking the word stress.

2 Students match jobs to qualities.

Give students time to do this in their groups and then check their ideas open-class. Accept any answers, provided they can be justified. Get them to extend some of their definitions by adding *because* to their original sentences eg. A manager has to be organised *because* s/he has so much to do.

3 Students find out about the qualities needed for fellow students' jobs or for jobs they might do in the future.

Check the questions for finding out about jobs: *What do you do?/What would you like to do?* Elicit and drill: *What qualities do you need for the job?*

Students mill around the classroom, asking as many people the questions as possible. Ask one or two students to report back to the class on anything interesting they found out.

4 Students prioritise the most important qualities of a teacher.

Elicit and write on the board some qualities that everyone agrees are important for a teacher.

Tell students to work in their groups to come up with an order of importance for these words.

As groups come to a consensus, put them to

work with another group. Their task now is to reach another consensus. Depending on the size of the class, you can keep joining groups together until the whole class form one large group with one list of qualities in an agreed order. If your class is too large for this, combine groups only once or twice and then get class feedback and have the final discussion open-class.

6 Reading

AIMS

- To develop the skill of reading for specific information based on prediction.
- To provide further practice of *should* and *don't have to*.

1, 2+3 Students work in pairs to answer the questions on time management. They then discuss a variety of management problems, using *should* and *don't have to*. Finally they check their solutions against ideas in a checklist written by management consultants.

Introduce the subject of time management by asking the questions in Exercise 1 open-class. (Tell students things which make time pass slowly or quickly for you eg. when someone is late or you are waiting at the dentist's. Tell them ways you waste time, like making another cup of coffee before correcting homework, or how you manage time well by marking work before you leave school.)

Put students in pairs to answer the questions. Ask them to cover the management checklist while they do this exercise.

When they have made their decisions, they uncover the checklist and compare their answers.

At feedback, encourage discussion of any of the problems where students don't agree with the consultants.

7 Speaking

AIMS

- To provide further practice of verb + *ing* form and *have to*.
- To revise *going to* for future plans.

Elicit a few activities students do regularly. Ask one or two students if they enjoy a particular thing or if they feel they have to do it. Check that they use the *-ing* form after *enjoy* and the infinitive (without *to*) of the verb after *have to*.

Refer them to the list of activities in their book. Put them in pairs to decide which they enjoy doing and which they have to do.

Ask a few students for their answers to a random selection of the activities listed and elicit other activities they have thought of.

2 Students complete a diary for the next day and then tell their partner about some of the things they plan to do.

Demonstrate what they have to do by talking about your own plans and completing a timetable on the board. Give students time to complete a timetable of their own. Encourage them to write short entries rather than whole sentences and then to talk about their plans in more detail.

8 Listening

AIMS

- To develop the skill of listening for general and specific information.
- To stimulate discussion on the topic of good/ bad managers.
- To revise the use of *should/shouldn't* for advice.
- To teach and give practice of possessive pronouns.

1-4 Students briefly discuss the question of punctuality. They listen to two recordings of a manager dealing with an employee who is late for work and answer the questions in their book.

Tapescript

2

MANAGER: Ah, there you are, Jim. Late again.

JIM: I'm sorry, but . . .

MANAGER: Well sorry's no good, is it? This is the third time in three weeks. The company doesn't exist for you, you know. Everyone else gets here on time. Look! All here, working away. Doing your work, as well as theirs. It's not fair, is it?

JIM: No, but . . .

MANAGER: No, it's not fair. What have you got to say for yourself?

JIM: Nothing.

MANAGER: Nothing. Well, if you come in late again, you won't have to come back. We don't want people who can't be punctual.

3

MANAGER: Ah, Jim, there you are.

JIM: I'm sorry but . . . I can't manage . . .

MANAGER: Now, what's the trouble?

JIM: I'll go and start work.

MANAGER: No. I want to know why you are late.

JIM: I'm tired.

MANAGER: Yes?

JIM: Well, I live with my old mum and I look after her without any help but the week before last she had a bad fall, (Oh dear) she fell down the stairs. She's eighty-one you know and she can't be left alone. I've got someone to come and look after her every morning at eight o'clock but sometimes she's late and I have to wait for her.

MANAGER: Yes. I see. Well, you organise things at home, so if you have to be late a few mornings, that's OK, we'll cover for you.

Answers

2

1 No, he's been late before. Yes it does.
2 If Jim is late again, he'll get the sack.

3

1 Because he had to wait for the woman who looks after his mother.
2 She tells him not to worry, that they will cover for him when necessary.

Ask the questions in Exercise 1 open-class to introduce students to the topic of punctuality.

Before playing the first interview, establish that the office worker's name is Jim. Give students time to read the questions and query any vocabulary

Play the tape. When students have told you how they feel about the manager's attitude, tell them to listen to the alternative interview and answer the next set of questions.

After playing the tape again, if necessary, get the students to discuss the two management styles open-class. Put them into groups of three to list advice for the 'bad' manager using *should*.

Grammar: possessive pronouns

1-4 Students study examples of possessive pronouns in sentences to deduce rules for their use and form. They complete a chart and then play a memory game to practise the new language.

Answers

1
1 theirs - their work
  hers - her letters
  his - his phone
  mine - my clients
2 the possessive pronoun is used to avoid repetition of the noun.

2

my - *mine*	our - *ours*
your - *yours*	your - *yours*
her - *hers*	their - *theirs*
his - *his*	

Either write the model sentences on the board or refer students to them in their book. Students answer the questions open-class and then work individually or in pairs to complete the chart. They check their answers with another student. At feedback, confirm that generally they add '*s*' to the possessive adjective to form the possessive pronoun.

Organise the next activity as a game. Ask everyone to give you a personal belonging (a pen, a wallet, a comb, etc.) and put them out around the class. Students then circulate in pairs checking they remember who each thing belongs to. Demonstrate the activity by pointing at one or two things and then at the students you think they belong to, saying: *This is hers.*

That is his. Pairs could check things they are unsure of by asking the student concerned: *Is that yours?*

After the activity, hold up each object eliciting its name (*It's a pen.*) and then asking: *Whose is this?* Encourage students to say *It's mine* to reclaim their possession.

English in action

AIMS

- To provide freer practice of language from the unit.
- To revise/teach ways of making suggestions using *Let's . . ./Why don't we . . .?*

1 Students consider advertisements for unusual products and answer the questions in their book.

Set the situation for the roleplay, asking if any students have their own business and what products they sell. Refer students to the products advertised on the page and give them a few minutes in pairs to answer the questions together.

2–4 Students work in groups of business people or bank managers, following the instructions for their role. They use *Let's. . ./Why don't we . . .?* to make suggestions.

Divide the class into groups of four or five. One person in each group is a bank manager, the others are business people. The business people work together in their group and all the bank managers form one group and work together.

Tell students to read the appropriate role card, checking that they have understood the instructions with someone who has the same role.

Elicit ways of giving suggestions, drilling the model sentences in the book.

These expressions can now be used by students as they work in their groups to prepare for the interview. Circulate in the class as they do this, feeding in vocabulary or repairing breakdowns in communication, as necessary. (You could note common errors for a correction spot at the end of the activity. See page 16.) The business people need to list their qualities individually but can complete the rest of the form as a group. The bank managers need to make questions they can ask during the interview.

Bank managers interview groups separately. They speak to each group in turn, noting their answers and changing groups every five minutes. Finally they confer as a group to decide who to award the money to. While they are doing this, put the business people into new groups so that they can tell one another about *their* group's product.

Finally the bank managers explain their decision to the whole class.

Language review 4

a
1 don't have to
2 should
3 doesn't have to
4 do (you) have to
5 should
6 has to
7 don't have to

b
1 It's his.
2 It's mine.
3 It's hers.
4 It's theirs.
5 It's ours.
6 It's yours.

c Suggested answers
1 B: Me too. Why don't we go to the cinema?
2 B: OK. Let's have a drink.
3 B: Yes. Why don't we try to meet some English people?
4 B: Let's go to that new shoe shop in town.
5 B: Why don't we go for a run?

5 Consolidation

LANGUAGE REVISED

- Vocabulary of countries, nationalities, transport, restaurants and languages
- Superlatives
- Ways of deducing unknown vocabulary
- Word order in inverted questions and questions with auxiliary verb *do*

- The alphabet
- *Should/have to/don't have to* (obligation)
- Past Simple and *used to*
- *Going to* vs *will* (decisions)
- *Let's . . . /why don't we . . .?* for making suggestions
- Classroom equipment

1 Across cultures: lifestyles

AIMS

- To revise vocabulary of countries/nationalities/languages/transport.
- To revise superlatives.
- To provide an opportunity for personalised spoken practice.

1 Students read the headings in the newspaper article and answer the questions in their book.

Answers

British (English)
German (German)
Portuguese (Portuguese)
Irish (Gaelic and English)
Spanish (Spanish, Castillian, Catalan, Basque, Galician)
Belgian (French and Flemish)
Dutch (Dutch)
Luxemburger (French, Letzeburgesch and German)
Italian (Italian)
French (French)
Greek (Greek)
Danish (Danish)

Lead in by asking students to name the first twelve countries to join the European Community. Then refer them to the article to check their answers and to name the nationalities and languages of each country with a partner. Refer students to the introductory paragraph to help them predict the content of the article.

2+3 Students read the article and answer questions a)–l).

Answers

a) Britain	g) Portugal
b) Holland	h) Italy
c) France	i) Belgium
d) Greece	j) Spain
e) Denmark	k) Ireland
f) Luxembourg	l) Germany

Give students time to check their predictions and the vocabulary in the questions. They then find the answers to the questions in the text and compare their answers with another student, before confirming them open-class.

4+5 Students read the text again to find other interesting information. They then name three other countries they know and make superlative sentences about them.

Give students time to read the text more thoroughly to find something they find surprising to tell the rest of the class. As they tell the class their interesting fact, encourage them to explain to one another any words which other students find problematic.

Put students in groups of three to name three further countries. They should check they know the nationality and language of these countries.

They then pool information in order to make sentences about the countries, using superlatives.

They read their sentences out to the class, who have to guess which country each sentence is about.

6 Students say when and how they last went to any of the countries mentioned.

Do this open-class encouraging students with particularly interesting experiences to say more.

2 Thinking about learning: strategies

AIMS

- To help students deduce unknown language from context.
- To revise question formation.
- To provide practice in using the alphabet.

1 Students match the definitions to the new vocabulary in the article

Answers

a)	sweet-toothed	h)	to go on strike
b)	housing	i)	single-parent (families)
c)	EC	j)	unemployed
d)	health-conscious	k)	dishwasher
e)	consume	l)	rainfall
f)	illiterate	m)	smoker
g)	pet	n)	illegitimate

Demonstrate what students have to do by eliciting the answer to the first question open-class.

Students work in pairs to find the vocabulary and then compare their answers with another pair before checking with the class as a whole.

At feedback, make sure pronunciation of new vocabulary is accurate and ask students what clues, if any, helped them find the words.

2 Students match the new vocabulary to the linguistic clues in their book.

Answers

a) sweet-toothed – 2
b) housing – 3
c) EC – 5
d) health-conscious – 2
e) consume – 3, 4
f) illiterate –1
g) pet – 4
h) to go on strike – 4
i) single-parent (families) – 2
j) unemployed – 1
k) dishwasher – 2
l) rainfall – 2
m) smoker – 1
n) illegitimate – 1

Again, begin the exercise open-class so students understand what to do. Ask them which two words they can see in the new word *sweet-*

toothed and ask them which linguistic clue refers to this (the parts of a compound word). They then work with their partner to list which clues they used to find the other new words.

3 Students rearrange words to make questions.

Answers

1 Can I say X?
2 What is the English for X?
3 How do you spell that?
4 How do you pronounce this word?
5 Can you say that again, please?
6 What is this called in English?
7 Can you say that more slowly, please?

Refer students to the jumbled words and re-order the first one on the board as an example. Give them time to rearrange the words individually and then to check with their partner.

As you check their answers as a class, make sure that students use correct stress and intonation.

4 Students list the questions they have made in the correct category.

Answers

Questions with auxiliary do
How do you spell that?
How do you pronounce this word?

Inverted questions
Can I say X?
What is the English for X?
Can you say that again please?
What is this called in English?
Can you say that more slowly please?

Use the examples to remind students about the two types of question form. Students then work together to categorise the questions they made from the jumbled words in the previous exercise.

5 Students ask questions to learn the names of any classroom vocabulary they don't know.

Give an example by having the dialogue in the example with one student. Then sit students in circles of about six or seven. Tell them to hold up or point to classroom objects they want to know the name of. Anyone in the group who knows can answer and everyone should compile a list of the vocabulary. If nobody knows, then students should put the object to one side and ask the whole class or teacher at the end. As students run out of items, refer them to the illustrations in the book.

At feedback, check spelling, pronunciation and word stress. Supply the vocabulary for any objects the class were unable to name.

3 Language in context: eating out

AIMS

- To check/teach restaurant vocabulary.
- To revise the grammatical structures introduced in Units 1–4.
- To provide an opportunity for freer spoken practice.

1 Students discuss things they should/shouldn't do when first eating out with a new friend.

Use the photograph to establish the theme of restaurants. Set the scene of taking a new friend to a restaurant. Ask students to discuss the ideas listed in pairs.

Lead from their answers in feedback to set the scene for the listening exercise to come.

2+3 Students listen to the people ordering food and answer the questions in their book. They listen again for particular expressions which incorporate a variety of the language from the last four units.

Tapescript

WOMAN: I really enjoyed seeing Paula last week, didn't you?
MAN: Yes, she seems to love her work.
WOMAN: Yes, it's great. She used to have problems with her boss, you know.
MAN: I know but things are better now and she . . .
WAITRESS: Excuse me. Are you ready, or would you like a few more minutes?
WOMAN: No, I think we're ready, aren't we, Paul?
MAN: Yes, I think so.
WAITRESS: Fine. Now, what would you like?
WOMAN: Oh dear. I can't remember what I de . . . Oh yes, I'll have the minestrone soup to start with and then . . . what's today's special?
WAITRESS: Um, it's Spaghetti Carbonara.
WOMAN: What is that, exactly?

WAITRESS: It's spaghetti with bacon in a cream sauce.
WOMAN: Hm. That sounds nice. I'll have that. And a green salad please.
WAITRESS: Right. And what would you like, Sir?
MAN: I'll have the soup too, please. And then the Lasagne.
WAITRESS: Fine. Now, what would you like to drink?
WOMAN: A bottle of house red, please, and can we have some . . .

Answers

2
1 Italian (spaghetti carbonara, lasagne, etc.)
2 A friend, the wine
3 The waitress
3
b), d), e), f), i), j)

Refer students to the couple in the photograph and explain that they are going to listen to them. Give students time to read the questions. Play the tape and let them confer before you check their answers.

Give them time to read the expressions a)–j). Make sure they realise that their task is to find the ones which are *exactly* the same as those they hear. Play the tape then check answers open-class.

4 Students listen again to change or complete the incorrect or incomplete sentences.

Answers

a) I really *enjoyed* seeing Paula last week.
b) She used to have problems with *her boss*.
c) Things are *better* now.
f) I'll have the minestone soup *to start with*.
g) What is *that*, exactly?
h) That sounds nice. I'*ll* have that.
i) I'll have the soup *too, please*.

Once students are sure which sentences they need to listen out for, play the tape again as a dictation. You will need to stop the tape every few words to allow students time to write.

Invite individual students to the board to write up the sentences as others dictate what they heard on the tape.

5 Students order a meal from an English menu, asking for clarification if they don't know what particular things are.

Establish that this is a menu of typically English food. Check they understand *starters, main courses* and *sweets* by eliciting typical examples from the students' own country. Elicit students' experiences of eating English food. (They often feel strongly about this, especially if they are studying in Britain.) Explain that the best traditional food is found in homes but also in pubs and some specialist restaurants. Elicit that food from a lot of other countries is widely available (Indian, Chinese, Italian, etc.)

Set the scene: students imagine they are in Porters restaurant. Tell them you are the waiter/waitress and will deal with questions about any dishes they don't know when you take their order. Refer them to the example dialogue.

If possible, arrange the classroom so that small groups are seated round each table as if they were in a restaurant. Give them time to consult the menu and one another as they would in a real restaurant. They need to discuss, in English, what they would like to eat but they can also chat more generally while they wait for their order to be taken. As they do this, study the extended menu below to check you know what is in each dish.

Go from table to table taking their orders. Supply further information about the dishes when they ask.

NB If your class is very large, choose other waiters/waitresses to work with you. While the rest of the class decide what to eat, they also familiarise themselves with the extended menu.

PORTERS
STARTERS
PRAWN COCKTAIL
(prawns and mayonnaise on a bed of lettuce)
FRESH TOMATO SOUP
FARMHOUSE PATE
(coarse chicken liver paté)

MAIN COURSES
All served with roast or new potatoes
and a selection of fresh vegetables (carrots, green beans and courgettes)
STEAK AND KIDNEY PIE
(steak, kidney and mushrooms, cooked with a pastry top)
LANCASHIRE HOT-POT
(stew of potatoes, carrots and lamb)
ROAST BEEF AND YORKSHIRE PUDDING
(a small, savoury pudding made of flour, egg and milk)
CHICKEN AND MUSHROOM PIE

SWEETS
BREAD AND BUTTER PUDDING
(a mixture of bread, butter, sultanas and egg custard)
APPLE CRUMBLE AND CUSTARD
(stewed apples, covered with a fine mixture of sugar, butter and flour. Custard – a sauce made of egg, sugar and milk)
FRESH FRUIT SALAD AND CREAM

---

6 Students decide which restaurant is most appropriate for the six groups of people.

Possible answers

a) Taste Of India
b) The Tageen
c) Italian Graffiti
d) Rose Mango
e) Café Fish
f) The Original Carvery

Put students in pairs and give them time to quickly read the advertisements. Get them to check what type of food each one offers.

Then refer them to the groups of people who want to eat. Give them time to read and check they understand the information about each group.

Make sure they realise that they can allocate each restaurant once only, that there is no one correct answer and that they must reach a group consensus on the answers.

As they finish, put pairs together. They explain their decisions to one another and try to come up with a final agreed answer.

Encourage further discussion at feedback when individual students tell you and the class about their group decisions.

NB In this freer activity, students will use English as best they can. If you wish to correct persistent mistakes, note examples as you hear them and have a correction spot at the end. (For advice on correction, see page 16.)

7+8 Students plan an outing to a restaurant together.

This activity will be all the more motivating if it really ends up in a class outing. If students are studying in London, they could choose between the advertisements in their book or other restaurant advertisements available in newspapers and entertainment magazines.

Students studying in other towns/countries could look at restaurant advertisements from the area they are in. If it is not possible to use advertisements in English, we suggest you use the advertisements in the book as a practice activity. Then use local advertisements to arrange the outing, encouraging students to discuss their preferences in English.

At feedback, students will either need to try to persuade other groups to accept their choice of restaurant, or go out in separate groups. They may like to set up a series of outings in order to try out a variety of restaurants.

Check what you know 1

1 LISTENING

Tapescript

I can't really believe how my life used to be. When I came out of university I just did the logical thing and went into advertising. I didn't really think about it, I got offered this job, the money seemed incredibly good. Everyone I knew thought I was really lucky – expensive sports car, big expense account, lots of business lunches and so on.

One day I saw a terrible car accident. It made me stop and think – what was I doing with my life? Was I working to live or living to work? I decided to change everything and went to live in Spain where I met my wife Rosa. We found this fantastic villa in the country. It was very old, very big but needed a lot of work. I used to live in this tiny flat in the centre of London – about twenty minutes from the office, very convenient but very small. I seemed to be travelling or working all the time, the job was very demanding, I worked terribly hard, basically all day every day.

Now life is just about perfect as far as I'm concerned. I get up when I like, I go into town to do some shopping or go and see friends. We've made lots of friends. I work on the house or on the land. We grow a lot of our own food. The climate is marvellous, not like London. Sometimes I find it hard to believe that my life was ever any different.

1
Now
no expense account
living in Spain
an easy life
lots of friends
fresh, homegrown food
Before
in advertising
lots of money
restaurant food
small accommodation
long working hours
worse weather

2
a) He used to be in advertising.
b) He used to have lots of money.
c) He used to have an expense account.
d) He used to eat restaurant food.
e) He didn't use to live in Spain.
f) He used to live in small accommodation.
g) He used to have long working hours.
h) He didn't use to have an easy life.
i) He didn't use to eat fresh, homegrown food.
j) He didn't use to have lots of friends.
k) He used to live in a country with worse weather.

2 PRONUNCIATION

a'ccountant (3) cre'ative (3) re'porter (3)
ad'vertisement (4) 'interesting (3) inde'pendent (4)
'sunglasses (3) 'camera (2) 'photograph (3)
mus'eum (3)

3 VOCABULARY

a) a toothbrush
b) a hairdresser
c) fit
d) suntan lotion
e) a hat
f) (to be) punctual
g) hardworking
h) awful

4 GRAMMAR

1	quite	6	as
2	most	7	bought
3	used to	8	instead
4	really	9	going
5	had		

5 READING

1 A taxi-driver
2
1 What time does he have to get up?
2 What time do all the people come into the centre of town?
3 What time does a normal day finish?
4 Why does he like picking up foreign tourists?
5 Does he enjoy his job?
6 Why can't he open the window?
7 Is he going to do this work for long ?
8 What is he going to do then?

6 *Obsessions*

LANGUAGE CONTENT

Productive language
• Present Continuous (describing pictures)
• Present Simple (habits)
• Adverbs of frequency
• Present Simple vs Present Continuous

• Don't mind + -*ing* form
• Verbs (everyday actions)

Receptive language
Sports and football vocabulary

1 Preparation

AIMS

• To revise the use of the Present Continuous for describing pictures, the Present Simple for talking about present habits, *used to* for talking about past habits and the adverbs of frequency *always, never* and *sometimes.*

1 Students describe the newspaper illustration in their book, using the Present Continuous.

Answers

A woman is hoovering (vacuuming) her flat. A man is washing his hands. A woman is checking her gas oven.

Elicit the names of the items in the picture (cooker, vacuum cleaner, scrubbing brush, etc) and ask individual students to tell the class what each person is doing. It is only necessary to highlight the use of the Present Continuous if students are not able to use it correctly.

2 Students read the newspaper quotes and answer the questions in their book.

Establish that the quotes are from the same newspaper article as the illustration by asking students to scan them to find which quote goes with which person in the picture. This will give you the chance to clarify any vocabulary problems.

Put students in pairs to discuss the questions in their book.

Elicit the view of a variety of students at feedback, encouraging inter-student discussion.

3+4 Students ask their partner about their present and past habits, using the quotes as a basis for their questions.

Check that students can form Present Simple questions open-class, before they take it in turns to ask about each habit in the quotes. If your class has problems doing this, elicit and drill each question. Otherwise, one or two examples should be enough. Elicit short answers to the first question from a couple of students and refer the class to the examples in speech bubbles for possible natural sounding answers.

As they talk in pairs, listen and interrupt only if commmunication breaks down completely.

As students finish, direct them to Exercise 4, encouraging them to give details about any past habits they may have had using the *used to* structure.

At feedback, ask what interesting things they have found out about their partner's habits.

2 Speaking

AIMS

• To practise the Present Simple form for asking about present habits and routines.
• To revise/teach the adverbs of frequency: *very, quite often* and *occasionally.*

1+2 Students add questions to the questionnaire, then ask another student the questions.

Use the first question in the questionnaire to check students understand the adverbs of frequency. Begin by asking a student open-class *Do you often watch TV?* then ask *How many times a week?* Use the student's answers to help the class decide if this is *very often, quite often, occasionally* or *never.*

Students copy the questionnaire and questions into their notebook. Give them time to write more questions to ask their partner. Encourage them to ask about things they really want to know. If necessary, pair students with someone they don't usually work with.

Students ask all the questions in the questionnaire and tick the column that corresponds to their partner's responses.

At feedback, ask a few students about their partners, eliciting adverbs of frequency in response.

Writing

AIMS

- To highlight and provide written practice of the word order in sentences containing adverbs of frequency.

1+2 Students deduce 'rules' for word order from the examples in their book.

Answers

1
1 often and never   2 never
2 always

Elicit answers to the questions in Exercise 1 open-class.

Remind students that adverbs act differently with the verb *to be*. (It is possible to say: *I am often/never late*, with the adverb coming *after* the verb.)

Use the chart in their book to elicit that the adverbs *never* and *always* can only go before other verbs in the sentence.

3 Students use the information from the questionnaire to write sentences about their partner using adverbs of frequency.

Refer students to the example in their book and give them time to write complete sentences from their questionnaire.

As they finish, they show their work to another student and help correct each other's work.

3 Grammar: Present Continuous vs Present Simple

AIMS

- To highlight the difference between the Present Continuous and the Present Simple.

1 Students deduce the difference in meaning between the two forms, from examples .

Answers

1
1 b)   2 a)

Either refer students to the example sentences in their book and elicit the answers to the questions open-class, or use pictures or mime to elicit the sentences first.

2 Students categorise examples of the two forms.

Answers

Present Continuous	Present Simple
She is smoking.	She smokes 20
Is she smoking?	cigarettes a day.
No, she isn't.	Does she smoke?
Yes, she is.	Yes, she does.
She isn't smoking a cigar.	She doesn't smoke
	cigars.
	No, she doesn't.

Give students time to do this individually and then to check their answers with a partner.

At feedback, invite students to write examples in columns on the board. Remind them of the two question types they studied in Unit One: questions with *do* and inverted questions. Elicit that the Present Simple forms questions with *do* but that the subject and the verb *to be* are inverted in the Present Continuous.

4 Pronunciation: contrastive stress

AIMS

- To introduce and practise the use of contrastive stress to highlight new information in sentences and to correct misinformation.

1+2 Students listen to a dialogue and locate the words with main stress. They then practise the dialogue in pairs.

Answers/Tapescript

A: Are you wearing my jacket?
B: No, it's my jacket, not your jacket.

A: Well, it <u>looks</u> like my jacket.
B: But it <u>isn't</u> your jacket. It's <u>blue,</u> not <u>black</u>.

Give students time to read the dialogue to themselves before they listen. Ask them who they think is speaking.

Point out that the word *jacket* provides the important information in the first sentence and is therefore stressed and underlined. With a strong class, ask them to predict in pairs which other words will be stressed in each sentence or group of words. They then listen and see if they were correct. Weaker classes should listen immediately to locate the sentence stress.

At feedback, elicit that stress changes as new information is given, particularly when one piece of information corrects another piece. Ask students to repeat each sentence as they hear it then practise the dialogue, taking it in turns to begin.

3 Students deduce the habits of a particular student from a photograph of her room.

Answers

She plays tennis. She drinks coffee. She smokes. She plays the guitar. She watches TV. She reads novels. She likes Monet. She likes pop music. She wears black clothes. She listens to tapes.

Do this activity open-class. Refer students to the list of verbs in their book to help them talk about the photograph. If students make the mistake of using the Present Continuous, then correct them on the spot, asking if Jan is actually doing the particular activity *now*.

4 Students find out what Jan is doing at this moment by asking and answering about another photograph.

Answers

She is sitting on her bed. She is listening to tapes on her walkman. She is drinking Coke. She is wearing light blue jeans and a red T-shirt. She is reading a magazine.

Direct students to the instructions and prompts in their book. Highlight the use of the Present Continuous for action going on at the present time. Establish that Student A is looking at what Jan is doing *now*.

At feedback, select an A and a B student to ask and answer the questions open-class. Check they are stressing contrastive information correctly.

5 Listening

AIMS

- To develop the skills of listening for specific information and inference.

1+2 Students describe the illustration and write six sentences saying what is happening in the picture, using the Present Continuous.

Possible answers

2
A young woman is sitting at a table. She is reading a newspaper. A man is holding a coffee cup. A woman is coming into the café. She is shaking her umbrella. A woman outside is looking at her reflection in the café window and straightening her stockings.

Introduce the song by eliciting anything anybody knows about Suzanne Vega. Tell them the picture in their book illustrates the song *Tom's Diner* and check that they know *a diner* is a type of café in America.

Students work in pairs to describe as much as possible in the picture. Circulate in the class and supply vocabulary if necessary.

Refer students to the example sentence in their book to remind them to use the Present Continuous when they write their sentences

3+4 Students collect as many sentences describing the illustration as possible and then listen to see which ones are referred to in the song.

Answers

4
2 The woman who is sitting at the table.

Invite a student to read out one of their sentences. Write their sentence on the board, eliciting the correct form and spelling as you do so. If other students have described the same thing in different words, check these are also acceptable but do not write them on the board.

Invite another student to contribute a sentence describing something else in the picture and proceed as before. When you have as many different Present Continuous sentences as possible on the board, ask students to copy those they have not already written into their notebooks.

Students then listen to the tape, having closed their books, and tick the sentences in their notebook as they are referred to in the song. At feedback, check which of their sentences, if any, are not referred to.

Finally, ask them to decide which person in the picture is singing the song.

At the end of these activities, ask students for their opinions on the singer's feelings, asking them to justify their answers with words from the song.

Play the song again if students would like to hear it, this time following the words in their book.

6 Reading

AIMS

- To revise the names of sports.
- To preteach vocabulary related to football.
- To provide practice in reading for general and specific information.

Ask the first question open-class and write the names of sports they suggest on the board. If a particular word is not understood by someone in the class, ask the student who suggested it to explain or mime to the student who doesn't understand. If possible, have pictures of some sports available to show the class. Before students write any of the vocabulary in their notebooks, check and mark word-stress on the words on the board.

Put students in groups of four or five to answer the other questions. They should explain words to one another where necessary and make a list of any words none of them can understand to ask you later.

At feedback, check all their answers and encourage student-student explanation of problem words before explaining yourself.

Encourage speed reading by setting the task as a competition to see who can find the information most quickly.

Give students time to read the true/false statements before they read the article again. Clarify problems of vocabulary before they read. Elicit the information from the article which shows the example statement is false. (*Glenys . . . will travel anywhere in Britain to see her team in action.*)

As students finish, get them to compare their answers with another student, justifying answers they disagree on, using the text.

Grammar: *don't mind + -ing* form

AIMS

- To highlight and practise the meaning and form of *don't mind*.
- To revise other verbs which take the same form.

1 Students deduce the meaning of *doesn't mind* from the example and answer the question in their book.

Answer

It isn't a problem.

Do this open-class. Write the example on the board and highlight the meaning of *doesn't mind* by eliciting that Glenys travels great distances and this is not always an easy or cheap thing to do. Then ask if this is a problem for Glenys.

2 Students listen and repeat the sentence, differentiating between the sounds /n/ and /ŋ/

Write the phonemic symbols on the board. Encourage students to nasalise the /n/ sound to produce /ŋ/. Get them to mumble the sentence. Then hear one or two examples from individual students.

3 Students put Glenys' activities into the correct columns.

Answers

She enjoys: seeing Swansea play; watching cricket; watching football
She doesn't mind: leaving her son with her parents; having no social life; staying in cheap hotels
She hates: travelling by coach; missing a match

Copy the columns and their headings onto the board and ask students where to put *travelling to see Swansea City play.* As you write it up, ask again *Is 'travelling a long way' generally a positive or negative thing? Is it a problem for Glenys?*

As students list the ideas from the article in the correct columns, circulate in the class and prompt students who have difficulty, asking if the activity they are considering is generally considered a positive or negative thing and whether it's a problem for Glenys.

As students finish the exercise, get them to compare their answers with a partner.

At feedback, ask one student to tell you which things Glenys enjoys doing, another student which things she doesn't mind doing, and another student which things she hates doing.

Highlight the use of the *-ing* form by asking students to tell you the name of the verb in each example. Elicit that the verb + *ing* is used after *don't mind.*

4 Students say how they feel about the activities listed.

Put students in pairs to discuss the situations in their book.

At feedback, ask if anyone found out anything surprising from their partner.

English in action

AIMS

- To encourage autonomous language work outside the classroom.
- To encourage communicative student-student interaction.

1 Introduce the topic of this section by encouraging students to discuss the photographs and answer the questions in their book.

Answers

1 painting, fishing, skiing and collecting memorabilia

Do this exercise open-class. Ask students to name the hobbies they can see and elicit some related vocabulary to the board. If any students seem particularly interested in one hobby, lead to the second question in their book and encourage other students to question them about it.

2 Students listen and decide which hobby is being talked about and why the speaker enjoys it.

Tapescript

Well, it became a serious hobby about six years ago. I went skiing with my family in the Alps and found I preferred watching and painting to going on the ski slopes. I'd always enjoyed art at school but after that holiday it became a passion. I spend my time on holidays now visiting art galleries and collecting postcards of pictures I particulary like. I paint seriously at the weekends but I usually draw or sketch something every day. I particularly like drawing people and landscapes – the countryside – using watercolours and oil paints. This means I can be sociable and go out with my friends. For example, one of my friends goes fishing a lot and I go with him. He fishes and I paint. That's one of the things I like about this hobby – you can do it indoors and outdoors so I can take advantage of the good weather too. I take private lessons once a week with a really good teacher. It's expensive but I don't mind spending money on this – I enjoy it so much.

Answers

2 Painting. He enjoys it because he can be sociable, do it indoors or outdoors and take advantage of the good weather.

Make sure they know why they are listening. Give them time to check their answers together before you ask them as a class. Play the tape again if there are discrepancies.

3 Prepare students to give short talks on one of their particular interests.

Explain that everyone should give a short talk on something that interests them. Refer them to the instructions and answer any questions. You may like to give time for initial preparation in class but most of this work can be done outside class.

You need to decide how the talks will fit into your future lessons. You may decide to begin or end the next series of lessons with this activity. We recommend limiting the talks to one or two a

lesson as whole lessons devoted to this one activity can become demotivating. If your class is very large then students with interests in common could work together, sharing the preparation work, the talk itself and the questions from the class.

Point out to students that the best talks are those that reflect their own enthusiasm for a subject and pictures/slides/objects will help keep their fellow-students interested.

Students need to know, in advance, how much time they can have, though be flexible – if something is going well allow longer.

4 Students give their talk and others listen and ask questions.

Students will probably want to refer to notes but shouldn't read a speech. Let them decide whether they want fellow-students to interrupt with questions as they are speaking or whether they prefer questions at the end.

This is a fluency activity, so don't correct students as they talk.

Language review 6

a
1 I sometimes visit friends at the weekend.
3 I always play golf on Saturday afternoons.
5 I never do the shopping during the week.
6 I always take my children to the park on Sundays.
8 We usually go to the cinema on Fridays.

b
1 is having	4 clean
2 plays	5 visit
3 am painting	6 are doing

c
1 A: Excuse me, *do you speak* English?
   B: Yes, I do, a little. Can I help?

2 A: Hi! Where are you?
   B: I'm in the living room. *I am watching* TV.

d
1 She doesn't mind doing the washing-up.
2 He doesn't like sharing his office with people who smoke
3 He doesn't like going home in the rush hour.
4 He doesn't mind working late if it's necessary.

7 *Spotlight*

1   Preparation

AIMS

- To revise and practise the use of the Present Perfect, +/– *ever*, to talk about experiences.
- To revise a variety of country and nationality words.

1 Students say which countries they think the owner of the travel souvenirs has been to.

Possible answers

I think she has been to Russia because she has got some Russian dolls.

I think she has been to Africa because she has got an African mask.

I think she has been to Egypt because she has got an Egyptian papyrus.

I think she has been to Tunisia because she has got a Tunisian pottery lamp.

I think she has been to Libya because she has got a Libyan carpet.

I think she has been to Pakistan because she has got a Pakistani horse.

NB There is also an Ecuadorian parrot on the page.

Refer students to the travel souvenirs and ask them to name them open-class. Elicit nationality adjective with the object. If students have problems pronouncing the nationality words, this is the time to correct them. As you do so highlight shifting word-stress on country and nationality words. (Ja'pan vs Japan'ese, 'Egypt vs E'gyptian and 'Ecuador vs Ecua'dorian.)

Elicit the example sentence from their book by asking an individual student which country they think the owner of the kimono has been to.

Get students to repeat the example sentence, stressing the country in the first part of the sentence and the name of the object in the second part eg. I think she's been to *Russia* because she's got some Russian *dolls.*

Put students in pairs to make similar sentences about other objects before checking open-class.

2 Students find out about their partner's travel experiences.

Refer them to the example question in Exercise 2 and elicit Y*es, I have* and *No, I haven't* in reply. Then refer them to the speech bubbles for alternative, more informative answers, clarifying meaning if necessary.

Tell them they have two minutes to ask their partner questions about past travel experiences. This can be organised as a competition with the winner being the student who finds out information about the most countries. Each student needs to make two columns headed *yes* and *no* in their notebook. As they ask about a country, they write it in a column according to the answer their partner gives.

At feedback, ask the student who says they have asked about the most countries to tell the class what they found out eg. *X has been to Japan and Germany but she hasn't been to China, Russia or Italy.* As other students listen they should tick off countries they also asked about. When the winner has named all her/his countries, ask other students to tell you which other countries they asked about and what their partner said.

3+4 Students complete questions in their book to ask about other interesting experiences. They ask as many people their questions as possible to find out how many students in the class have/haven't done these things.

Make sure students understand that the word *ever* can be used or omitted in Present Perfect questions and that there is no one correct way to complete the questions. Encourage them to ask about things that really interest them. Circulate in the classroom as they write their questions, checking their work informally.

Before they ask their questions, get them to extend the yes/no columns in their notebooks. By numbering each line to correspond with each of their questions and by marking the appropriate column as students answer, they can record how many have or haven't done the things they ask about.

If possible, students should stand up and mill around the classroom, asking other students their questions. If this is not possible, then get them to ask as many students as possible sitting near them.

At feedback, ask students to give you an example of a question they asked and to tell you how many students they spoke to had/hadn't had this experience.

2 Grammar: Present Perfect vs Past Simple

AIMS

- To check/teach the use of Past Simple and Present Perfect for talking about general experience or specific time and detail.
- To revise the Past Simple and past participle forms of common regular and irregular verbs.
- To highlight the Present Perfect form of *have*.

1 Students study the examples in their book and answer questions.

Answers

1 Past Simple = Where did you go?/Who did you go with?
  Present Perfect = Have you ever been abroad?
2 Past Simple
3 Present Perfect
4 *have* + past participle; *have* + *not* + past participle; *have* + subject + past participle

Elicit the example questions and answers to the board. Since students invariably find using the two forms difficult, you may like to get maximum practice by building the model questions and answers up into a connected dialogue like this:

1 Ask students what question you ask to find out if someone has been abroad.
2 If necessary, mould their contribution into an

acceptable Present Perfect question and drill it, checking stress, sounds and intonation.
3 Elicit the affirmative short answer, followed by information saying when they went abroad. Then recap by getting an open-class exchange of the question and answer from two students in the class.
4 Continue to build the dialogue in this way, recapping on the complete dialogue so far, each time another line is added.
5 Finally, get students to practise the complete dialogue in pairs and to add other questions asking for further detail eg. *How did you go?*

Refer students to the model dialogue in their book and ask the questions open-class.

2 Students complete the verb chart.

Answers

Present	Past Simple	Past participle
go	went	been/gone
see	*saw*	seen
do	did	*done*
eat	*ate*	eaten
meet	met	*met*
hear	heard	*heard*
taste	*tasted*	*tasted*
visit	*visited*	*visited*

The Past Simple and past participle of *meet, hear, taste* and *visit* are the same.

NB Answers

a) 2
b) 1 – *Have*

Students copy and complete the verb chart in their notebooks. As you check their answers, elicit that the Past Simple and past participle forms of regular verbs are the same.

Refer students to the NB box *Present Perfect of have* and check their answers to the questions open-class. Highlight the use of *have* with food/drink by asking students how else you could say the question in the NB box to elicit *Have you ever eaten/tasted Chinese food?*

59

Pronunciation

AIMS

- To highlight features of Present Perfect pronunciation.
- To provide spoken practice using the Present Perfect and Past Simple forms.

1 Students listen to a Present Perfect question on tape and answer questions about the pronunciation they hear.

Tapescript

How many countries have you been to?

Answers

1 countries
2 have = /əv/; been = /bɪn/

Either refer students to the model question in their book, elicit it to the board or use the tape to dictate it to them. Highlight the position of the preposition *to* at the end of the question.

Give students time to read the questions before they listen (again) to the tape.

Tell students to repeat what they hear and ask them the questions in their book. Check that they say the question with falling intonation, as some students have a tendency to make questions rise.

2 Students use the word prompts to make Present Perfect and Past Simple questions.

Answers

1 How many jobs have you had?
  How many schools have you been to?
  When did you start your present job/school?
2 What types of food have you eaten?
  When did you last eat out?
  Where did you go?
  What did you eat?
3 Have you seen any of these films?
  When did you see them?
  What did you think of them?

Elicit the first question open-class then get students to write the Present Perfect and Past Simple questions in their notebooks.

They check their questions with a student sitting next to them before you correct the exercise open-class.

3 Students ask and answer the questions.

In a small class, students can mill around and ask everyone the questions, noting answers.

In a larger class, put students in groups of five or six to ask their questions. At feedback, students listen to find out who has done these things most in the whole class.

3 Listening

AIMS

- To develop the skill of listening for general and specific information.
- To extend the range of expressions students can use to express likes and dislikes.
- To revise/introduce a lexical set of adjectives ending in *-ing*.

1 Students listen to the tape and complete the chart in their books.

Tapescript

1 It was very frightening. I love horror movies. I think they're great!

2 It was disgusting. All that sex and violence. Films like that shouldn't be allowed!

3 It wasn't very good, a bit long and boring really. I wouldn't want to see it again. It was disappointing. I thought it would be better.

4 It was good. The beginning was exciting. Other people's problems are always interesting even if they are a bit depressing.

5 It was all right, quite an amusing film. Not fantastic but not bad.

Answers

Person 1 loved the film. Person 2 couldn't stand the film. Person 3 didn't like the film. Person 4 liked the film. Person 5 quite liked the film.

Following on from the last exercise, ask students if they enjoy going to the cinema. Explain that the people they are going to hear on tape are coming out of the cinema at the end of different films. Give students time to check the instructions and chart in their book and to copy it into their notebooks if necessary. Ask them which expressions at the top of the chart express positive feelings and which express negative feelings. Make sure they understand that they go from most negative to most positive, left to right and that each feeling will be expressed once only.

Students check their answers together after the first listening and listen again if necessary.

2 Students listen to the tape again and decide which adjective each person uses.

Answers

Person 1 - frightening; Person 2 - disgusting; Person 3 - boring and disappointing; Person 4 - exciting, interesting and depressing; Person 5 - amusing

Refer students to the adjectives and example in their book before they listen to the tape again.

At feedback, repeat their correct answers, saying the word with feeling and using facial expression and/or mime (eg. drumming fingers to suggest boredom) to reinforce the meaning of each adjective.

3 Students listen again to identify main word-stress and the number of syllables in each adjective.

Answers

'frightening (2 syllables); dis'gusting (3 syllables); 'boring (2 syllables); disa'ppointing (4 syllables); ex'citing (3 syllables); 'interesting (3 syllables); de'pressing (3 syllables); a'musing (3 syllables)

Stop the tape immediately after each adjective so students can locate the stress and decide how many syllables they hear. Check their answers at each stage.

Finally, ask them to take the part of different people they heard and to say in one sentence what the film was like (eg. Person 1: *It was frightening!*) Encourage them to say the adjective with feeling, facial expression and/or mime.

4 Students list the adjectives in positive/negative columns.

Answer

Positive	Negative
exciting	frightening
amusing	disgusting
interesting	disappointing
	boring
	depressing

Students work in pairs to do this, thus repeating the adjectives again.

4 Grammar: Present Perfect (recent past)

AIMS

- To introduce the Present Perfect for talking about the recent past, +/– *just* and *recently*.
- To provide personalised practice.
- To provide further practice of contrastive stress.

1 Students deduce this use of the Present Perfect from the example and by answering the questions.

Answers

1 The Present Perfect is used here to describe what happened recently.
2 *just* means a short time ago.

Do this exercise open-class, asking the questions in the book yourself.

2 Students use the Present Perfect to say what kind of film each cinema-goer has just seen.

Answers

The first person has (just) seen a frightening film.
The second person has (just) seen a disgusting film.
The third person has (just) seen a boring and disappointing film.
The fourth person has (just) seen an exciting, interesting but depressing film.
The fifth person has (just) seen an amusing film.

Refer students to their answers to Exercise 3 Listening and to the example in their book. Check they reduce *has* to *'s* or its weak form /əz/. Point out that the number of the person and the adjective will be stressed as they are contrasted in each sentence.

Make sure students realise that *just* stresses the recency of the event but is not a necessary part of the structure.

Students work in pairs, drilling themselves.

3 Finally, they ask another student about a film she/he has seen recently.

Have the example dialogue with an individual student open-class, with you asking the questions and encouraging the student to tell you more. Students then have a similar extended dialogue with their partner.

Pronunciation: /æ/ vs /ʌ/

AIMS

- To introduce a set of past participles.
- To highlight the difference in sound between /æ/ and /ʌ/, showing its effect on meaning.
- To provide further practice of the Present Perfect for recent past.

1 Students complete the verb chart.

Answers

1 Present	2 Past Simple	3 Past participle
swim	swam	swum
run	ran	run
drink	drank	drunk
ring	rang	rung
begin	began	begun
sing	sang	sung

Ask students to copy and complete the chart into their notebook. As they do this, write it on the board.

As you check their answers, write the present forms in and highlight the consistency of spelling in the Past Simple and past participle columns.

2,3+4 Students listen to a model showing the difference in pronunciation between the /æ/ and /ʌ/ sounds. They then listen and recognise the verbs they hear before producing them for recognition by their partner.

Tapescript

2

1	swam	4	rang
2	run	5	began
3	drunk	6	sung

Answers

3

Column 2 – swam, rang, began
Column 3 – run, drunk, sung

Get students to listen and imitate *swam* and *swum*. If they have difficulty, encourage them to open their mouth wider and to move their tongue further down at the front of their mouth for *swam*.

As they listen to the Past Simple and past participle forms they note the number of the column each word appears in.

At feedback, ask students to say a word they heard and you circle the one they say on the board. If they mispronounce and you circle the wrong verb, this should prompt other students to correct the sound. Return to the original student to see if they can pronounce the sound more acceptably now.

Demonstrate what they have to do next with an individual open-class. Say one of the Past Simple or past participle forms and elicit the number of the column it is in.

Students then work in pairs, taking it in turns to say one of the verbs or to say which column it is in.

5 Students use the new past participles in sentences to describe the film stills.

Answers

She's just swum across the pool.
He's just drunk some whisky.
He's just run a race.
She's just sung a song.

Refer students to the film stills and the example sentence in their book.

They work in pairs to decide on a Present Perfect sentence to describe the other stills. Check their answers open-class.

5 Vocabulary: *-ed/-ing* adjectives

AIMS

- To contrast adjectives ending in *-ing* with adjectives ending in *-ed.*

1 Students read film reviews and answer questions to deduce the difference in meaning between adjectives ending in *-ing* and *-ed.*

Answers

1 *-ed* describes how people feel.
2 *-ing* describes what makes them feel this.

Introduce the concept of two forms for the same adjective by miming tiredness and eliciting *You're tired.* Then ask students why they think you are tired; is your work relaxing or tiring? Write the complete sentence on the board. *I'm tired because my work is tiring.* Ask which adjective says how you feel to elicit *tired* and which adjective describes what makes you feel this, to elicit *tiring.*

Refer students to the film reviews at the foot of the page to find examples of *-ing* and *-ed* adjectives. Put them in pairs to consider the adjectives in the reviews and to answer the check questions in their book.

Ask the check questions again, as you hear which adjectives they found in each review. Refer back to the tired/tiring example if there is a problem.

2 Students complete the unfinished reviews.

Answers

1 Really *amusing.* I laughed till I cried!
2 Don't be *disappointed.* Book your tickets early!
3 Horrific! Very *frightening.* You won't sleep for a week!
4 A very *depressing* film. Everybody dies or lives a life of misery.
5 *Disgusted* parents want violent film banned.

Students work in pairs to do this, checking their answers with another pair as they finish. Deal with any discrepancies open-class.

6 Reading

AIMS

- To develop the skills of reading for general and specific information.
- To provide further practice in using *-ed* and *-ing* adjectives.

1+2 Students talk about scandal in general, then read the review of the film to answer the questions.

Answers

1 A scandal is something the general public thinks is shocking or immoral. It can be political, social, sexual, financial, etc.
2 The review is positive.
1 The scandal was a political/sex scandal.
2 In Britain in June 1963.
3 A member of parliament - John Profumo
   A showgirl/callgirl - Christine Keeler
   A doctor - Stephen Ward
   A Russian diplomat - Ivanov
4 John Profumo resigned/Christine Keeler went to prison/Stephen Ward committed suicide/It doesn't say what happened to Ivanov but he was expelled from the country.
5 Possibly a cause of the Conservative government defeat in the 1964 election.

Write the word *Scandal* on the board and ask students what it means. Elicit that there can be political, social, sexual, legal and financial scandals by asking what kind of scandal it is if a) a bank manager takes money from the bank or b) young people have nowhere to sleep but the streets or c) innocent people are put in prison, etc.

Introduce the subject of the film by referring to the photograph and name of the film in the review. Ask what type of scandal they think this film is about and if any students have seen the film. If they have, ask them if they liked it and what they remember about it.

Warn students that two adjectives are given in certain places in the text but that their first task is to answer the comprehension questions and not to worry about the form of the adjective at this point.

At feedback, encourage students to justify their answers from the text.

3 Students choose the correct adjective from the pairs given at each place in the review.

When you are satisfied that comprehension is checked, ask students to read the text carefully again in order to choose the correct adjective. They then compare their answers with a partner before you check them as a class.

7 Writing

AIMS

- To revise possessive adjectives and object pronouns.
- To provide written practice incorporating this and other language from the unit.

Answers

1

Subject pronouns		Possessive adjectives		Object pronouns
I		my		me.
You		*your*		you.
She		her		*her.*
He	passed	*his*	secrets to	him.
It		*its*		it.
We		our		*us.*
You		your		*you.*
They		*their*		them.

2

it - the film	his - Ward
his - Ward	his - government
she - Keeler	minister
her - Keeler	(Profumo)
them - members of	it - the scandal
high society	it - the film
she - Keeler	it - the film

Tell students that they are going to revise these basic parts of speech in order to improve their writing skills. Let them complete the chart individually and then compare their answers with a partner. You need only check them if discrepancies occur.

Put students to work in twos or threes to complete the second exercise. Deal with any problem areas at the end.

3 Students write a short review about a book, a film or a play they have seen.

You may like to set this for homework but it's a good idea to give students some time to prepare their work in class. Refer them to the questions in their book to guide them. If a number of students have seen the same play/film/book, they can work together. Their reviews could form the basis of a new class magazine.

English in action

AIMS

- To introduce a lexical set of film vocabulary.
- To introduce expressions for talking about films.
- To extend students' ability to make suggestions.

1+2 Students find examples of the different types of films listed in the advertisements in their book. They listen to check their answers and to locate word-stress on each type.

Tapescript/Answers

Casablanca is a 'love story.
There isn't a 'western.
Nightmare on Elm Street is a 'horror film.
The Silence of the Lambs is a 'thriller.
2010 is a science 'fiction film.
Tom and Jerry is a car'toon.
The Best of Laurel and Hardy is a 'comedy.

Tell students to find the title of the film in the advertisements which represents each type of film listed. Elicit the first example: *Casablanca is a love story.*

Put students in pairs to make similar sentences about the other films.

Play the tape for students to check their answers and to locate word-stress. Then check the answers open-class.

3 Students say which type of film they like best and answer the questions in their book with another student.

Answers

3 Example answer *The Silence of the Lambs* starring Jodie Foster and Anthony Hopkins is on at Screen 4 of the Plaza Cinema, at 12.05, 2.25, 4.45, 7.05 and 9.30 daily, with late shows at 11.50 pm on Friday and Saturday.

When students have made their decision, ask one pair open-class what they want to see and who is in it.

Invite a number of students to ask these questions across the class, beginning with: *X, which film would you like to see? Where is it on? When is it on?* thereby drilling the questions.

4+5 Students decide which film to see as a group, using the expressions on the page to make suggestions and then try to persuade other students to join their group.

Remind students of the aim of this activity: to plan a cinema outing with people from the class. Their task is to persuade people to go to the film of their choice. Elicit the language they can use to make suggestions. They will probably volunteer *Let's . . ./Why don't we. . .?* Get them to use the name of the film they have chosen to complete the suggestion.

Get a student to ask you which film you would like to see so that you can introduce *What about + -ing?* and *How about. . .?* Drill these forms.

Refer students to the tables in their book to highlight the use of these expressions with either the infinitive or *-ing* form.

This activity will be more motivating if it really leads to a class outing. You could substitute the advertisements in the book for a selection of films (English-speaking, if possible but not necessarily) showing in your area.

Put students in groups of four or five. Give them a few minutes to make their choice individually and then let them discuss together. When they agree on a film they should note who is in it, where it is on and what time/s it is on.

Finally, each group tells the other students what they have decided and any information they have on the film. Some individuals may wish to change their plans and go with another group. You may want everyone to agree on one film so encourage full class discussion or compromise by suggesting one film this week and another the next.

If you accompany the group to the cinema, encourage them to speak English when they meet or talk afterwards. If you can't go with them, you could ask them to write short reviews of the film for you to read. In any case, use some future class time to hear about their impressions of the film/s they saw.

Language review 7

a
I: So, tell me a little about the things you *have done*.
C: Well, I *studied* French and German at university. Then, I *taught* in secondary school for a few years.
I: *Did you enjoy* teaching?
C: No, not really. I *didn't like* the discipline problems. So, I *started* working for a large drug company.
I: *Have you worked* abroad at all?
C: Yes, well about three years ago I *got* a job in France, selling advertising space for a science magazine.
I: *Have you been* anywhere else?
C: Yes, I *worked* in Germany in 1990.
I: Oh really? What *did you do* there?

b
1 He's just woken up./The alarm clock has just rung.
2 He's just had a shower.
3 She's just written a letter.
4 They've just got married.

c
1 interested
2 embarrassed
3 exciting
4 frightened
5 shocking
6 boring
7 disappointed

d
I took *my* car round to my sister's house last night. She wasn't at home but *her* husband was. He asked *me* to wait because she was on *her* way home. I started looking at *their* photo albums and found all the old photos of *us* as children with *our* parents. There were also some photos of our parents before we were born. There was a lovely one of *them* with *their* dog, Bess.

Movie time

AIMS

- To provide students with an opportunity to use the language introduced so far.

1-3 Students look at the film stills and arrange them to make a story of their choice, including what has happened before each picture and what they think is going to happen next.

Put students in groups of five. If you have odd numbers increase a group/s by one other student. Tell them they are moviemakers (check they know that *movie* is another word for *film*) and that they have to use these pictures in their film. Make sure they realise that there is no one correct way of ordering the pictures.

As they discuss their order, they should be imagining a storyline for their film. Encourage them to discuss what happened immediately *before* each picture and what they think will happen *next*. Circulate as they work and help them with vocabulary. They can also use dictionaries to find vocabulary they need.

4+5 Students write a dialogue for each photograph and show it to you for correction.

Encourage them to name their characters and to write what they think they are saying in each picture.

As they finish, correct their work. If possible, talk to each group and ask questions where you need clarification. Work on accuracy but also on ways to get what they want to say across.

Give them time to rework their dialogues, checking them again for accuracy.

6+7 Students learn a part in their film and then act it out to the whole class.

How you deal with this part of the activity will depend on your students' motivation:

a) If you decide to finish the activity in one day, then you could get groups to read out their lines rather than learn them. Their story probably has four or five people in it so each student takes one part. Where there is an extra student, they could provide sound effects or some narration between scenes.

b) If you have time and students are very motivated, ask them to learn their lines at home. They may also like to find costumes or props. They could then act out their film and discuss the different stories and scripts at the end. They may like to look at one another's work in detail and the scripts and perfomances could be written up for an issue of the class magazine (see English in Action, Unit 1). Alternatively, they could invite students/teachers from other classes or friends/family to see their films.

This is intended as a fluency activity with students using the language at their disposal as they work. Except for the written scripts, it is not intended that teachers should correct students.

8 Consequences

LANGUAGE CONTENT

Productive language
- *So* and *because* to introduce reason and result
- *If/When* + future time
- *If* + present +*will* (first conditional)
- *Definitely/probably* (word order)
- Education and qualifications
- Words that collocate with *exams* (*take/pass/fail/retake*)

Receptive language
- Selected vocabulary from newspaper articles
- The passive form of verbs in questions

1 Preparation

AIMS

- To introduce the theme of the unit.
- To develop the skill of listening for specific information.

1+2 Students play the game of *Consequences*, following instructions on tape.

Tapescript

1 Take a piece of paper to write on.
2 Write the name of a famous woman at the top.
3 Fold the paper over so you hide the name. Pass the paper to the person on your left.
4 On the new piece of paper, write the word *met* and the name of a famous man.
5 Fold the paper over and pass it to the person on your left.
6 Write the words *She said to him* and add what she said.
7 Fold the paper over and pass it to the person on your left.
8 Write the words *He said to her* and add what he said.
9 Fold the paper over and pass it to the person on your left.
10 Write the consequence beginning *And the consequence was* and add what happened next.
11 Fold the paper over and pass it to the person on your left.
12 Unfold the paper and read the complete story.

Explain that students are going to play a game called *Consequences*. They need a loose piece of paper to write on. To give them an idea of what is involved, refer them to the examples in their book.

Play the cassette or read the instructions out yourself. Students write what they are told then fold over the paper to hide what they have written. They pass their paper to the student on their left and write, according to the next instructions, on the paper they are given, fold it over and pass it on. When the instructions are finished, students unfold the paper they have in their hand and read the complete story out loud.

Do this open-class, getting a number of students to read their versions out at the end.

2 Writing: *so* vs *because*

AIMS

- To revise/teach and practise *so* and *because* for linking sentences.

1+2 Students deduce the difference in meaning between *so* and *because* by answering questions about sentences in their book. They then join half-sentences using *so* and *because*.

Answers

1

1 because   2 so

2

They went to Greece by boat
- *because* it was more romantic.
- *so* it took a long time.

They stayed in a cheap hotel
- *because* they didn't have much money.
- *so* the room wasn't very comfortable.

It was very hot in Greece
- *because* it was the middle of August.
- *so* they went to the beach a lot.

They decided to go to a disco on their last night
- *because* it was the end of their holiday.
- *so* they woke up late and missed the boat home.

Elicit the model sentences to the board or refer students to them in their book. Ask the check questions open-class.

Use the example to show how they can join the sentences in the left and right hand columns. They do this in pairs, saying the examples as they write. Remind students that sentences on the right can be used once only.

Hear some of their sentences open-class.

3+4 Students write possible reasons for and results of the social situations in their book.

Put students in groups of three or four to do this exercise. They should suggest a few reasons and results for each situation listed and then write the most interesting reason and result down.

When they have finished, ask them to compare their answers with another group and decide which group's answer is the most interesting for each question.

At feedback, hear the examples one group think are most interesting and encourage other groups to disagree.

For further conversation practice list some of the reasons for one of the social problems thought of by the class. In groups, students should then rank the reasons in order of importance, putting what they think is the main cause of the problem first. As they need to agree as a group, this will provoke discussion. Comparing one group's decisions with those of another group will provoke further discussion.

3 Reading

AIMS

- To preteach vocabulary for the reading exercise.
- To develop the skills of reading for general and specific information.
- To encourage students to deduce vocabulary from context.

1+2 Students match words to pictures and then find the connection between the objects and the newspaper articles.

Answers

2

1 The objects are mentioned in the newspaper articles as things put in the time capsules.
2 To help future generations understand present life more fully.

Give students a couple of minutes to do the matching exercise in pairs, before checking their answers with the class.

Make sure students read the questions before they read the articles and that they know they can answer these even if they don't understand every word in the articles.

At feedback, as students discuss what a time capsule is, take the opportunity to highlight the verb *bury*, in preparation for its appearance in the next set of questions.

3 Students read the questions and look for more detailed information in the articles.

Answers

1 At Castle Howard in Yorkshire.
2 Nearly 800 items.
3 1982.
4 To mark the BBC's 60th birthday.
5 3982.
6 1938.
7 The American Westinghouse Company.
8 They could be misled by the time capsules.
9 Compact discs and pictures of a man and a woman.
10 People could believe that the Earth was full of perfectly-formed, white, Beatles fans.

Give students time to read the questions and to ask you for clarification, if necessary.

After reading the articles, encourage them to compare their answers with another student. At feedback, deal with any discrepancies, referring students back to the articles to clarify points of disagreement.

4 Students match definitions to words underlined in the articles.

Answers

a) clues   e) lifestyle
b) mislead   f) contents
c) cross-section g) convince
d) Earth   h) proof

Do the first example open-class and ask students to find the vocabulary with their partner.

Check their answers open-class, getting them to repeat the words after you.

4 Grammar: *If/when* + future

AIMS

- To show the difference in meaning between *if* and *when*.
- To introduce and practise the Present Simple form used after *if/when* when talking about the future.
- To highlight the pronunciation of 'dark' /l/ after *Wh-* question words.

1 Students deduce the difference in meaning between *if* and *when* by answering questions about example sentences in their book.

Answers

1 b)	3 the future
2 a)	4 the present

Elicit that the example sentences are based on information in the time capsule articles. Ask the check questions open-class.

2 Students rearrange jumbled words to make sentences about the future.

Answers

1 If you are late this evening I won't wait for you.
2 If you don't eat lunch you will be hungry later.
3 When I see her I will tell her.
4 When I finish the report I will bring it into your office.
5 If they ask me to stay I will refuse.
6 When she rings you she will tell you the problem.

Students either do this alone and check their answers with a partner or work with a partner from the start.

At feedback drill their correct sentences, with rising intonation at the end of the first clause and falling intonation at the end of the second clause.

3-5 Students complete questions with *if* or *when*. They then listen to the questions on the cassette and practise saying the dark /l/ after *what* and *where*. Finally they ask and answer these questions with other students.

Answers/Tapescript

1 What will you do *when* you get home this evening?
2 What will you do *if* there's a transport strike tomorrow?
3 What will you do *if* it rains this weekend?
4 What will you do *when* this course finishes?
5 Where will you live *when* you are old?

If students have problems with this exercise, prompt them with check questions asking if the outcome in each question is most likely/will definitely happen or if it is only a possibility.

Drill the completed questions, stressing the main information word and using falling intonation.

Direct students to have short conversations with a few other students. They should use their completed questions and begin each new conversation with a different question.

When they have finished, ask individual students what they found out about one of the students they spoke to.

5 Speaking

AIMS

- To revise some of the language introduced so far in the unit.
- To highlight the word order in sentences using *will* + *definitely/probably*.
- To provide written practice of first conditional sentences.

1+2 Students decide what to put in their own time capsule and explain their reasons to other students using *because* or *so*.

Put students in pairs to answer the questions.

As they finish, put pairs together to explain their choices using *so* or *because*. As they listen they should make a list of the other pair's items.

3 Students say what they think people in the future will surmise because of the other students' time capsule choices.

Direct students to the table in their book showing the position of *probably* and *definitely* in positive and negative sentences. Use the pictures with the time capsule articles on page

49 to elicit sentences based on this model and drill them.

Now tell each pair to consider the things the other pairs chose to put in their time capsules, and to discuss what people in the future are likely to think.

When they have discussed their ideas, ask them to write their opinions for the other pair to read. Direct them to the model first conditional sentence in their book.

Finally, pairs exchange their written opinions and read what other students thought about their choices. Alternatively, they could display their work on classroom walls or in the class magazine so everyone can see what people chose and the conclusions that could be drawn.

6 Vocabulary: education

AIMS

- To introduce/revise vocabulary of school subjects, types of schools and exams.
- To highlight that stress falls on the penultimate syllable in words ending in -ic.

1 Students use their previous knowledge and context to deduce the meaning of education vocabulary. They use their mini-dictionary to supplement this if necessary.

NB Answers

The stress goes on the penultimate syllable.

Summarise the ways to learn what unknown words mean:

a) Their partner can explain.
b) They can deduce from the question; what two types of school could they be asked about?
c) They can look the word up in a dictionary/ their mini-dictionary.
d) If all else fails, they can make a note of a word to ask you afterwards.

Allow a good amount of time for students to do this exercise. Make sure they realise they only have to understand, not answer, the questions.

As pairs finish, get them to check any difficulties with other pairs.

At feedback, deal with problems only and refer students to the NB box *Word families* and check their answer to the question in it.

2 Students discuss the questions.

As the vocabulary of school subjects is likely to be revision (see *The Beginners' Choice* Unit 20), deal with the questions in Exercise 2 open-class. Ask students about the subjects they studied at school, making sure their word stress is acceptable. (If you should find that the vocabulary is completely new to your class, then spend more time on this. Put students into groups, mixing nationalities in a multilingual class, to discuss the subjects they took at school and how they felt about them.)

Put students in groups of four or five to discuss the questions about exams. This activity will probably take longer with a multilingual class.

7 Listening

AIMS

- To develop the skill of listening for specific information.
- To provide further contextualised exposure to examples of *if/when* + future time.

1+2 Students listen to a school student to see which of the questions in their book are answered and what the answers are.

Tapescript

INTERVIEWER: So, tell me a little about the different schools you've been to.

GIRL: Well, I've always been to state schools ever since I started school. My parents never had a lot of money. Apparently they would like to have sent me to a private school but they couldn't afford it.

INTERVIEWER: What did you think of your very first school?

GIRL: I loved my primary school, our teachers were wonderful. We had a great time but we learnt a lot as well. I was very sad to leave it when I was ten.

INTERVIEWER: I know, it's hard isn't it?

GIRL: Yes, but I soon settled in to my new school. I didn't like the teachers so much but I made one or two good friends which meant it wasn't too bad. I've been at this school for nearly seven years now.

INTERVIEWER: Really? And what about exams? What exams have you taken?

GIRL: Um . . . I took GCSEs in Maths, English,

French, Science, and, um, Geography, Art and Religious Education when I was 16 and then I had to choose three subjects to study for A levels for the next two years. Those are the only really important exams, GCSEs and A levels. Anyway, I decided to do Maths, Physics and Chemistry for A level. It's been hard work but I've enjoyed it. My exams are in June.

INTERVIEWER: Right. Um, what then?

GIRL: Well, *if I pass my A levels I'll go to university.* Which university I go to will depend on the grades. *If I fail I don't know what I'll do. I suppose I'll have to retake them or maybe I'll just start looking for a job.* Anyway, *in July I'm going to hitchhike around Europe with my boyfriend* for a couple of months. I'm really looking forward to it.

INTERVIEWER: I'm not surprised. It sounds great.

Answers

1

Q: Did you go to a state school or a private school?

A: She went to different state schools.

Q: Which of these subjects did you study? Did you study them at primary or secondary school or in higher education eg. university ?

A: At secondary school she studied Maths, English, French, Science, Geography, Art and Religious Education for GCSEs and Maths, Physics and Chemistry for A levels.

Q: What are the names of the important exams in your country?

A: GCSEs and A levels.

Q: At what age do you take them?

A: GCSEs at 16, A levels at 18.

Q: What happens if you fail them? Can you retake them?

A: You can either retake them or look for a job.

Q: What difference does it make if you pass them?

A: If you pass A levels you can generally go to university or college.

Q: Are the exam grades important?

A: Yes.

2 See the sentences in italic in the tapescript.

Set the context for the listening by referring students to the photographs in their book.

Students listen the first time to see which questions she answers. When they have checked this with another student, get them to listen

again and note her answers.

They listen again and note what she says about her future.

Pronunciation

AIMS

- To heighten students' awareness of falling and rising intonation patterns.
- To provide spoken practice of first conditional sentences.

1+2 Students listen to model first conditional sentences and identify the intonation patterns. They then repeat the sentences.

Tapescript

If I pass, I'll go to university.
I'll go to university, if I pass.

Answers

1 Up, because the sentence is not finished.
2 Down, because the sentence is finished.

Give students time to read the check questions before you play the tape. Ask them to predict the pattern they are going to hear.

They listen and answer the questions, conferring with a partner before checking their answers open-class. Point out that the clauses in these sentences can go in any order so it is not their meaning that completely dictates their intonation. Point out that the 'unfinishedness' is signalled by rising intonation.

3 Students who are taking other exams and courses tell the class what they will do if they pass/fail the exams and when the courses finish.

Elicit which students are taking other exams/ courses open-class. Encourage them to give as much information as possible. Prompt someone to ask another student the questions in the book but do not insist on complete first conditional answers as these are often repetitive and unnatural. If students can use each of the clauses independently and correctly then they are doing well.

71

English in action

AIMS

- To provide practice in writing formal letters.
- To develop the skill of listening for specific information.

1 Students prepare the content of a letter asking for English exam information.

Write the names of some English language exams on the board. Elicit what students already know about them.

Explain that they are going to find out about exams they might take one day. Make sure they realise that they can *really* send their letters as a realistic outcome should increase motivation.

Establish that this is formal letter writing. You may like to prepare them for a more formal style by putting informal sentences, words or contracted forms on the board for them to change to formal style. For example:

How about sending me . . .?	exam
I want to know . . .,	maths
I'm a student.	TV
I've got . . .	yeah

2 Students decide which expressions go at the beginning and which go at the end of their letter.

Answers

At the beginning of a letter: Dear Sir/Madam, I am writing to . . . At the end of a letter: Please send me information about . . . Thank you for your help in this matter. Yours faithfully,

Make sure students realise that we only write *Dear Sir/Madam* if we don't know the name of the person we are writing to. Give them time to plan their own letter, using these expressions.

Students will probably want their letter to be as correct as possible before sending it so encourage them to check spelling in a dictionary. Circulate in the classroom as they work, making suggestions for correction where necessary.

3+4 Students write their address and the date at the top of their letter and then write the address of the examinations board, dictated to them.

Tapescript

English Language Information Service
The British Council
Medlock Street
Manchester
M15 4AA

Give out sheets of writing paper for the final version of their letter. (They may wish to write a rough in their notebook first.)

Elicit that their complete address, without their name, should appear in the top right-hand corner of the letter, with the date beneath it.

Explain that a formal letter often also includes the address of the person the letter is going to and that this goes under their own address but on the other side of the letter, directly above *Dear Sir/Madam*. Show where on the board.

Dictate the address they should send their letter to. If you know the address of a central examinations authority in your country or a particular exam board, then dictate this address, making sure you include *The Department for English Language Exams* (so that receiving a letter in English is not too much of a shock!). (In case no suitable local exam authority exists, the tape gives the address of the British Council in Britain which should have details of all British exam boards offering international English language exams. You may have a local British Council office in your country, in which case you could dictate their address instead.)

Language review 8

a
Possible answers
1 I really didn't like the film *because there was so much violence.*
2 I didn't have enough money to pay the bill *so I asked Jon to lend me some.*
3 I decided to change my job *because I didn't like my boss.*
4 I stayed in bed all morning *because I didn't feel very well.*
5 The party next door was so loud I couldn't sleep *so I called the police.*
b
1 When she arrives   3 When it finishes
2 If he feels better   4 If I see him
c
Possible Answers
If the ball hits the window, the glass will break.
If the glass breaks, the dog will jump out, etc.

9 *Face value*

LANGUAGE CONTENT

Productive language
- *Must be/might be/can't be* to express degrees of certainty (deduction)
- Adjectives for describing people
- *Look* vs *look like*

- *Really/very/quite* + adjectives
- Present Perfect +/– *yet/already* (indefinite time)

Receptive language
- Vocabulary related to concerts/music

Preparation for this unit

In the English in Action section of this unit, students are asked to tell the class about an English or American song they like. Ask them in advance to choose a song, find out interesting information about the singer(s) and bring a tape/record into class.

1 Preparation

AIMS

- To provide speaking practice to revise Present Continuous, Past Simple, Present Perfect, *going to* and *will*.
- To introduce the theme of prejudice.

1-3 Students look at the photograph in their book and speculate about the story behind it. They then look at another photograph on page 126, and discover the complete story.

Answers

3 The photographs form an advertisement for *The Guardian* newspaper. (The young man is not, in fact, trying to attack the businessman. He wants to push him out of the way of the car.)

Encourage students to describe the photograph in the Present Continuous open-class. Provide vocabulary as it is required.

Put students in groups of four or five to answer the questions and to make a complete story.

As they finish, they tell their story to another group and listen out for similarities and differences to report to the class.

Refer them to the second photograph on page 126 and elicit open-class the prejudice it is trying to expose and the purpose of the advertisement.

2 Grammar: *must be/might be/can't be*

AIMS

- To introduce degrees of certainty using *must/might/can't be*.
- To highlight the dropping of /t/ at the end of *must/might/can't* before *be*.

1+2 Students match definitions to example sentences, and then listen and repeat the example sentences, linking the two words in the modal expression.

Answers

1
He is definitely a criminal – He is a criminal.
I'm sure he's a criminal – He must be a criminal.
Perhaps he's a criminal – He might be a criminal.
I'm sure he isn't a criminal – He can't be a criminal.
He definitely isn't a criminal – He isn't a criminal.
2 No. The /t/ sound disappears.

Tapescript

2
He must be a criminal.
He might be a criminal.
He can't be a criminal.

Elicit the three sentences containing *must be/might be* and *can't be* to the board by asking students how sure they are that the young man in the picture is a criminal.

Refer students to the chart in their book and give them time to match the sentences and compare their answers with a partner.

Ask students to listen to see if they can hear the /t/ at the end of each sentence. When they have recognised the elision, ask them to mumble drill *must be/might be/can't be* a few times. Then play the tape again for them to repeat the complete sentences.

Put students in pairs to make sentences based on the prompts in their book. Hear their examples open-class.

Elicit the examples with *could* and *may*, asking how sure the speaker is when these expressions are used. (This is to provide alternatives to *might be* for passive recognition. Any differences between *might/could/may* do not need to be highlighted at this stage.)

3   Speaking

AIMS

- To provide further practice of *must/might/can't be.*
- To practise question forms.

Either refer students to the story in their book or ask them to close their book and elicit the story to the board. To do this mark 34 spaces, one for each word in the story, on the board. You could use computer software such as *Storyboard* or *Quartext* for this, or write on the board in the classroom and proceed as follows. Explain that each space represents one word in a story. Put the three full stops in their appropriate places and tell students what the marks represent. Their job is to suggest words to fill the spaces and thus

discover the story themselves. If they offer a word that is in the story, write it in the correct spaces on the board. Encourage students to spell words for you as you write them up. If they get really stuck, then mime words (to point, a bar, or a gun). When the complete story is on the board, ask them to read it and tell you what is strange about it.

Put students in pairs to answer these questions. Give them time to read the questions and to ask you for clarification if necessary. Make sure they realise that they are giving their *opinions* rather than finding the exact answers at this stage.

As students finish discussing, put pairs together to justify their opinions. Refer them to the example sentence in their book to encourage them to use modals of deduction.

Find out if anyone in the class knows the solution to the problem. If they do, suggest they take your place and answer the class questions.

Make sure the class understand that they can't ask questions requiring more than the three answers you are allowed to give.

Give students time to write three or four questions together before they begin questioning you. Circulate in the classroom as they do this, making sure all questions can be answered by *yes, no* or *not important*.

Establish the rules of the game. The aim is for them to find out why the man said 'thank you'. The class can ask up to 15 questions before you win and tell them the answer. If someone thinks they have the answer first, they should stop the game and say what they think. If they are wrong, the game continues without them. As they hear a question on their list, students tick it off so that you are asked new questions each time.

When the game ends, you or another student will explain that the man had hiccoughs. Elicit the appropriate sound and write the word on the board so that they can learn the word and try the problem on someone in another class.

4 Vocabulary: describing people

AIMS

- To introduce vocabulary to describe personality.
- To provide further practice of the language of deduction/degrees of certainty.
- To highlight the difference between the verbs *look* and *look like*.

1 Students match the definitions to the adjectives in their book.

Answers

a) mean	e) gentle
b) sociable	f) unthreatening
c) patient	g) shy
d) vain	h) romantic

Do the first example open-class, saying the definition and eliciting *mean* and its opposite. Make sure they realise that only one in a pair of adjectives will be used so they can now tick off the *mean/generous* combination. Then refer the students to the exercise in their book and put them in pairs to complete the task.

Hear their answers open-class, checking their pronunciation and encouraging them to put the new vocabulary in sentences eg. *Tell me about someone who doesn't like spending money* to elicit: *He's mean/He's a mean person.*

2 Students speculate on the characters of the people in the photographs.

NB answer

looks is followed by an adjective on its own.

Refer students to the photographs in their book

and ask if anyone looks particularly friendly. Ask them how they would compare one of the characters to a film star and elicit *She/He looks like a filmstar*. Now, refer the class to the NB Box *look vs look like* and ask the question.

Begin Exercise two open-class to encourage group speculation. This is a good place to feed in number +*ish* eg. *thirtyish* for talking about approximate age.

Students work in their pairs to answer the other questions. They compare their answers with another pair as they finish.

5 Reading

AIMS

- To develop the skill of reading for general and specific information.
- To revise superlatives.

1, 2+3 Students read an article, written by a panel of judges, about the characters of the people in the photographs. They then read what the characters themselves think.

Answers

1
a) Tina
b) Elizabeth
c) Mark

3
1 The people think that the panel was generally fairly accurate.
2 Elizabeth thinks that she is more complicated than she initially looks.
  Mark doesn't think that he is vain or threatening and insists that he is in fact very romantic.
  Tina thinks that the panel were misled by her physical appearance and that in fact she is sociable and friendly and not at all aggressive.

Establish that a panel of judges also imagined the characters of the people in the photographs for a magazine article. Direct students to read the texts quickly just to answer the questions in the first exercise.

Check their answers open-class. Refer them to the questions in Exercise 2. They should read the article again, more closely, and discuss their answers with their partner. Ask one or two people to tell the class what surprised them about the panellists' analysis.

Give students time to read the questions in Exercise three before directing them to the final part of the article on page 124.

At feedback, ask how accurate their predictions were.

6 Writing

AIMS

- To revise/teach the use of adverbs of degree to modify adjectives.
- To provide personalised written practice of some of the language of the unit.

1-3 Students complete the chart with the adverbs of degree and then write a description of their own character.

Answers

1 quite shy/shy/very shy/really shy

There are examples of these adverbs in the article, particularly on page 124. Students could find and underline these first. However, they have already seen the use of *really/quite* + verb in Unit 3 so these words should cause little problem. The difference between *very*, which can't be used with verbs, and *really* can be seen here as one of degree.

Elicit the adverbs to columns on the board as a final check.

Direct students to write a paragraph about their own character using she/he instead of their name. Remind them that use of the conjunctions *and/but/or/so/because* as well as adverbs of degree + adjectives will make their work more interesting to read.

Circulate as they write, helping with vocabulary if required. It is a good idea to have dictionaries available so students can be independent too. As they finish, look at the work of individual students, giving suggestions to make their writing clearer.

Collect their paragraphs and read a selection of them for others to guess who is being described. You could encourage them to use *must/might/can't be* by suggesting students in the class eg. *What about Youssef?* to elicit eg. *No, it can't be. He loves children!*

7 Speaking

AIMS

- To provide freer personalised speaking practice.

1 Students discuss how they judge people when they first meet them.

Give students a few minutes to think about the suggestions in their book individually. Then put them in groups of four or five to discuss their order of priorities and come to a consensus.

As groups finish, get them to compare their ideas with another group to encourage further discussion.

2 Students talk about how they met a particular friend and what attracted them.

Tell students about one of your friends to give them an idea of what to do. Then put students in pairs to discuss the questions in their book.

8 Listening

AIMS

- To introduce a lexical set of vocabulary to do with concerts/music.
- To provide further practice of *must be* to express degrees of certainty.
- To develop the skill of listening for general and specific information.
- To introduce and practise the use of *yet* and *already* with the Present Perfect.
- To provide spoken practice of adjectives describing character.

1 Students complete the diary.

Answers

1 concert	6 stage
2 sang	7 played
3 songs	8 band
4 audience	9 tape
5 applauded	

Introduce this section of the unit by referring students to the photograph of Phil Collins and eliciting what students know about him. (He used to be lead singer/drummer of the 1960s group Genesis and since then has had a number of hits on his own and has starred in a few films.) As the class/you talk about this, try to introduce the vocabulary for Exercise one, naturally, as it occurs.

Refer students to the diary and put them in pairs to complete the gaps. Tell them the words are in the mini-dictionary on page 138 if they need to check their meaning as they do the exercise.

Students check their answers with another pair. Deal with any discrepancies at the end.

2 Play the tape of the Phil Collins' song. Students decide what it is about and write the chorus.

Tapescript

Chorus
It must be love I'm feeling
This must be love
This must be love I'm feeling
This must be love

Verse 1
Well, I wait in every day
Oh just in case you decide to call
And I can hardly wait
'Cos I never thought time could pass so slowly

Verse 2
Happiness is something I never thought I'd feel again
And now I know
Oh, it's you that I've been looking for
And day by day, more and more

(Chorus)

Verse 3
Well, I know what you think
You've heard it before
Don't tell me I know
That this feeling inside my heart
Well, you know, never letting go

(Chorus)

Verse 4
Words can only say so much
It's hard to express
Oh, the things you do to me
You're everything I could ever dream you would be

(Chorus)

Answers

The song is about love.

The chorus is:
It must be love I'm feeling
This must be love
This must be love I'm feeling
This must be love

Set the task, establishing that the chorus is repeated many times so they should listen to it once or twice before trying to write down the words. Play the tape.

Elicit that this is a love song and let them check the words of the chorus together.

3 Students look at the words of the song in the tapescript at the back of the book and answer more specific questions in their book.

Answers

1 Because he is waiting for his friend to call him.
2 Yes, because of his friend.
3 That the feelings expressed are just words and only superficial *You've heard it before.*
4 No. *It's hard to express.*

Give students time to read the questions and to guess the answers first. Then refer them to the tapescript on page 132 to check their answers.

Play the tape again with students following the words in their book and joining in the chorus if they wish.

4, 5+6 Students listen to an interview with Phil Collins and answer the questions in their book. They then listen again to complete the chart. They use the information in the chart to ask and answer about countries Phil Collins has visited, using *yet* or *already* with the Present Perfect.

Tapescript

PHIL: Oh, where haven't I been would probably be quicker. Actually, there's an awful lot of ground that we haven't travelled. We've never been to Russia, for instance, never been to China, Africa. So, there's been lots of large expanses of area we've never, never, sort of, managed to get to.
INT: Have you been to Japan?
PHIL: Oh yeah. Japan we've been to three or four times and it's a very interesting place to play. I

mean I love the food there anyway, Japanese food's one of my favourite foods. And, um, it's so different that it's so interesting.

INT: How do the audiences differ say in Latin America to Japan?

PHIL: Well, in Japan they all sing along to the records, they all sing along to the songs when you're singing them in concert but they don't really understand what they're singing I don't think. Um some of them do I suppose because they've, they're taught English and some of them speak very good English considering its culture you know, completely different sort of culture. Um. They're very rowdy in South America, in Latin countries, I mean, that's including places like Spain and what have you. Er, each country's got its own type of reaction, um. But we've played in so many different places and we've all got a soft spot for lots of them: Italy is always great to play, um most of the European countries now are really good. Germany was a bit of a problem for us in the early days but it's strong for us now so . . . they've all got their own little identity to be quite honest.

Answers

4

1 What different countries have you been to?
2 Russia, China, Africa, Japan, Latin America, Spain, Italy, Germany.
5 Countries he has already visited - Japan, South America, Spain, Italy, Germany, most European countries.
  Countries he hasn't visited yet - Russia, China, Africa.

Before students check their chart in pairs, direct them to the example in their book. Elicit that *yet/ already* refer to any time up to the present. In these examples *yet* is used in the question and negative sentences and comes after the verb. *Already* is used in positive sentences and generally goes between the auxiliary verb *have* and the past participle in Present Perfect sentences.

Speaking

AIMS

- To provide freer practice of adjectives to describe national characteristics.

1+2 Students discuss typical characteristics of their own nationality.

Refer students to what Phil Collins says about the identity of different nationalities. You may like to play the tape again so that students recall what he says about them. Before you do so, write the following on the board:

Which nationalities does he say:
a) have wonderful food? b) sing along at concerts? c) are very different culturally? d) are rowdy? e) used to be a problem for the band?

When they have listened and answered these questions, see if they agree with him or if they think national stereotypes reveal prejudice.

Give them time to think about the image people from other countries have of their nationality and what they think themselves.

Put students in groups of four or five to discuss this. In a multilingual class, mix nationalities to encourage maximum discussion. In a monolingual class, get students to compare what they think and then to talk about other nationalities they are familiar with.

English in action

AIMS

- To expose students to a variety of songs in English.
- To encourage autonomous work outside the classroom.
- To develop the skill of listening for specific information.

1-7 Students find out information about a song in English that they particularly like. They tell other students about it, play the song and finally vote on all the songs they have heard.

Either set this up in advance so that students are ready to tell the class about their songs in the lesson. Or, use the first lesson to set the situation telling them about a song and singer *you* particularly like. Either way, make sure they know that they need to come to class with the words of their song and information on the singer/s. Encourage students to find information in libraries or from other people. It doesn't matter if they have to do this in their own language as long as they speak English in class. If your students cannot find songs in English, you can do the activity with other songs and talk about them in English.

You may like to spread this activity over a number of lessons, with one or two students beginning/ending each class with their song. Or you could devote a complete lesson or class magazine to the activity (see English Action, Unit 1).

(see English Action, Unit 1).

8-9 Students listen to a conversation in a record shop and answer the questions in their book. They then practise the conversation, substituting their own song for the one on the tape.

Tapescript

WOMAN: Excuse me.

MAN: Yes?

WOMAN: I'm trying to find a particular song. Can you help me?

MAN: Well, I can try.

WOMAN: Have you got 'Angel' by The Eurythmics?

MAN: The Eurythmics? Which album is it on? Do you know?

WOMAN: No, sorry, I don't.

MAN: Well, let me see. Oh yes, here it is. It's on 'We Too Are One'. I think we've got that. Do you want CD, tape or record?

WOMAN: CD, I think.

MAN: Right. They're over there on the right. The album's called 'We Too Are One' under *E* for Eurythmics.

WOMAN: Great, thanks.

MAN: That's OK.

Answers

8

1 'Angel'	3 'We Too Are One'
2 The Eurythmics	4 CD

Give students time to read the questions before they listen. They can compare their answers with another student. Play the tape again, if necessary, for students to hear the answers themselves.

When comprehension has been checked, elicit the conversation line by line orally. As students suggest how to say each new line, mould their contribution into acceptable English and drill it. Then get students to practise the conversation, first in open pairs, then in closed pairs.

Get them to practise it again, taking it in turns to be the customer and asking for their favourite song.

Language review 9

a

Students will use *might be/must be/can't be* + name of object, depending upon how sure they are.

1 a shoe   2 a lamp   3 a pair of glasses
4 a camera   5 an alarm clock   6 a toothbrush

b

1 Isabel might be late for the cinema.
2 It can't be 6 o'clock.
3 They must be Maria's brothers.
4 He must be really stupid.
5 He can't be your friend.
6 She might be tired.

c

1 looks like	6 look
2 look	7 look like
3 looks	8 looks
4 look like	9 look
5 looks like	10 looks

d

1

A: Have you seen Cher's new film *yet*?

B: No, not *yet*. Have you?

A: No. But Françoise has *already* seen it and says it's wonderful.

2

C: I have *already* told you, you can't have a new bike *yet*. We haven't got enough money.

D: I know but I'm trying to save the money myself. I've *already* got more than half the money I need.

C: How much have you got?

D: Not enough *yet*. But I've told the man in the shop I'll buy it before Christmas!

10 *Consolidation*

1 Across cultures: money

AIMS

- To provide an opportunity for freer speaking practice.
- To revise the use of the Present Simple (+/- adverbs of frequency) to talk about habits.
- To revise the use of the Present Continuous to describe pictures.
- To revise the use of the Present Perfect to talk about the recent past.

1 Students discuss attitudes to money in their country based on the situations in their book.

Put students in groups of four or five, mixing nationalities in a multilingual class, to answer the questions in their book.

As they talk, circulate, noting any typical mistakes which they should be able to self-correct. Use these as the basis for a correction spot either at the end of this activity/lesson or at the beginning of the next lesson. (For advice on correction, see page 16.)

2 Students listen to a discussion and identify the situations referred to.

Tapescript

SUE: You seemed really surprised in that restaurant the other night. Do you think I left a too big a tip?

BETH: No, I thought you left too little.

SUE: Too little?

BETH: Yes.

SUE: But I left ten percent.

BETH: Yes, but Americans tip fifteen and that's what I'm used to.

SUE: Fifteen?

BETH: Yeah.

SUE: Oh, that seems a lot. You don't do that in England do you?

BETH: I try not to but it's difficult.

SUE: Goodness! What about when you go out with men in the States? Who pays?

BETH: Usually the man, if, if he invites me to go out then I expect him to pay.

SUE: Really, even if he's another student?

BETH: Yeah, if I want to pay we can talk about it and usually there's no problem.

SUE: Right, but you must talk about it before you offer your part.

BETH: Absolutely.

SUE: Oh, that's strange.

BETH: It needs to be clear.

SUE: I think in Britain probably if you're students you pay half and half, er, not all couples but students I think. Yeah, yeah, that's really quite different. Um, if for example I borrowed some money from you say, something very little, to buy a packet of cigarettes for example and I didn't give you the money back the next day, how would you feel about that?

BETH: Um, a bit anxious. I would expect you to pay me back.

SUE: But I'm a friend Beth!

BETH: Well I know, and I know that you would pay me back but I would expect you to pay me back even for a packet of cigarettes.

SUE: Yeah, I think the British are like that too. Let me ask you another thing. If you found ten dollars in the street.

BETH: Uh huh.

SUE: Only ten dollars right. If money's important would you take it to the police station?

BETH: Not ten dollars no.

SUE: Ah you see. So what would you do?

BETH: I'd keep it. If I found a lot of money I'd take it to the police but not ten dollars.

SUE: No, I think it's the same here.

Answers

They discuss questions 1, 5, 7 and 9.

Explain that the discussion is between an American and a British person. Make sure they realise that the first time they listen they only need to note the number of the questions discussed.

3 They listen again for the answers to the questions discussed and say which answers surprised them.

Answers

1 The British usually tip 10%, Americans 15%.
9 The man usually pays for both of them in America. In Britain, students probably pay half each.
7 Yes, in both countries.
5 No. In both countries, people don't usually hand small amounts of money to the police.

Encourage students to write notes about each answer.

Give them a chance to discuss their answers with a partner and to listen again, if necessary, before you check what they heard with the class.

At feedback, encourage discussion of anything the students find interesting or strange. Get students to tell the class anecdotes about things they have heard or seen which reinforce or refute the information on the tape.

4+5 Students read the cartoon in their book and retell the story by answering questions.

Answers

4
1 They are husband and wife.
2 That the woman should ask for the money back from her husband.

5
1 The woman is reading from her old diary. The man is reading a newspaper and listening to her.
2 She has just read that she lent him money on their honeymoon.
3 He is laughing because he remembers; it isn't a very usual thing to do on your honeymoon.
4 He isn't laughing because she wants her money back now.

Do the first part of the exercise open-class. Ask students to read the cartoon. You should see whether they have understood it by their reaction. Ask individual students whether they think it's funny. You may like to feed in expressions like *I don't get it./British humour!/ What's funny about that?* Encourage them to ask one another about any words they need clarified and check that they realise that the couple are husband and wife.

Give students time to read the questions

before they read the joke again. Then put them in pairs to answer the questions and come up with a summary of the story.

Check one pair's version of the joke open-class, getting other students to add anything they think has been misunderstood or left out.

6,7+8 Students identify the items in the photograph and then put them in order by price and discuss their relative expense with another student.

Ask students, in pairs, to identify each item in the photograph by pointing at it and saying its name. Encourage them to ask other students open-class about anything they don't know, by referring to something else in the picture eg. *What's that, next to the banana?*

Give them time individually to number the things in order of growing expense (1 = the cheapest, 13 = the most expensive). They then compare their answers, either talking about the differences between countries or arguing over discrepancies with someone from their own country.

9+10 Students discuss present-giving in their family or country, based on the prompts and questions in their book.

Put students in groups of four or five to discuss the questions. In a multilingual class, mix nationalities and encourage discussion of the customs in different countries. In a monolingual class, encourage discussion of the habits in different families.

At feedback, get students to ask you about Britain or other English-speaking countries you know.

Answers

In Britain, generally, presents are given at all the times listed to family and friends, children generally getting the most presents. Typical gifts include books and cassettes (or socks and handkerchiefs) for birthday/Christmas; household goods for weddings (with the couple often preparing a list of acceptable gifts beforehand!) and housewarming parties; baby clothes for new babies; souvenirs from holidays; money or a specially chosen present when people leave jobs; wine when you are invited for dinner;

dinner; and plants or chocolates when you visit elderly relatives. The British and Americans also send greeting cards to a vast range of people on almost any occasion; many people believe present-giving has become very commercialised.

2 Language in context: shopping

AIMS

- To revise the language of deduction (*must be/ might be/can't be*).
- To revise the use of the Present Perfect for recent past.
- To develop the skill of reading for general and specific information.

1+2 Students speculate about what is in each person's package in the article and then skim each text to see if they were right.

Answers

2

Ian has just bought a packet of coffee and some bananas.
Bayo has just bought a ticket for a holiday.
Kate has just bought a book.
Jeanne has just bought a skirt.

Establish the task by holding up your own shopping bag and get students to tell you what might be in it. Encourage disagreement so that *must be/might be* and *can't be* are all practised.

Refer students to the article in their book and put them in pairs to do the task from the pictures only.

As they finish, get them to read the texts quickly to see if they were right.

At feedback, establish what each thing is. Beware of students saying *It must be an X.* when they know what it is. Remind them that if they are 100% sure, then they say *It's an X.*

3+4 Students read the article again to answer the more detailed questions. They then discuss what they've bought recently and their own attitude to impulsive shopping.

Answers

3

1 Ian - Not planned. He buys as he needs.
  Bayo - Planned. He worked for months to be able to afford it.

Kate - Quite planned. She's wanted to read this book for ages.
Jeanne - Probably planned, as she buys an item of clothing every month.
2 Ian buys when he needs.
  Bayo is able to decide what he wants and then work for it.
  Kate likes spending money.
  Jeanne spends all she earns and doesn't save.
3 Jeanne seems quite extravagant and Bayo and Ian seem fairly careful.

Get students to compare their answers as they finish reading and to direct each other back to the text if discrepancies occur.

At feedback, highlight the language they may need for their discussion. For example, contrast *to plan your shopping* with *to buy on impulse* and focus on the expressions *to be careful/ extravagant with money*, by asking which expression is most likely to refer to a mean or a generous person.

Put students in small groups to discuss what they have bought in the last week. Elicit from them that *in the last week* means any time from a week ago to the present and therefore requires use of the Present Perfect.

3 Thinking about learning: approaches

AIMS

- To encourage students to recognise and evaluate different ways of learning languages.
- To extend the use of verb + *like* to include ways of talking about all five senses.

1 Students discuss skills they have learned and how they learned them.

Refer students to the list of skills in their book and elicit which they can and can't do. Make sure *can* is pronounced /kən/ in ´complete sentences and /kæn/ in short answers. To get maximum practice of this vocabulary and revision of *can/can't*, set up a 'Find Someone Who' exercise as follows.

Get students to prepare a chart, with six to ten questions like these on it:

... can cook Italian food.
... can ski.
... can drive.
... can dance.
... can swim.
... can speak more than 2 languages.

Students mill round the class asking different people each question until someone says *Yes I can*. This person's name is then put on the questioner's chart. The winner is the student who completes their chart first.

Put students in small groups to discuss the remaining questions.

At feedback, ask for examples of students who learned something in a particularly interesting way.

2+3 Students listen to people talking about their experiences of language learning and answer the questions in their book. They listen again for greater detail and complete the chart.

Tapescript

1

INTERVIEWER: Liz, what language have you learnt?

LIZ: Um, I've just finished doing a course in Russian.

INTERVIEWER: Russian! That sounds really exciting. Where did you learn it?

LIZ: That was, er, that was a course of evening classes at a local college here.

INTERVIEWER: And how many evenings did you go?

LIZ: Um. Just one evening a week, we went for two hours every week, which wasn't really enough, I don't think.

INTERVIEWER: You'd need to go more often to make it worthwhile?

LIZ: I think so, if you were going to learn the language properly, yes.

INTERVIEWER: Mm. How did they teach it?

LIZ: Um. It was quite a traditional method really. We did a lot of grammar exercises, um, obviously the grammar's quite different, quite important in Russian. Um. That was OK. I didn't mind that. I actually quite like grammar.

INTERVIEWER: Any other techniques?

LIZ: Um. Yeah, there was, er, a video course.

INTERVIEWER: What did that involve?

LIZ: That was, it went with the book we were using and, er, we used to watch a one hour video each week of people talking Russian, real Russians, um so that was good, that was an interesting way to learn.

INTERVIEWER: You really enjoyed that?

LIZ: Yeah. I think it was a more valid way to learn, really.

INTERVIEWER: Was there a part of the course then that wasn't very satisfactory?

LIZ: Yeah, we did a lot of translation in class, really again it was the traditional approach, um, reading around the class, taking turns to translate things around the class, which, basically was too difficult, um, for our level, we couldn't do it at all really.

INTERVIEWER: Mm. So if, um, you know, if someone else was going to study at an evening class would you recommend it as a way of learning?

LIZ: I think it depends on the course, um, and the teacher obviously. I don't think I'll be going back to that particular college next year.

2

INTERVIEWER: Steve, what language have you learnt?

STEVE: German.

INTERVIEWER: German? And how did you learn it?

STEVE: Self-taught.

INTERVIEWER: You taught yourself? Now, what does that involve?

STEVE: Well, in my case that involved using phrase books, dictionaries, and parallel texts.

INTERVIEWER: Parallel texts? What are they?

STEVE: Well, parallel texts are when you have a story and the story is in two languages, in this case of course, German and English. And you would have the German on one side of the page and the English on the other side of the page. Um, I used to, understandably, I used to buy stories I liked, and stories in fact that I'd already read in English and so then I could read the German, remembering what I'd read in English.

INTERVIEWER: So, um, you really enjoyed that way of learning really?

STEVE: Very much.

INTERVIEWER: Yeah. And, OK, you were learning from dictionaries and and parallel texts and and phrase books, but when you were in conversation with people, did you find any difficulties at all?

STEVE: Um, I often found difficulties, um, but I had a number of friends who used to correct me, um, and that was in fact very helpful, I, I didn't mind being corrected.

INTERVIEWER: That was OK?

STEVE: That was a great assistance, yes.

INTERVIEWER: Mm. And so, I mean I suppose if you're teaching yourself, um, there must be a lot of motivation about it all - are there any negative things at all, anything you didn't enjoy doing?

STEVE: Certainly, certainly, yes. I didn't like studying the grammar by myself and, I think as a result of that, my German isn't as good as I would like it to be.

3

INTERVIEWER: Janet, do you speak a foreign language?

JANET: Mm, yes, yes I do. I'm fluent in Spanish.

INTERVIEWER: Really? How did you learn it?

JANET: Well, I went and lived in Spain for, er, two years. Um, I lived in Madrid.

INTERVIEWER: Sounds great.

JANET: Yeah, it was

INTERVIEWER: Did you know people there?

JANET: Yes, I had, I had, some friends out there, um, which was great when I first arrived, to know some people there.

INTERVIEWER: How did you go about learning the language, um, you know, did you just talk to people or where there other ways?

JANET: No, lots of ways. Um, I used to watch television. Um, I'd watch the news in Spanish for example and try to work out what was going on, um and of course I watched lots of other programmes, that was very useful, watching television.

INTERVIEWER: What other ways?

JANET: I also used to buy cassettes of, um, pop songs, you know, modern pop songs and, um, I'd learn the words and sing along in Spanish to the words.

INTERVIEWER: And which of those did you really like doing?

JANET: I loved the songs. That was great, and I learnt a lot.

INTERVIEWER: Right.

JANET: But, um, another thing I did which, um, which was useful, but not so much fun as singing songs, was, um, I used to write lists of vocabulary, you know, long lists of words, yeah, it was hard work but, um, I didn't mind that because it was so useful. I learnt a lot.

INTERVIEWER: I suppose if you were going out there and learning it the way you, you know, really wanted to there wasn't a lot that you perhaps wouldn't enjoy, but is there something that really, you know, was the most boring thing?

JANET: Oh, what I didn't like, the worst thing, um, was being corrected by my friends, you know, you're sitting in a bar or café and, um, and everything you say they're correcting. I didn't like that.

INTERVIEWER: Right.

JANET: But over all, I mean, going to the country, going to Spain to learn Spanish was wonderful. I'd recommend anybody to do it.

INTERVIEWER: Yeah.

Answers

2

1 Liz – Russian; Steve – German; Janet – Spanish

2 Liz – evening classes; Steve – self-taught; Janet – lived in Spain

3 Liz – negative; Steve – positive; Janet – positive

3	liked	didn't mind	didn't like
1	watching videos	grammar	translation
2	parallel texts	being corrected	grammar
3	singing songs	learning vocabulary	being corrected

This exercise is made up of three separate recordings which together provide for extended listening practice. If you think your class is not yet ready for this, we suggest you limit their listening to one or two of the recordings only. In this case, draw an abridged version of the chart in the Student's Book on the board for them to copy and complete. Alternatively, treat the exercise as a jigsaw activity.

Set the scene by asking individual students open-class how they began to learn English or another foreign language. Did they take formal lessons, go to the country or learn by themselves from a book? Did they feel generally positive or negative about the experience?

Refer them to the questions in their book to establish what they need to listen out for during the first listening.

Once the questions have been answered, refer them to the chart which they should copy into their notebook. Elicit examples of the type of vocabulary which could go in each column eg. dictation, watching videos, etc. and play the tape again for them to complete the chart.

Students compare their answers and listen again if they can't agree on what they heard.

At feedback, remind students to use the verbs in the chart + noun or *-ing* form. (eg. *She liked watching videos.*)

4 Students discuss their own feelings about the learning activities written on the chart.

Elicit an example open-class, inviting a student to tell you how they feel about one of the activities in their chart. Then students discuss each activity in turn with their partner.

Finally, encourage students to say what they particularly like/dislike to the class as a whole. This will give you insight into this group's preferred learning approaches for future lessons.

5 Students answer questions about the language learning advertisements in their book.

Answers

1 Language courses
2 BBC – your children will enjoy the course.
  Accelerated Learning – you'll speak confidently in 3½ weeks.
3 BBC – return your money.
  Accelerated Learning – accept the course back at no cost.
4 BBC – sight and sound
  Accelerated Learning – all your senses

Refer students to the advertisements and ask if they have heard of these or similar language learning methods.

Give them time to scan the advertisements to find the answers to the questions.

At feedback, encourage them to give natural short answers to sum up the promises in the advertisements.

Ask students what they think about the claims in the advertisements. How long do *they* think it takes to learn a language?

6-7 Students match verbs expressing the senses to the parts of the body involved and complete a gap-fill exercise with the verbs.

Answers

6	7
look like - eyes	1 feels like
feel like - hands	2 looks like
taste like - mouth	3 tastes like
sound like - ears	4 smells like
smell like - nose	5 sounds like

Introduce the idea of using all your senses. Point to different parts of the body as you ask what you do with each one eg. *eyes* to elicit *look/see/watch*; *ears* to elicit *hear/listen*; *hands* to elicit *touch* and *feel*; *nose* to elicit *smell*; *mouth/tongue* to elicit *eat/taste*.

Students now match the verbs + *like* to the parts of the body.

Students complete the exercise in their book and check their answers with a partner.

At feedback, make sure the verb, and not *like*, is stressed in the new expressions and that main stress is on the final noun in the sentences.

Check what you know 2

1 LISTENING

Tapescript

B: Hello?
A: Hi. Debbie. It's Alan.
B: Hi Alan. How are you?
A: Fine. Listen. Are you doing anything at the moment?
B: No, just watching TV.
A: Well, why don't we go and see the new film at the Rio?
B: Oh yes, I mean no, I've already seen it. How about going into town to see the new Madonna film? It's on at the Odeon.
A: Mm. Have you heard anything about it?
B: My sister says it's very exciting, so it must be good. She doesn't normally like thrillers.
A: Madonna in a thriller! OK, I'm just looking in *Time Out*. The Odeon. Yes it's on at 5.20 and 7.45.

B: Not the 5.20. The later one is better. Let's meet in front of the cinema.

A: OK. You get the tickets if you arrive first.

B: Fine, so the Odeon at 7.45. Don't be late!

1

Type of Film: *A Thriller*

Cinema: *The Odeon*

Times: *5.20 and 7.45*

Actors/actresses: *Madonna*

2

What type of film is it?

Where is it on?

What time is it on?

Who is in it?

2 PRONUNCIATION

Tapescript

1 He's very *angry*.
2 *She sang* it lots of times.
3 Has he *run* yet?
4 Is this your *cup*?
5 He *rang* home.
6 Where is the *hat*?
7 Her *uncle* is very large.
8 What a terrible *cat*.

3 READING

1 It can't be a routine job because it's exciting and different.
2 It must be a temporary job because it's for three months.
3 It might be a job for a doctor because they ask for medical experience.
4 It might be a dangerous job because you need a lot of nerve.
5 It can't be in England because it is in a tropical climate.
6 It must be a demanding job because you have to work hard.

5 VOCABULARY

Sports
football
tennis
swimming
Adjectives to describe people/things
interesting
depressing
polite
Types of films
western
horror
comedy

Education
university
qualification
subjects

6 GRAMMAR

1	when	6	did you go
2	quite	7	don't mind
3	yet	8	phones
4	looks	9	can't be
5	goes	10	Sometimes

Images

- To introduce guided visualisation as an approach to language learning.
- To revise the use of verb + *like*.
- To revise basic countryside vocabulary.

1+2 Students imagine what things are like and award themselves points depending on the clarity of their image. They tell their partner which sense they were able to evoke most strongly.

Remind students of the claims of the Accelerated Learning advertisement on page 63. Elicit the names of the five senses and ask them which they think is most important for learning a language.

(Other humanistic language learning approaches, such as Suggestopedia and Inner Track Learning also emphasise the importance of involving the whole person in learning. Visualisation activities are used in these methods.)

Refer the students to the questions in their book and the marking system. Tell them to read the first question and shut their eyes to imagine birds flying. Allow them time to imagine the picture. Tell them to open their eyes and to put the number 1, 2 or 3 next to question 1a) depending on the clarity of the picture in their imagination.

Proceed as above for the other questions.

Students total their marks and compare their results with those of another student.

At feedback, ask students which group of questions they could imagine most easily.

3-5 Students listen to the cassette and imagine a scene based on the picture in their book. When the cassette tells them to, they close their eyes and continue to imagine the scene on the other side of the door.

Tapescript

The tapescript for this activity is on page 157. If you wish, you can photocopy and distribute it to students at the end of the activity. It is not intended students should read the tapescript as they listen.

Make sure the students understand what to do. Tell them that they are going to listen to a description of the picture in their book. They should look at the parts of the picture as the tape describes them. When the tape tells them to close their eyes they should do so and continue to imagine the scene. Finally, ask an individual student to tell you what they are going to do, as a final check that your instructions have been properly understood.

Tell students to relax and take a few deep breaths.

Make sure they are looking at the picture in their book and start the tape. To gain maximum effect, follow the picture in your book yourself and close your eyes when instructed to do so by the tape.

6 Students return to reality and tell another student what they remember of the scene they imagined beyond the door.

When the tape finishes, everyone will have their eyes open. Proponents of visualisation as a teaching device emphasise the importance of a very definite return to reality and the classroom at the end of the experience. Tell the students they are no longer in the garden but back in the classroom. Put them in pairs to tell each other what they can remember of the garden on the other side of the door.

At feedback, ask a few different students what they imagined. Finally ask them what they thought of the experience. Do they think that reference to their feelings and senses is helpful in learning English?

11 Changes

1 Preparation

AIMS

- To develop the skills of listening for general, specific and inferred information.
- To revise the use of the Present Perfect for indefinite past time.
- To highlight the difference in meaning between the past participles *been* and *gone*.

1+2 Students describe the photographs on the page and predict what the song will be about. They listen to the song to identify which things in the photographs are mentioned in the song.

Tapescript

See the Students Book, page 133 for tapescript.

Answers

Possible answers

1
1 Evacuees are probably waiting at a station.
2 Young girls are carrying bunches of flowers.   3 A newly-wed couple are walking along a street.
4 Lovers are kissing goodbye as the man goes off to war.   5 Soldiers are carrying a coffin in a graveyard.   6 An old woman is crying.
2 flowers, girls, husbands/soldiers, graveyard

Refer students to the photographs and ask them to name the people/things they see open-class. Elicit sentences describing what the people in the photographs are doing, thereby checking the vocabulary needed for the song.

Ask students to listen to the song and tell you which people or things in the picture are mentioned. They compare their answer with another student before confirming with you.

3+4 Students listen to the song again and answer the questions in their book. They then infer the singer's attitude to war from the words in the song.

Answers

3
Verse 1: Question: Where have all the flowers gone?
           Answer: Young girls have picked them.
Verse 2: Question: Where have all the young girls gone?
           Answer: Gone for husbands.
Verse 3: Question: Where have all the young men gone?
           Answer: Gone for (to be) soldiers.
Verse 4: Question: Where have all the soldiers gone?
           Answer: Gone to graveyards (died).
Verse 5: Question: Where have all the graveyards gone?
           Answer: Gone to flowers (have become covered with flowers).

4
1 It is an anti-war song.
2 *When will they ever learn?* She is pessimistic.

NB Answers
1 been
2 gone

Elicit the name of the song and tell students to listen again for the changes in each verse. They note the question and the answer in each verse.

Play the tape as many times as necessary for both students to agree in each pair.

When you check their answers open-class, encourage them to contract the questions and to use their notes to produce full Present Perfect sentences. (eg. *Young girls have picked them every one.*)

Play the song again so students can answer the final set of questions. Give them time to confer before they tell you what they think. Refer them to the words on page 133 if they find this difficult and let them work from the tapescript.

Elicit/tell the class that this song was written by the British singer Pete Seeger in the early 1960s when anti-war songs were popular. They were often sung on anti-Vietnam demonstrations.

Find out if students know a version of the song in their own language.

Finally, if the class would like you to, play the tape again and encourage students to sing along. In a multilingual class, if the students are willing, you could finish with verses in different languages.

Refer students to the NB Box *been vs gone* and ask the questions. As a further check, ask students to copy the time-line from the Language Review on page 71.

2 Speaking

AIMS

- To provide personalised speaking practice revising the Past Simple + *ago*.

1-3 Students complete the chart, first with their dates and then with their partner's dates. Finally, they tell the class something interesting they found out.

Before students ask their partner for their dates, check the question form of the first question open-class. (*When did you last move house?*)

At feedback, encourage students to give as much information as they can remember.

3 Grammar: Present Perfect: unfinished past

AIMS

- To introduce and practise the use of the Present Perfect for talking about things that began in the past and continue into the present.

1 Students use the example sentence in their book to deduce the new concept of the Present Perfect.

Answers

1 Yes.   2 In 1991   3 Moved

Elicit/write the example sentence onto the board. This should clarify that the Present Perfect is used to describe an action that began in the

past but continues into the present. (In other languages, the Present Simple is often used to express this.)

Ask the check questions open-class.

2 Students write positive and negative sentences about their partner, based on the information in the chart.

Make sure students realise it is not necessary for them to express each piece of information in both the positive and negative forms. They should choose a form/s that makes sense. (*She hasn't been on holiday since . . .* doesn't lend itself to a positive form.)

3 Students find out where other students live and work and how long they have done so.

Answers

Where do you live/work?
How long have you lived/worked there?

Elicit the two questions open-class, reinforcing the difference in concept between the Present Simple and this use of the Present Perfect.

Make sure students say the questions with falling intonation, stressing *live/work* in the first question above and *long* in the second question. Get students to pronounce unstressed *do you* as /dʒʊ/ and *have* as /əv/.

If possible, students mill around the classroom, asking the questions to as many students as they can. If not, get them to ask the students sitting near them. Give them the task of finding the person who has lived in the same house and/or worked in the same job for the greatest length of time.

4 Vocabulary

AIMS

- To teach students nouns related to life changing events.
- To encourage students to organise their vocabulary in word families.
- To provide personalised speaking practice incorporating the new vocabulary and the Present Perfect (unfinished past).

1+2 Students match nouns to definitions in their book. They then make the opposites of the nouns based on the first two letters of each one.

Answers

1		**2**
1 d)	4 b)	birth/death
2 a)	5 c)	divorce/marriage
3 e)		redundancy/employment
		illness/health
		wealth/poverty

Put students in pairs to do these exercises. Remind them of their mini-dictionary on page 138 in case they have problems.

3 Students pool their knowledge and use their mini-dictionary to find related adjectives and verbs.

Answers

marriage (*n*), married (*adj*), to marry (or get married) (*v*)
divorce (*n*), divorced (*adj*), to divorce (or get divorced) (*v*)
employment (*n*), employed (*adj*), to employ (*v*)
redundancy (*n*), redundant (*adj*), to be made redundant (*v*)
health (*n*), healthy (*adj*), to be healthy (*v*)
illness (*n*), ill (*adj*), to be ill (*v*)
poverty (*n*), poor (*adj*), to be poor (*v*)
wealth (*n*), wealthy (*adj*), to be wealthy (*v*)

Ask students to make three columns, headed *nouns, adjectives* and *verbs* in their notebook.

Put students in small groups to pool what they already know and to decide what to look up in their mini-dictionary.

As groups finish, get them to compare their lists and then elicit the answers open-class. Encourage students to put the vocabulary in sentences eg. *Tell me about your children, Alicia, when were they born?*

4 Students tell each other about the things that has changed their life the most in the last five years.

Refer students to the prompts in their book and give them a chance to ask you about this or other vocabulary for the task. As an example, tell

students about something that has changed your life recently. Then put them in pairs to talk together.

5 Reading

AIMS

- To develop the skills of reading for general and specific information.
- To provide speaking practice (as students exchange information).

1+2 Students read about one of the couples in the article to answer the questions.

Answers

1
Bill and Jane
1 Bill was made redundant.
2 They were worried when it happened.
3 They are still worried.

Debbie and Martin
1 Debbie got a better job.
2 They were excited when it happened.
3 Debbie is worried and he tolerates the situation.

2
Bill and Jane
1 Last year.
2 They have had a baby; Jane has given up work; her father has died; they have moved house. Since Bill was made redundant, he has spent more time with the baby but lost confidence and self-respect; he has recently begun to enjoy the free time; they have had to borrow money and they are both worried about this.

Debbie and Martin
1 18 months ago.
2 They have had more money but less time together; she has worked and travelled a lot; she has bought new clothes etc.; she has had less time for her family and friends; he has become less happy about the whole situation.

Divide the class into two groups, A and B. Make sure that each group knows which section to read and understands to answer the first set of questions for that section only. As they finish, they check their answers with another student in the same group. If they don't agree on the answers, they should refer each other back to the text and, if necessary, ask for your help.

They then read the article again to answer the more detailed questions.

3,4+5 Students check they have understood the details of their section. They then work with a student who read the other section and exchange information. Finally, they answer questions referring to both couples.

Get two or three students who have read the same section to make sure they agree on the answers to their questions.

Pair students from group A with students from group B. They tell each other about their couple and then discuss the questions in Exercise 5. Make sure they realise that they should give their opinions and that there are no correct answers.

Finally, ask one or two students to tell the class what they and their partner thought and encourage further discussion.

6 Grammar: *for/since*

AIMS

- To contrast the use of *for* and *since*.
- To provide further practice of the Present Perfect for talking about the unfinished past.
- To revise/extend the students' range of words and expressions relating to time.

1 Students deduce the difference in use between *since* and *for* by referring to example sentences and answering the questions in their book.

Answers

1 This depends on the date at the time you are using the book!
2 *since*
3 *for*

Put the example sentences on the board and elicit the number of years after *for* as you do so. Take the present year date as your starting point so if you do this exercise in 1995 the answer will be *for five years*.

Ask the check questions open-class.

2 Students complete a time-line to reinforce the meaning of *for* and *since*.

Answers

for three days   *since* Monday

Ask students to copy the time-line into their notebook and to complete the gaps, checking with a partner.

As a pair finish, invite one of them to the board to draw the completed time-line for the class to see.

3 Students put the expressions in their book in the *for* or *since* column.

Answers

For: many years, three days, ten minutes, two weeks, a few months, a long time, ages, a while
Since: 1990, April 29th, yesterday, we last met, last night, 3.30, 1987, the summer, January, Monday

Students do this alone or in pairs, checking their answers with other students when they finish. Deal with any discrepancies open-class.

Pronunciation

AIMS

- To highlight the pronunciation of unstressed *for*, with or without the final /r/ sound.
- To provide controlled practice of time expressions with *for*.

1+2 Students listen and repeat the expressions. They listen again and mark the final /r/ where they hear it.

Tapescript/Answers

for three days	for a long time
for ten minutes	for ages
for two weeks	for a while
for a few months	

Elicit the first example, *for many years*, from the *for* column in the last exercise. Make sure students say the weak form /fə/.

Play the tape, stopping it after each example for choral and then individual repetition.

Put the example *for a few months* on the board and ask an individual student to say it. Highlight the /r/ sound at the end and mark how it links to the next word.

Tell students to look at the other expressions using *for* in their notebook and to mark them in the same way if they hear the final /r/.

Play the tape again and then elicit that /r/ is heard when *for* precedes a vowel sound. Get students to tell you the relevant expressions.

3 Students make up other expressions of time using *for* based on those in their book.

Make sure students understand that they should make up other expressions around the basic unit of time. Put them to work on this in pairs, then hear their expressions in feedback.

7 Speaking

AIMS

- To provide personalised freer practice of Present Perfect + *for/since*.
- To revise/introduce personal possessions vocabulary.

1 Students say which things listed they or their family have/haven't got and how long they have had them.

Check the question forms for this activity open-class. Get an individual student to ask you if you have got one of the possessions listed and then how long you have had it.

Put students in pairs to ask their partner in turn about each thing on the list.

2 Students answer the questions in their book to talk about the last present they received.

Give an example of this yourself. Show students something you have got on you (eg. a brooch, a pen) and tell them on what occasion you got it and who gave it to you.

They tell each other about their last present, though not necessarily showing it to their partner.

Ask individual students about their partner's present open-class.

Grammar: *give* + two objects

AIMS

- To revise/introduce two ways of combining *give* with direct and indirect objects.

1 Students work out the 'rules' for this grammar point by looking at example sentences and answering the questions in their book.

Answers

1 a watch	4 the thing she gave
2 him	5 *to*
3 the person she gave it to	

Either copy the example sentences from their book onto the board or elicit two similar sentences about a particular student's present from the last exercise.

Ask the check questions open-class. Encourage students to use the most common form of *give* + indirect object without *to*, + direct object, as shown in sentence a). Get them to use this form to tell you about their last present. Who gave them what?

Highlight that when the pronouns *it/them* are used instead of the direct object, we often use the other form, as shown in sentence b). Get students to use this form by asking individual students eg. *Who gave you your watch Paolo?*

2 Students rearrange jumbled words to make sentences.

Answers

1 Give it to me tomorrow.
2 Her brother gave me some chocolate.
3 She gives them socks every Christmas.
4 He has given his mother expensive perfume.

Students do this individually and check their answers in pairs.

At feedback, get them to repeat the correct answer as it is suggested.

3 Students tell one another about their most treasured possession, answering the questions in their book.

Put students in groups of three or four. Make sure they realise that this time they talk about their favourite, not their most recent, possession.

Encourage students to ask questions to get more information as they listen.

Tapescript

1

INTERVIEWER: Margaret, what's your most treasured possession?

MARGARET: Um, I think, I think it's probably a pen.

INTERVIEWER: A pen? What kind of a pen?

MARGARET: That's, er, it's a rather nice old-fashioned kind of fountain pen, one of the ones you have to put the ink in yourself.

INTERVIEWER: And who gave you that?

MARGARET: That was my mum.

INTERVIEWER: Your mother gave it to you?

MARGARET: Yep.

INTERVIEWER: That's nice. When did she give it to you?

MARGARET: Well, let's think. It would be about seven years ago now, I suppose, while I was at university.

INTERVIEWER: And why did she give it to you?

MARGARET: It was a time I was doing my final exams and I was feeling a bit uncertain about them, I wasn't sure if I was going to pass or not so she gave me the pen as a sort of a good luck charm.

INTERVIEWER: And that's really why it's so special to you, because it's a lucky charm.

MARGARET: Uh huh. Yeah, and it actually worked because I did pass the exams in the end and it's also a very nice pen.

2

INTERVIEWER: Richard, what's your most treasured possession?

RICHARD: I think, probably it would be my Pentax camera, actually, yeah.

INTERVIEWER: Was it a present?

RICHARD: Yes it was. Um. My grandfather gave it to me, er, a while ago now, in fact.

INTERVIEWER: How long ago?

RICHARD: That must be ten years ago, I think, yeah.

INTERVIEWER: Why did he give it to you?

RICHARD: It was just before I got my first job abroad. It was in Cairo, in Egypt and, er, he gave it to me because I was leaving.

INTERVIEWER: And why is it so special to you?

RICHARD: I think it is really special because I've been travelling, um, quite a bit in the last few years and it's always gone with me everywhere I've been and it's, er, with it I've been able to take lots of

photographs and they're memories for me so it's really been the source of a lot of special memories.

3

INTERVIEWER: Susannah, what's your most treasured possession?

SUSANNAH: Um, I think it's my car.

INTERVIEWER: Was it a present?

SUSANNAH: No, I bought it myself, but I had to save a lot of money for it first.

INTERVIEWER: Right, and so you're very fond of it?

SUSANNAH: Yes, I am. It was, it was quite cheap and nothing special but it's got a lot of character.

INTERVIEWER: When did you buy it?

SUSANNAH: Um, I bought it about a year ago, so it still feels quite new and exciting.

INTERVIEWER: So what makes it so special for you?

SUSANNAH: Um, well it gives me my independence. I don't have to rely on my friends to drive me to places. I can go wherever I like. I like travelling, um, and so I can take it on holiday with me.

Answers

	Person 1	Person 2	Person 3
1	a fountain pen	a camera	a car
2	a present from her mother	a present from his grandfather	no, she bought it herself
3	to bring her luck in her exams	because he was leaving Britain to go abroad	–
4	about 7 years	10 years	a year
5	it is a good luck charm	the source of a lot of special memories	gives her independence

Ask students to write the number of each question, 1-5, three times in their notebooks.

They listen to the tape and write short/one-word answers by each number in their notebook. They listen more than once, if necessary, conferring with their partner between listenings.

When they have all the information they need, give them a couple of minutes to recode their notes to one another, in order to tell the class what they heard.

Alternatively, treat this as a jigsaw activity (see page 16).

English in action

AIMS

- To provide an opportunity for freer speaking practice.
- To give written practice of the Present Perfect +/- *for* and *since*.

1 Students roleplay an interview between a prospective emigrant to Australia and an Australian immigration official.

Set the scene for the activity by asking students which country is depicted in the photographs. Divide the class into two groups, explaining that half the class want to move to Australia permanently. The others are Australian immigration officials.

Refer the immigration officials to their instructions on page 125 and the would-be emigrants to their instructions on page 70. Give them time to read the instructions and to ask you if there is anything they don't understand.

When students have completed their first task, they compare their ideas with another student playing the same role.

They then have the interview in pairs with an emigrant talking to an immigration official.

2-6 Students write character references for each other, based on the model in their book. They read the reference written for them and comment on its fairness.

Tell students that whether they emigrate to Australia or not, they will all need character references to go to live abroad. Refer them to the model, asking them to list the sort of information that is included in this character reference.

At feedback, elicit any other areas they might include, stressing that this reference is for general character and not for a particular job. Elicit how these references are headed and how each paragraph deals with a new subject area.

Put students in pairs and give them time to think of questions they need to ask their partner. Then tell them they have three minutes each to ask their questions.

Students can either write the reference in class or for homework. In either case, encourage them to hand in the final version to you. Remind them that this type of writing usually demands more than one draft. They will probably appreciate your comments before the final draft is written; since references need to be accurate, suggest linguistic corrections as well as suggesting where the content needs to be clearer for the reader. However, individual style makes references more interesting so try to keep the flavour of the original reference.

Get students to swap their references and to decide how true/fair their own reference is.

Language review 11

a
1 gone   3 been
2 been   4 gone

b
1 lives
2 works
3 has he worked
4 have you known
5 do not (don't)
6 have got ('ve got)
7 have had it ('ve had it)

c
1 We have known Carlos since 1990.
2 They have been married for a long time.
3 He has lived in San Francisco for 18 months.
4 She has been in hospital since Saturday.
5 She has been a teacher for three years.

d
1 Sally gave Christopher a pen and a book.
2 Tony gave Sophie a camera.
3 José gave Ali a shirt and tie.

e
1 Sally gave them to Christopher.
2 Tony gave it to Sophie.
3 José gave them to Ali.

12 *Memory*

1 Preparation

AIMS

- To introduce the theme of memory.
- To revise a variety of basic vocabulary.
- To highlight the weak forms of *was/were*.

1+2 Students look at the photograph in their book for two minutes and then list the objects they remember. They check their answers with another student, using *There was/were* . . .

Answers

a biro	some keys (5)
a watch	a spoon
a rubber	some stamps (8)
two apples	a cassette
a tea cup and saucer	a dictionary
a pencil	two bars of chocolate
a map	a wallet
a ruler	a cheque book
a calculator	six credit/telephone cards
a camera	two ten pound notes

Make sure students know what to do and what the time limit is. Ask them to shut their books when you say *Stop!* and write as many things as they can remember.

Elicit an example from one student and check that they pronounce *was* or *were* as weak forms.

Put students in pairs to check their lists together.

At feedback, find out which pair has the greatest number of objects between them. As they list their objects, others should tick them off their list and volunteer any that haven't been mentioned by the winning pair at the end.

2 Speaking

AIMS

- To provide an opportunity for speaking practice.
- To develop the skill of reading for specific information.

1-3 Students decide which type of things they are likely to remember/forget . They discuss these with another student before reading the article to find out what scientists think.

Answers

3
1 Most pleasant experiences, things that interest us, things we have a special reason to remember (eg. the death of a President), things we think about just before we go to sleep and unpleasant things we would like to forget.
2 Names, numbers, dates, information learned for exams and things we do not understand or find interesting. Also things when we are embarrassed, ill or very tired and routine, everyday things.

Check the key vocabulary *to remember* and *to forget* by asking students if they have a good or bad memory. Then ask them to read the list of things in their book and to decide which they remember easily and which they forget.

Put them in pairs to compare their answers. Elicit which things they agree on and which they don't. Then direct them to the article to see who is right according to the scientists.

Encourage students to express any disagreement with the article open-class.

3 Listening

- To develop the skills of listening for general and specific information.
- To provide contextualised examples of the Past Continuous for interrupted actions in the past.
- To revise year and month dates.

1 Students match historic events to dates.

Answers

Elvis Presley died in August 1977.
There was a big earthquake in San Francisco in April 1906.
The Berlin Wall came down in November 1989.
Nelson Mandela was released in February 1990.
Marlene Dietrich died in April 1992.

Check students' ability to say month and year dates by asking one person when they were born. Get them to ask someone else in the class and so on until any problems in pronunciation have been ironed out.

Refer students to the dates in the chart and elicit how to say each one.

Ask which events are portrayed in the photographs on the page and then give students time to match each event in the chart to its date. Students compare what they think with a partner and then check their answers as a class.

2 Students listen to the cassette and number the events as they are talked about.

Tapescript

1
I remember exactly what I was doing when I heard Marlene Dietrich had died. I was at the theatre in London. I went to see *The Phantom of the Opera*. We heard the news in the interval. I was buying an ice-cream at the time. It made me feel rather old.

2
When I heard there had been another big earthquake in San Francisco I was playing tennis with my father. We were on vacation and my mother came running to tell us the news. Our house had been completely destroyed. There was nothing left.

3
There were a lot of changes in many countries at the time but I really didn't think it could happen in Germany so quickly. I couldn't believe it when I heard people were knocking the wall down. I turned off the radio and phoned my German friend Birgit to tell her.

4
I wasn't really surprised. We were expecting Mandela's release from prison, but when my friend told me I was so pleased for a minute I couldn't do anything. I was shaving, in fact, which was a shame because I stopped dead and cut myself.

Answers

Marlene Dietrich died (1)
Earthquake in San Francisco (2)
Berlin Wall came down (3)
Mandela released (4)

Get students to copy the names of the people and events in their notebook. They then number them in the order they hear them. At feedback, also elicit which event/s are not referred to (Elvis Presley's death).

3 Students listen again and number the activity of each speaker at the time the event took place.

Answers

b) buying an ice-cream (1)
g) playing tennis (2)
a) listening to the radio (3)
e) shaving (4)

Students listen and note which activity the four people were doing at the time of the event.

At feedback, check the answers open-class, without insisting that students form complete Past Continuous sentences at this point.

4 Grammar: Past Continuous (interrupted action)

- To highlight the use and form of the Past Continuous for talking about interrupted action in the past.

1 Students deduce this use and form of the Past Continuous by looking at example sentences and answering the questions in their book.

Answers

1 shaving/telling news
2 shaving started first, telling news interrupted it
3 *told* is in the Past Simple, *shaving* is in the Past Continuous
4 Past Continuous: *was/were* + present participle
   negative: after *was/were* + *not*
   question: invert *was/were* and the subject

Elicit to the board the first sentence in the grammar box and ask the first two check questions to establish the sequence of events.

Check the concept again by drawing a time-line on the board, like the one in the Language Review on page 77, but using the model sentence.

Ask one student how to talk about the time shown by the wiggly line. Then add the Past Continuous sentence to the diagram.

Refer students to the chart in their book which shows that the Past Continuous sentence can be in first or second position in the sentence.

Get them to answer questions 2 and 3 in pairs before eliciting the answers open-class.

Pronunciation

AIMS

- To highlight a typical stress and intonation pattern for Past Continuous sentences.
- To highlight that unstressed *was* is pronounced /wəz/.

1 Students listen to the example sentences and locate main stress in each clause and the weak form /wəz/.

Tapescript

I was shaving when he told me the news.
He told me the news when I was shaving.

Answers

1 The information words *shaving* and *news* are stressed in each clause. *Was* is weak and pronounced /wəz/.

Ask students the two questions in their book before they listen to the sentences on cassette.

2 They listen again to identify the intonation pattern.

Answers

1 The voice goes up at the end of the first clause; the sentence is unfinished.
2 The voice goes down at the end of the second clause; the sentence is finished.

Ask students if the first part of each question goes up or down and play the tape again. When they have identified the movement of the voice, remind them that a rising intonation often suggests incompletion (cf Unit 3 and Unit 8).

3 Students practise saying similar sentences.

Answers

The first person was buying an ice-cream when she heard about Marlene Dietrich.
The second person was playing tennis when he heard about the earthquake.
The third person was listening to the radio when she heard about the Berlin Wall.
The fourth person was shaving when he heard about Nelson Mandela.

Refer students to the example in their book and put them in pairs to create the sentences.

Hear their sentences open-class.

4 Students mime activities until the teacher says *Stop!*. They then write down what other people in the class were doing.

Either refer students to the list in their book to choose an activity to mime, or give each student a strip of paper with one activity for them to mime written on it. They mustn't show anyone else their strip of paper.

Give students time for their mime to become quite obvious and for them to have a good look round. Then say *Stop!*.

Students work in pairs, as quietly as possible, to remind each other what other students were doing. One of them writes down the example sentences.

Say *Stop!* again once students begin to dry up.

Find out which pair has the most sentences. Ask them to read their sentences to the class, while others listen and tick off the sentences they also have. If wrong information is given then the student named says what she/he was actually doing. Finally, get anyone with a sentence not referred to by the winning pair, to contribute their sentence.

5 Reading

AIMS

- To pre-teach selected vocabulary for the reading text.
- To develop skills of reading for general and specific information and of inferring information from text.
- To highlight the difference between *to remind* and *to remember*.

1 Students answer the questions about the slate in order to understand the words *slate*, *item, cellophane, to clear* and *to cross off*.

Answers

1 To write things on that you want to remember.
2 Because they have been done.
3 By lifting the cellophane and separating it from the board below.

Refer students to the picture of the slate/memory board and say it is important to the text they are going to read.

Elicit open-class that *the slate* is used to write things on that you want to remember eg. a shopping list. We *cross off items* to show action has been taken. *To clear* the slate you lift up *the cellophane*. As a further check ask students what we call the thing to write lists on (the slate); what we do to show we have done something on the list (cross it off); another word for the thing on the list (an item); why we lift the cellophane (to clear the slate); and what we lift to clear the slate (the cellophane).

2 Students read the page from the novel for general understanding.

Answers

1 Because Constance can't remember things and uses it to know what to do each day.
2 Diana, Constance and David. Diana and Constance are friends who live together. David is Constance's (twin) brother.

Refer students to the book cover and elicit the name of the novel and the writer. Tell them that Jane Rule is a twentieth century American writer. Assure them that the page they are going to read is not difficult and that it isn't necessary to understand every word. There is a glossary of difficult words under the text.

From the picture on the cover of the book students can see there are three important people in the book. Ask them to read the page and answer the questions in their book.

Give them a chance to confer with a partner before you ask for the answers open-class.

3 Students read again and infer the answers to the more detailed questions.

Answers

1 Because she suffers from extreme loss of memory.
2 Every day.
3 She reminded her to get dressed. It isn't usual to need to remind people of this and the consequences of forgetting could be funny!
4 He usually comes round for dinner.
5 Because she can't remember the bad things that happen.

NB answers

1 *remember*
2 *remind*

Give students time to read and clarify the questions before they read the text again. Refer them to the text again and encourage student discussion if there are discrepancies at feedback.

Refer students to the NB Box *remember vs remind* and ask the check questions. This is intended for clarification so students can recognise *remind* in context. We do not suggest you spend time getting students to produce comparative examples at this level.

4 Students match Constance's activities to the words on her memory board in the novel. They number the activities in the order she did them.

Answers

a) 6 b) 2 c) 5 d) 9 e) 3 f) 4 g) 8 h) 1 i) 7

Put students in pairs to do this activity and check their order as a class.

6 Writing

AIMS

- To revise/teach/practise the use of sequencers for writing paragraphs.
- To revise the Past Simple and *going to* future.

1 Students pool their knowledge to answer the questions about the sequencers in their book.

Answers

1 first
2 finally
3 next, then, after that

Elicit/provide the answers to these questions open-class.

2 Students use the sequencers to write a paragraph saying what Constance did, based on the information in her memory board.

Students work in pairs to organise Constance's activities into a paragraph. Make sure they know to write their paragraph in the past, using the sequencers provided.

Either collect in their work to mark or get students to swap their paragraphs and check one another's work.

3-4 Students write a chronological list of things they have to do tomorrow. Another student reads the list and, using sequencers, tells the class what their partner is going to do.

Encourage students to write as complete a list as possible, in note form, putting their activities in the order they expect to do them.

NB This list will be needed for the English in Action activity at the end of the unit, so make sure students keep it safely.

7 Vocabulary: shops and products

AIMS

- To revise/teach the names of a selection of shops and associated products.
- To focus on the pronunciations of *s* in plural nouns.
- To highlight and provide practice in the pronunciation of consonant clusters at the end and in the middle of words.

1 Students listen and repeat the words in their book. They identify the pronunciation of the final *s* in each word.

Answers/Tapescript

ice-creams /z/	lamb chops /s/
sandwiches /ɪz/	crisps /s/
traveller's cheques /s/	stamps /s/
aspirins /z/	

Use pictures or the actual items to elicit the singular form of the products. (Use a picture of an ice-cream cone, not a bowl of ice-cream, to elicit the countable noun *an ice-cream*). Check that the students are using *a/an*, pronounced /ə/ and /ən/ appropriately.

Now ask them to say the plural forms of the words. They will probably find this more difficult to get their tongues round.

Suggest they listen carefully to the tape to hear how the final *s* is pronounced in each case. First, get them to copy this chart from the board into their notebook:

	/s/	/z/	/ɪz/
ice-creams			
sandwiches			
traveller's cheques			
aspirins			
lamb chops			
crisps			
stamps			

Do the first example open class, getting students to tick the /z/ column, then play the tape, stopping it after each word.

Check their answers open-class, getting students first to say the isolated *s* sound and then to add it to the singular noun.

2 Students match each product to a place in the photographs.

Answers

You can get ice-creams at the newsagent's.
You can get sandwiches at the baker's.
You can get traveller's cheques at the bank.
You can get aspirins at the chemist's.
You can get lamb chops at the butcher's.
You can get crisps at the supermarket.
You can get stamps at the post-office.

Check the names of each place in the photographs open-class. If students have problems saying the consonant clusters at the end of the shop names (eg. chemist's), get them to isolate the sound made by the final s and add it to the name of the shop-keeper.

Students make seven columns in their notebook, each one headed by the name of a place in the photographs. They choose one of the products in their book to write beneath each place. They should use each product once only.

Let them check their answers with a partner before you elicit complete sentences open-class.

At feedback, encourage students to say where else each product could be bought.

3 Students add other things to their list of possible purchases from each place.

Put students in pairs to add two more things to each column in their notebook.

As they finish they compare their answers with another pair, adding things they haven't already listed.

As this group of four finish, they compare their list with another group of four, and so on, until they have all the items suggested by their classmates on their list.

At feedback, check spelling and pronunciation of all the items and write them on the board.

4 Finally, Students make shopping lists, choosing at least one thing to get from each place, in preparation for the grammar activity to come.

NB Answer

any is generally used in questions and negative sentences.

Get students to write their own shopping list individually. Tell them to write the thing they most need to get next time they go to each place in the photographs.

Refer students at this point to the NB box *some vs any* and ask the check question. To get further revision of *some* and *any* with countable and uncountable nouns, refer students to the Language Review for homework andor use the dialogue in the NB box as a model for pairs practice, like this:

a) Student A looks at the list of items on the board and Student B looks at her/his own shopping list.

b) Student A asks Student B if she/he needs any of the things listed under a particular shop eg. *Do you need any aspirins, toothpaste or soap?* Student B responds according to her/his own shopping list: eg. *I need some toothpaste but I don't need any aspirins or soap.*

c) Students then change roles and Student A answers according to her/his own shopping list.

Grammar: infinitive of purpose

AIMS

* To introduce the use of the infinitive (with *to*) to answer the question *Why?*
* To highlight the use of the verb *get* to mean *buy*.

Students ask and answer about each other's shopping list based on the example in their book.

Get a student to ask you why you are going to a particular shop. Answer eg. *To get some meat.*

Elicit the two-line dialogue, based on the one in their book, to the board. Include the words, *because I want*, in brackets, to highlight the meaning behind the infinitive of purpose.

Put students in new pairs. Tell them to ask about each shop in their book and to make a note of the thing their new partner says they are going to buy.

At feedback ask individual students to tell you about their partner, like this: *She's going to the butcher's to get some steak.*

English in action

AIMS

- To provide further practice of language from the unit.

1-3 Students find out what the LOCI method is by reading a caption from a page of *The Sunday Times Magazine*. They then try to decipher an example of the method by interpreting the picture.

Answers

1 It's a way of remembering lists of things by visualising them.

3 Going down the left-hand side and up the right-hand side of the street, the artist wanted to remember to:
- cancel the newspapers (the elephant)
- check his wash bag for things like sticking plaster and aspirins (on roof)
- buy film for his camera
- get some foreign money in small change to use on arrival
- take out travel insurance (broken leg)
- buy books to read
- buy new ski-goggles
- start doing ski exercises (on chimney)
- find his passport
- find warm clothes
- buy suntan lotion (on the roundabout)
- decide what time to leave for the airport

Ask if anyone has heard of the LOCI method. If so, let them tell the class what they know and use the caption as a final check.

Elicit that *The Sunday Times* is a Sunday newspaper. Put students in pairs to decipher the map.

Hear some of the interpretations open-class, encouraging students to use prepositions of place, before sending students to the solution on page 125.

4-5 Students draw a LOCI map to remind them what to do tomorrow. They then ask about their partner's map to find out what it means.

Refer students to their own memory board list which they planned in Exercise 6 Writing on page 75. From this and the shops in a familiar shopping street, they construct their map.

Before they ask and answer about their maps in pairs, ask one student why they have drawn a particular item, to elicit an answer using the infinitive of purpose eg. *To remind* me to buy flowers for my mother.

Students may like to see more than one person's LOCI map. Either display them in the classroom or suggest they form a basis for an article in the class magazine. (For advice on making a class magazine, see English in Action, Unit 1.)

Language review 12

a
1 It started to rain when I was driving to work.
2 They were having breakfast when the post arrived.
3 He was dreaming of his girlfriend when the alarm clock went off.
4 He was making dinner when she told him the news.

b
Possible answers
1 To get some money, to open an account, etc.
2 To borrow books, to do research, etc.
3 To look at paintings, to buy new paintings, etc.

1 To read the news, to see what's on TV, etc.
2 To get fit, to save money on bus fares, etc.
3 To put up pictures, to mend a fence, etc.
4 To sew on a button, to make a dress, etc.

c
1 any 2 some 3 any 4 some 5 any 6 any 7 some 8 some 9 any

d
Possible answer
Yesterday Alfonso had a disastrous day. First, he was having a bath when he heard the doorbell ring. So he got out of the bath, put on a dressing gown and ran downstairs. Then, when he was running downstairs, he tripped over a magazine and fell to the bottom. He got up and went to open the door. But the telephone rang when he was opening the door so he went to answer it. Finally, he was speaking on the telephone when the bath ran over and water started pouring down the stairs.

13 Time for politics

1 Preparation

AIMS

• To introduce the theme of the unit.
• To revise the Past Continuous for interrupted actions.

1 Students match photographs of famous historical people to their quotes.

Answers

Hamlet - 'To be or not to be, that is the question'.
Martin Luther King - 'I have a dream'.
Marie-Antoinette - 'Let them eat cake'.
Winston Churchill - 'We shall fight on the beaches'.
Nixon - 'There will be no whitewash at the White House'.
Napoleon - 'Not tonight Josephine'.

Refer students to the photographs and check whether students have heard of the people. Encourage students who know who they are to tell the others about them open-class.

Put students in small groups to match the quotes to the people. If necessary, clarify vocabulary in the quotes with groups as they work.

2-3 Students match the quotes to the occasion they were said and then write explanatory sentences, using the Past Continuous.

Answers

2

a) Martin Luther King   d) Marie-Antoinette
b) Napoleon   e) Churchill
c) Hamlet   f) Nixon

3
Martin Luther King was speaking at a political rally when he said 'I have a dream'.
Napoleon was speaking to his mistress when he said 'Not tonight Josephine'.

Hamlet was speaking to himself when he said 'To be or not to be, that is the question'.
Marie Antoinette was speaking about the poor when she said 'Let them eat cake'.
Churchill was speaking on the radio when he said 'We shall fight on the beaches'.
Nixon was speaking to members of the government when he said 'There will be no whitewash at the White House'.

Elicit who said which words open-class. Refer students to the list of options in their book and ask them to match an occasion to each quote.

Put students in pairs to write sentences, based on the example in their book. Check their answers open-class.

2 Grammar: subject questions

AIMS

• To introduce/practise subject questions and revise object questions.

1 Students look at the subject and object questions and answer the questions.

Answers

1 a) Napoleon b) Josephine. 2 b) 3 a)

Elicit the examples in the grammar box to the board and ask the check questions open-class.

2-4 Students read the statements about Napoleon and make questions to find out more about him. They then answer the questions.

Answers

2
1 Who adored him?
2 Which battles did he win?

3 What went wrong?
4 Who captured Napoleon?
5 Where did he live in exile?
6 How did he die? When did he die?
3
He was Emperor of France from 1804 to 1814.
1 He was adored by the French.
2 He won, among others, the battles of Austerlitz,
   Ulm, Wagram and Borodino.
3 He lost the battle of Waterloo.
4 Wellington captured Napoleon.
5 He lived in exile on Elba and Saint Helena.
6 He died, either of cancer or poison, in 1821.

Put students in pairs and make sure they realise that the questions they make should ask for further information and should not simply turn the statement into a question form. Questions will be either object or subject questions depending on the information they want.

When you have checked the question formation open-class, put students in small groups to answer the questions. They make a note of questions they cannot answer.

Go through their answers, getting students to read out their questions at each stage. Encourage other students to answer the questions, before answering them yourself, if necessary.

Vocabulary: political leaders

AIMS

• To introduce and practise a set of nouns to describe political leaders.

1-2 Students match the new vocabulary to the people in the photographs. They then check their answers against the cassette and mark the stress on the new words.

Answers/Tapescript

Napoleon Bonaparte was an 'emperor.
Hamlet was a 'prince.
Winston Churchill was a prime 'minister.
Marie-Antoinette was a 'queen.
Richard Nixon was a 'president.
Martin Luther King was a poli'tician.

Put students in pairs to match the words. Make sure they realise that where a pair of words is given, only one should be used.

Play the tape, stopping after each example for students to mark word stress on.

3 Students brainstorm other people, past or present, who have had these political roles and name their nationality.

In a multilingual class, put students in groups of four or five, mixing nationalities. In a monolingual class, do the activity open-class.

3 Reading

AIMS

• To provide information about government in English-speaking countries.
• To encourage students to deduce the meaning of unknown vocabulary from context.
• To help students differentiate between the sounds /ɒ/, /ɔː/ and /əʊ/.

1 Students read the text and answer the questions in their book.

Answers

1 Britain, the United States and Australia.
2 Britain has 3, the United States has 2 and
   Australia has 4.
3 The United States has a president.
4 Britain and Australia have a prime minister.
5 New Zealand, India and Jamaica.
6 Britain, Australia, New Zealand, India and
   Jamaica all have the same queen/king.

Refer students to the photographs of parliament buildings in their book. Ask which ones they can identify. (Clockwise starting with large photo: Capitol Building, United States; Houses of Parliament, Britain; Parliament Building, New Zealand; Parliament Building, Canada.)

Give students time to read the questions before they read the text. Remind them that they will not need to understand every word in the text to do the task.

They check their answers with a partner. At feedback, deal with any questions they can't agree on and send them back to the text for confirmation.

2 Students match the definitions to the underlined words in the text.

Answers

1 leader 2 election 3 opposition 4 vote 5 party
6 Members of Parliament 7 laws

Students either do this together or individually
and compare their answers at the end.

Pronunciation: word families

AIMS

- To heighten student awareness of word families
  and the possibility of shifting word-stress.
- To highlight sound differences between /ɒ/, /ɔː/
  and /əʊ/.

**1 Students look at a list of words and decide
which form of speech they are.**

Answers

1 leader (*n*), lead (*v*), 2 election (*n*), elect (*v*),
elected (*adj.*), 3 opposition (*n*), oppose (*v*), 4 vote
(*v*), voter (*n*), 5 law (*n*), lawyer (*n*), 6 government
(*n*), govern (*v*)
2 leader, voter, lawyer all refer to a person

Elicit the example from the Students' Book to
show that the word *politics* is related to the
words *politician* and *political*. Ask students
which is a noun/adjective and which noun refers
to a person.

Put students in pairs to decide about the rest
of the vocabulary. As pairs finish, they check
their answers with another pair. At feedback deal
with any problems.

**2 Students listen to the cassette and mark
word-stress.**

Answers/Tapescript

Example: 'politics, poli'tician, po'litical
1 'leader lead   4 vote 'voter
2 e'lection e'lect e'lected 5 law 'lawyer
3 oppo'sition o'ppose   6 'government 'govern

Stop the tape after each family of words to give
students time to mark the stress. Draw attention
to stress shift eg. from 'politics to po'litical and its
effect on sound (/ɒ/ typically becomes /ə/ in
unstressed syllables.)

**3 Students listen again and identify the sounds
/ɒ/, /ɔː/ and /əʊ/ in the words.**

Answers

/ɒ/ comes in politics/politician, opposition,
/ɔː/ comes in law/lawyer
/əʊ/ comes in oppose, vote/voter

Highlight the difference between the three
sounds with a minimal pairs exercise, like this:
a) Write the three example words, *cot, caught*
   and *coat* on the board. Put the numbers 1, 2
   and 3 above them.
b) Say the words in random order and ask
   students to write down the numbers 1, 2 or 3
   as they hear the words.
c) As you check their answers, get them to
   repeat the sounds after you. Begin with /ɒ/,
   encouraging students to produce a short
   sound with rounded lips. For /ɔː/ begin with
   /ɒ/ and get students to lengthen the original
   sound. /əʊ/ is made up of two sounds. Begin
   with /ə/ and finish with /ʊ/.
d) Students test a partner as in stage b).
   Students listen to the political vocabulary again
to identify words with the target sounds in them.
Make sure they realise that the three sounds do
not appear in every word. Stop the tape after
each word and check what they heard.

**4 Students discuss the political system in their
own country, answering the questions in their
book.**

Put students in groups of four or five to do this.
In multilingual classes, mix nationalities so
students find out about different countries. In
monolingual classes, get students to pool their
ideas and allow slightly less time for the activity.

4 Vocabulary: political issues

AIMS

- To introduce and practise a set of vocabulary of
  political issues.

**1-2 Students match words to definitions and
then put them in order of importance.**

Answers

1
1 c) 2 g) 3 a) 4 e) 5 f) 6 d) 7 i) 8 b) 9 h)

In multilingual groups, put students into groups of three or four, of mixed nationalities. Between them they should recognise most of the vocabulary.

In monolingual classes, either they will recognise words which are similar in their own language or they will need more help from you. In either case, check their answers as they finish. Encourage them to predict word-stress on the new vocabulary.

Before students prioritise the political issues, make sure that they realise there is no one correct answer. Their task is to come up with an agreed order which means they will need to convince the others in their group that their ideas are right.

5 Reading

AIMS

- To develop the skill of reading for specific information.
- To allow for recognition of target vocabulary in an authentic context.

Students read the leaflets and answer the questions in their book.

Answers

1   The Liberal Democrat Party, The Labour Party, The Conservative Party
2   a) the economy, health
    b) education, childcare, pensions (Lib. Dem. and Lab.)
    c) unemployment (Lab.), the environment (Lib. Dem.), defence (Con.), taxation (Lib. Dem.)

Refer students to the election leaflets and elicit their purpose. Get students to name British political parties they have heard of and then ask them the questions in their book.

They check their answers with other students. Act as arbitrator if they can't agree, highlighting the part of the text they need to reread.

Grammar: *will* (promises)

AIMS

- To introduce and practise the use of *will/won't* for making promises.
- To introduce and practise *as soon as* + present + *will*.

1 Students look at examples of election promises using *will* and recognise the form of *will* sentences + *as soon as*.

Answers

1
1 future 2 when 3 a present form

Refer students to the sentences in the grammar box and ask them who they think is speaking to elicit that these are political promises.

Ask the check questions open-class.

2 Students work in threes and look at one of the election leaflets each. They tell each other the promises, using *will*, in their party's leaflet.

Answers

Example answers
The Labour Party will introduce a fair minimum wage. The Conservative Party will lower interest rates. The Liberal Democrats will improve education and training, etc.

Put students in threes: A, B and C and get them to take responsibility for one leaflet each. (In a class of mixed ability students, give your strongest students the Liberal Democrat leaflet to work on, and your weaker students the Labour Party leaflet.) Give students time to make their promises, based on the information in their leaflet and the example sentences in the grammar box.

6 Listening

AIMS

- To develop the skills of listening for general and specific information.

Tapescript

Part 1

I: Mr Blair, what party are you in?

TB: I'm in the Labour Party. I joined the Labour Party when I was aged about 20 years old and it's the only political party that I have joined and I came into Parliament for the Labour Party in 1983, so I've been in Parliament now for some considerable period of time.

I: Of these key political issues here, which do you think are the most important ones now?

TB: The economy is always of enormous importance. There have been great problems with, er, British industry and the fact that we have been importing very many more goods than we've actually been exporting abroad, and so it's important to build up our economy and build for future economic success. Unemployment is immensely important, particularly amongst young people because we have had large numbers of young people unemployed for long periods of time and the issues, I think the issues of the future revolve around the question of how women can both work and bring up a family which is the issue of childcare, and the environment, which I think is of much greater importance today than it has been traditionally.

Answers

1 The Labour Party
2 Since 1983
3 a) The economy and unemployment
    b) The environment and childcare

Use the photograph to tell students about Tony Blair, explaining that he is the MP for Sedgefield, a constituency in Durham, North-East England.

Give them time to read the questions before they listen. Check the answers open-class.

2 They then listen to the second part of the interview and complete his diary for next week.

Tapescript

Part 2

I: You must have a very full diary, can you tell me what you're going next week?

TB: On Monday I start at 10 o'clock in the morning with a speech to a conference in London about crime and the problems of crime particularly, um, in the London area. Later in the day, round about 4 o'clock in the afternoon, the government will publish its new proposals on immigration and I will be responding to those on behalf of the Labour Party. And then in the evening, round about 7 o'clock, I will be taking some constituents of mine from the north of England round a tour of Parliament.

I: On to Tuesday.

TB: On Tuesday, I will be going up to the constituency and I will be having lunch first of all, at around about 1 o'clock, with the Chamber of Commerce in my constituency, that looks after business interests there, and I will also be opening a new road to the airport in my constituency, which is something we have been asking for for a long time. And then in the evening I will be presenting awards at a local community college to those that have undergone education and training within our area.

I: What time will that be?

TB: That will be round about 8.30 but then there will be a social function after that, a dinner, and we will be eating with some of the students and so there will be a chance to talk with them too. And indeed I think also that day I'm fitting in a recording of a television programme about the coal industry as well, so I will be having a fairly busy diary. I think that's round about 6 o'clock in the evening.

I: OK. Then on to Wednesday.

TB: On Wednesday, I will be holding surgeries in my constituency, that is where my constituents will come to me with particular problems that they have, problems say with housing, or with, um, difficulties in finding work, and I will see them, and then later that day there is, er, what is called an open day at a local factory which means that the factory allows people to come in and see what is happening in the factory, see the products of the factory and those that work there will take part in that.

I: That's at what time?

TB: And that will be round about 2 o'clock in the afternoon.

I: Right, let's move to Thursday, then.

TB: On Thursday, I'm having a meeting with the fire brigade in the London area because there have been a lot of difficulties in the London area recently with fires and in particular with the additional funding that is required, the money that is needed by the fire brigade to carry out their duties in London. And then I will also be having a meeting a little bit later, round about 12 o'clock, er, that morning, with those that are concerned with the reform of our prison system in Britain because we have had a very serious problem with overcrowding, with too many people in the prisons and I will be meeting those that are campaigning for changes in the prison system, and then later that day, at 4 o'clock, I will be meeting with the heads of various department stores to talk about whether Britain should allow trading in shops, shops to be open on Sundays.

I: And finally Friday?

Answers

Monday: 10am – *conference on crime*
               4pm – respond to government's
                      immigration proposals
               7pm – tour of Houses of Parliament
Tuesday: 1pm – *Chamber of Commerce lunch*
                    – open airport road
               6pm – *TV recording*
            8.30pm – present education and training
                      awards
                    – *student dinner*
Wednesday: am – constituent's surgeries
               2pm – *factory open day*
Thursday: – fire brigade meeting
              12am – *prison reform meeting*
               4pm – *Sunday trading meeting*

Refer students to the diary in their book and the appointments to be inserted. Make sure they realise that the dashes marked on the diary show where appointments should go and students need to listen out for the times involved too.

They compare their notes and listen again, if necessary, until they are satisfied that they understand what Tony Blair has arranged to do next week.

7 Grammar: Present Continuous (future)

AIMS

- To introduce the use of Present Continuous for future arrangements.

1 Students consider two sentences in the Present Continuous and answer questions to highlight the difference in concept.

Answers

1 a) 2 b) 3 *on Monday*

Elicit the two sentences to the board and ask the check questions open-class. Students will get

practice in using the Present Continuous for future arrangements in Exercise 8 Speaking.

8 Speaking

AIMS

- To revise telling the time and days of the week.
- To highlight the sounds /θ/, /t/ and /f/.
- To provide speaking practice of the Present Continuous for future arrangements.

1 Students say the times listed in two different ways, paying attention to the pronunciation of /θ/, /t/ and /f/.

Answers

three – three o'clock
three fifteen – a quarter past three
three twenty five – twenty five past three
three thirty five – twenty five to four
three forty five – a quarter to four
three fifty – ten to four

Assume students can tell the time in English and focus on pronunciation. First, get them to say the time in the example. If students have a problem saying the /θ/ sound, get them to put their finger in front of their mouth and touch it with their tongue as they try to say it.

When you/they are satisfied they can say 3.30 accurately, get them to work in pairs to say the other times in both ways.

Listen to some of their examples open-class, checking their pronunciation.

2 Students say the days of the week and isolate the ones with the target sounds.

Answers

/θ/ – Thursday /t/ – Tuesday /f/ – Friday

Students say the days with their partner. Check the answers open-class.

3 Students look at Tony Blair's diary and check what he is doing next week.

Elicit the example given in their book.

Put students into new pairs to take it in turns to check the other information in the diary. Make sure they realise that they shouldn't show each

107

other the completed diary but should use their notes to make questions/answers.

4 Students work together, looking at diaries on different pages, to find a time to meet.

Before they begin, elicit a variety of ways of inviting people out eg. *Are you free on Saturday? What are you doing on Monday? How about meeting on Monday? Let's go out next week,* etc.

Set the scene and give students time to read the instructions in their book.

Put students in pairs and refer Student Bs to their diary on page 125. If students find a solution quickly, get them to organise where they will go, and when/how they will meet.

At feedback, find out what time the students have found to meet.

English in action

AIMS

- To provide an opportunity for freer speaking practice, referring to future time.
- To develop the skill of reading for specific information.

1 Students read about an imaginary country and plan their own political party, prioritising the political issues they will work on.

Set the scene for this activity. Give students time to read the text about their country and to ask you for clarification.

Put students in groups of four or five, mixing nationalities if possible. Students will need time in class or at home to plan their party in detail. Their first task is to decide on six priority issues to concentrate on.

2-3 Students make five laws for their country and decide on the punishment for people refusing to keep them. They also decide on three promises they can make to the people. They plan an identity for their party based on the instructions in their book, producing a notice to advertise a public meeting.

Students continue to work in their groups. Make sure students know how much time they have at each stage.

4-5 Students hold their meetings and vote for the party they think would be best in power.

Encourage all students in each group to take a role at the meeting. One student could introduce the party; another could present the political issues they would work on; another could explain the laws, and so on.

Before they hold their meetings, remind students that they will be asked to vote at the end so they should question politicians as they listen to them and evaluate their ideas. (They cannot vote for their own party!)

Language review 13

a + b
1 What did he find? All the lights were on.
2 Who ran past Mike? A young man.
3 What did Mike do? He tried to stop him.
4 What did the young man do? He hit Mike.
5 Who fell to the floor? Mike.
6 Who ran out of the door? The young man.
7 Who phoned the police? Mike.
8 What did Mike tell the police? What happened.
9 Who did the police look for immediately? The young man.

c
1 I will phone you when I arrive at the airport.
2 If you give me your address I will send you the information.
3 I won't come home late if I go to the party.
4 I will tell you as soon as I stop using the computer.
5 They will go to bed when they finish watching TV.
6 I will help you as soon as I get there.

d
1 . . . what *are you doing* this evening?
2 I'm probably *having* a quiet evening . . .
3 I *am inviting* a few friends over . . .
4 . . . my brother *is coming* here . . .
5 . . . we *are putting* up some new wallpaper . . .
6 I *'ll help* you.

14 Generation Gap

1 Preparation

AIMS

- To revise ways of talking about age, numbers and life stages.

1-3 Students guess the ages of the people in the photographs and check their answers on page 126.

Put students in pairs to answer the first question. Feedback should provoke discussion and establish that *young*, *middle-aged* and *old* are subjective terms.

Before they work in their pairs again, refer students to the photographs in their book. Establish that the average of the ages is 38 and that stress generally falls on the second number. (eg. thirty 'eight.)

Get one student to guess the age of one of the people, encourage disagreement and then leave students in their pairs to guess the ages of the other people. They should make sure their six answers average out at 38 before they check at the back of the book.

2 Reading

AIMS

- To develop the skill of reading for specific information.
- To provide an opportunity for oral transfer of information.

1 Students read about three people in the article, then complete the chart in their book.

Answers

Name	Job	Activities/ Interests	Secret of Youth
Nikki Thomson	Make up artist	Going to the cinema and out with her daughter	Drink plenty of water, live one day at a time
Sophie Norton	TV actress	Taking photos, cooking, swimming	Swim regularly, have young friends
Georgia Downs	Photographer	Aerobics, running, art galleries, photographic exhibitions and antique shops	Do exercise, use eye cream, keep smiling!
Tom Conti	Actor	Food and drink	Work and not too much drinking!
Alistair Blair	Designer	Clothes and exercise	Exercise, a careful diet, plenty of sleep
Lucille Anderson	Boutique owner	Ballet, opera and concerts	Keep busy, do everything in moderation!

First, ask students to copy the chart into their notebooks leaving enough space to write the information about all six people.

Tell them to choose three people and to read and complete the chart with their information. Check that each person in the article is being read about. If this isn't the case, ask a student who finishes quickly to read the extra article.

As they finish, direct students to find someone who has read about at least one person they haven't. They sit with this student and tell each other about their different person/people, changing partners if necessary in order to fill the complete chart.

Finally, check their answers open-class.

3 Speaking

AIMS

• To revise *have to/don't have to* and *should/ shouldn't* for expressing obligation.

1-2 Students say what they think helps people stay young. They consider the ideas provided in their book and add three other ideas themselves.

Ask students to say how far they agree/disagree with the people in the article's secrets of youth. As they do this, elicit the ways they can express the different degrees of obligation.

Put students in groups of three or four to discuss the ideas. Get them to put a), b) or c) next to each idea depending on the general opinion of the group.

As they finish, they can add their three new ideas, then put two groups together to share these opinions.

At feedback, check their answers and encourage disagreement and further discussion.

List their new ideas on the board and take a vote to see which idea the students think is best.

4 Listening

AIMS

• To pre-teach some expressions and their stress pattern for recognition in the song.
• To develop the skills of listening for general and specific information.

1-2 Students match the new expressions to their definitions. They then check the pronunciation and stress patterns in their mini-dictionary on page 138.

Answers

1
1 d 2 a 3 e 4 c 5 f 6 b

2 Main stress is generally on the word at the end of these expressions, not on the verb.

Tell students that they are going to hear a song by the singer Cat Stevens (put his name on the board). Ask if anyone has heard of him. If so, let them tell the class what they know. If not, tell them Cat Stevens was a popular pop singer in the early 1970s and that he has since become a Muslim.

Put the name of the song *Father and Son* on the board and ask students what story they think the song will tell.

When they have suggested various scenarios, refer students to the picture in their book and see if they can predict more.

Explain that the expressions in column A are in the song and elicit the instructions for the first exercise from them.

As they finish, refer them to the second exercise and their mini-dictionary on page 138.

Let them check their answers with another student before you check them as a class, paying careful attention to pronunciation.

3-4 Students complete the gaps in the song with the new expressions. They then listen to the song in order to check their answers and decide who is singing each verse.

Answers

3
1 *make a change*
2 *take it easy*
3 *settle down*
4 *take your time*
5 *turns away*
6 *go away*
7 *make a change*
8 *settle down*
9 *go away*

4
1 Father: verses 1, 2 and 4
  Son: verses 3 and 5
2 Verse 1 is repeated as verse 4. The words which change are: *relax* changes to *sit down*; *take it easy* changes to *take it slowly*; *have to know* changes to *have to go through*.

Put students in pairs to read the song and speculate about where each new expression fits.

Play the tape, more than once if necessary, and let them check their answers.

At feedback, elicit the answers and as each verse is completed, ask students whether it was sung by the father or the son. Give them time to read each verse carefully in order to do this, and deal with any vocabulary queries as they arise.

Answers

1 They're unhappy because of their inability to communicate.
2 Relax, take it easy, find a girlfriend, appreciate what you have now, don't be impatient, settle down, get married, take your time, don't make a change, think about things.
3 His father doesn't listen to his point of view. His solution is to leave.

Refer students to the final set of questions in their book and give them time to read them before you play the tape again.

After listening, let them confer in twos or threes before you elicit answers from the class, getting them to justify their answers from the text.

Play the song again if they would like to hear it and encourage them to join in or follow the words in their book.

5 Grammar: *shouldn't/mustn't/ don't have to*

AIMS

- To introduce *must/mustn't* to express degrees of obligation.
- To contrast *should/shouldn't, must/mustn't* and *have to/don't have to*.
- To highlight the pronunciation of unstressed *should* and *must*, and elision between *shouldn't/mustn't* and the following verb.

1 Students look at the examples in the grammar box and answer the questions.

Answers

1 should 2 must 3 have to

Copy the examples from the grammar box in the Students' Book onto the board but leave gaps for *must/mustn't* and *should/shouldn't*.

Elicit the father's words to show he is offering advice and write *should/shouldn't* in the right-hand column.

Refer students to the words the son hears. Does he think his father is only giving advice? Elicit that he hears an order and that the missing words are *must/mustn't*. If students suggest the son hears *You have to listen,* accept this as a possibility and supply *must* as an alternative to *have to.* (We suggest that *must* and *have to* can be seen as straight alternatives at this level.)

Now, ask students the questions in their books to check meaning.

2 Students listen to the example sentences on tape again. They repeat them and answer the pronunciation questions in their book.

Tapescript

The son hears:	The father means:
You must listen.	You should listen.
You mustn't go away.	You shouldn't go away.

Answers

1 listen and away
2 Should and must are unstressed; should = /ʃəd/, must = /məst/. You can't hear the /t/ sound before the following consonant.

Do this in two stages if necessary. First get students to listen and repeat. Then get them to listen out for the pronunciation features.

Nominate individual students to read the sentences in the grammar box out loud, paying particular attention to their pronunciation.

Refer students back to the list they made of the father's advice in the song (Exercise 4 Listening 5 above). Get them to work in pairs, one of them saying what the son heard, the other saying what his father meant.

Listening

AIMS

- To allow students to practise the difference between *shouldn't, mustn't* and *don't have to* when expressing degrees of obligation.
- To develop the skills of listening for general and specific information.

NB Answer

b

Refer students to the NB box *mustn't vs don't have to*. Ask the check question open-class.

If you think your students need practice of this distinction before tackling the task in their book, ask them to use *don't have to* or *mustn't* to tell you about the following or similar situations:

1 Drinking and driving in Britain (You mustn't . . .)

2 Drinking a glass of water before you go to bed. (You don't have to . . .)

3 Drinking alcohol at a party in Britain. (You don't have to . . .)

4 Boiling all water before you drink it in Britain. (You don't have to . . .)

5 Drinking alcohol when you are a Muslim. (You mustn't . . .)

1 Students listen to the conversation and answer the questions in their book.

Tapescript

SUE: But surely you agree that young people in America have more freedom, can do more what they want than in Britain?

BETH: Well, yes but it varies from state to state?

SUE: Are there different laws from state to state?

BETH: There are very different laws and for example I come from Salt Lake City in Utah.

SUE: Oh! You're not from San Francisco.

BETH: No. No. Seventy-five percent of the people in Utah are Mormon and Mormon laws very much affect our lives.

STEVE: Gosh.

SUE: Ok so they are sort of religious laws.

BETH: Well they're religiously based laws, no, they're not religious laws per se.

SUE: Um, and what, give me some examples of things you can and cannot do.

BETH: Well for example we really shouldn't smoke or drink alcohol.

SUE: Not at all?

BETH: Not at all and for example my parents don't drink tea or coffee.

STEVE: But then you drink tea or coffee then?

BETH: Well the odd cup. Just the odd cup.

SUE: I'm surprised you can eat meat.

BETH: Well, Joseph Smith, the founder of the Mormon church, recommended against it. He said that it would be better to eat lots of fresh fruit and vegetables but now everything's in moderation and so we eat some meat.

SUE: Right, and is it true that men can have more than one wife?

BETH: No it's not true any longer.

SUE: Oh really!

BETH: It was only in the past that they can only have more than one wife.

STEVE: Um, how many could they have?

BETH: I think up to four.

SUE: Really. And can Mormons marry non-Mormons?

BETH: They can but, for example, if I married a non-Mormon my marriage would only be for life, not for eternity.

SUE: Oh really. And what age can you get married?

BETH: As early as fourteen.

STEVE: I see, and that's the same for boys and girls.

BETH: It is the same yeah. It's a bit early in Utah.

SUE: Yes it is - fourteen goodness! And that's if the parents agree?

BETH: That is if the parents agree, yes. If the parents don't agree then kids have to wait until they're eighteen.

SUE: Right, OK, and when can they leave school?

BETH: Sixteen.

SUE: That's the same here.

BETH: Yes, it's the same everywhere in the States, it's the federal minimum age.

SUE: Right, OK, and then I suppose the boys go in the army.

BETH: No, there's no military service in the States.

SUE: Oh!

STEVE: But there was wasn't there a few years ago?

BETH: There was, there was a draft during the Vietnam war but not any more.

SUE: But not now.

BETH: Uh uh.

SUE: So they don't go in the army at all?

BETH: No, not at all.

Answers

1 2 are British, 1 is American.
2 Utah.
3 The majority of people who live there are Mormons.

Put USA on the board and elicit that this stands for the United States of America. Ask students how many states there are in America (50) and get them to brainstorm as many as they can. Establish that the conversation they are about to listen to is about one of these states.

Refer them to the first set of questions in their

book and check they know what they are listening for. Make sure they know that they can listen more than once if necessary and that they don't need to understand every word in order to answer the questions.

Play the tape and let them confer with a partner. If they can't agree on their answers, play the tape again.

Check their answers open-class.

2-3 Students predict how to complete the sentences about Utah and then listen to the tape again to check their predictions.

Answers

1 shouldn't 2 don't have to 3 mustn't 4 doesn't have to 5 mustn't 6 don't have to 7 mustn't 8 don't have to

Make sure that the students realise they are not expected to remember the answers from what they heard on tape. They should predict what they think in pairs and then listen again to find out what they don't know.

Play the tape more than once, letting students confer between each listening. At each stage, ask the class what they think the answers are. Do not agree or disagree but at this stage encourage students to tell others what they heard.

Finally, if necessary, play the tape in sections, stopping after each piece of information so that everybody feels they have understood enough to complete the task.

6 Speaking

AIMS

- To give students freer, personalised practice in expressing obligation.
- To revise/introduce and practise *too* and *enough* + adjectives.

1 Students discuss age laws in their own country/countries.

Put students in small groups to discuss the given ideas. In a multilingual class, mix nationalities in the groups. In a monolingual class, get students to compare the laws in their own country with the laws in Utah. At feedback get them to ask you about Britain where you mustn't buy

cigarettes or alcohol before you are sixteen. You mustn't get married before you are sixteen (eighteen without your parents' consent). There are strict laws at the cinema with some films forbidden if you are under thirteen, some if you are under fifteen and others if you are under eighteen. Children mustn't go in most pubs and nightclubs and are often not welcome in cinemas, hotels or restaurants. There is no military service but you can join the army when you are sixteen.

2 Students express their own opinion of these laws, using *too young/old enough*.

Begin open-class asking students about smoking. When do they think you are *too young/old enough* to smoke? Drill answers the class find acceptable eg. *You are too young to smoke when you are eight./You are old enough to smoke when you are twenty-one.*

Put students back in their groups to discuss the other subjects. At feedback, encourage disagreement and further discussion.

7 Writing

AIMS

- To introduce/contrast and practise using the conjunctions *but, although* and *however.*

1 Students deduce when and how to use the conjunctions by answering questions about their use in the examples.

Answers

1 *But* generally goes in the middle of a complex sentence, effectively joining two simple sentences.
 Although generally goes at the beginning of a sentence. It can often also go in the middle of a sentence fulfilling a similar role to *but.*
 However generally starts a sentence.
2 With *but* there is generally no need for a comma in the sentence.
 With *although* a comma is needed at the end of the first part of the sentence.
 However generally follows a full stop, beginning a new sentence. It is also generally followed by a comma.

Put students in pairs to answer the questions and then elicit the answers open-class.

Students complete the gaps individually and then compare their answers with another student. Deal with any discrepancies open-class.

Ask a few questions about the text to check comprehension, then nominate students to tell you something similar about their country.

Students could write about their countries for homework. In a multilingual class, encourage students to read about one another's country afterwards and to ask more questions. Students may like to make this information the focus of a class magazine as suggested in Unit One. In a monolingual class, you could encourage students to write about other countries they know or are interested in. This would require some research in their own time and could again provide the focus of a class magazine (See English in Action, Unit 1).

English in action

AIMS

- To encourage students to read, infer information from, and evaluate simple poetry.
- To raise students' awareness of the use of sentence stress.
- To motivate students to create a simple poem of their own.

Make sure the students understand that at the end of this section they will write a poem themselves in English.

Give them time to read the questions before they listen and follow the words in their book. Get them to compare their answers with a partner before they tell you what they think.

Play the poems again and students underline the stressed words. (These are marked in the tapescript above.) Use the tape to dictate the first poem before they mark the stress on it. Then get them to predict the main information and stresses in the second poem orally, playing each line on tape after they have said their version. Get them to repeat the line as it is said on tape.

Get them to say a poem each to their partner and to critically assess each other's sentence stress.

Ask students how they would prefer to write their poem, individually, in pairs or in groups. They should sit accordingly.

Refer them to the instructions in their book. Circulate in the class as they write and answer any queries as they arise.

5 Students listen to further instructions and write their poem in the diamond.

Tapescript

On line 1, write the name of the first time of life you chose.
On line 2, write 2 adjectives from your first list of adjectives.
On line 3, write 3 verbs from your first list of verbs.
On line 4, in the spaces on the left, write 2 nouns from your first list of nouns.
- In the spaces on the right, write 2 nouns from your second list of nouns.
- In the middle space, write 1 new noun to link the two different times of life.
On line 5, write 3 verbs from your second list of verbs.
On line 6, write 2 adjectives from your second list of adjectives.
On line 7, write the name of the second time of life you chose.

Refer students to the diamond shape in their book. Tell them that they are going to write a diamond poem, putting words in the spaces. They first need to copy the diamond exactly into their notebook.

Play the tape or read the instructions yourself from the tapescript, pausing after each line to give students time to write and/or collaborate.

6+7 If they like, students make changes to their poem before reading it aloud and listening to the work of other students.

Give students time to read their poem through and change the odd word if they really want to. There is no real need for them to do this as the charm of this type of poem lies in its simplicity and spontaneity.

Give them time to think about/discuss how they will say their poem to the class.

The poems could go in a class magazine (for ideas on making a class magazine, see English in Action, Unit One) or be collated to make a short collection of poems, which could constitute a personal souvenir of their English class.

Language review 14

a
1 teacher to pupil
2 boss to secretary
3 parent to child
4 doctor to patient

b
1 I don't have to
2 mustn't
3 mustn't
4 doesn't have to
5 mustn't

c
Possible answers
1 It's too big.
2 It's too heavy.
3 It's too busy.
4 She's too young.

d
Possible answers
1 It's not fast enough.
2 He's not old enough.
3 It's not warm enough.

e
I passed my exam but I decided not to go to university.
Although I passed my exam, I decided not to go to university.
I passed my exam. However, I decided not to go to university.

She didn't have much money but she bought a new jacket, etc.

We looked for him for ages but we couldn't find him, etc.

It was an interesting job but the pay was terrible, etc.

15 *Consolidation*

1 Across cultures: attitudes to children

AIMS

- To revise *have to/don't have to/mustn't.*
- To provide further practice of *although/ however/but* in paragraph writing.
- To practise the skill of listening for specific information

1 Students discuss things children are expected to do in their country/family.

Introduce the subject of the unit by referring students to the photographs on this page. Elicit the general attitude to children in their country; are children treated specially or considered a nuisance?

Put students in small groups to discuss the ideas in their book. In multilingual classes, mix nationalities so students can learn about a variety of countries. In monolingual classes, get students to compare the situations in their different families.

At feedback, they can ask you about the situation in Britain. In Britain a lot of adults still think children should be seen and not heard! Young children often go to bed early, even before the father comes home. They have to ask permission to leave the table and go out, although they are often given quite a lot of freedom. They don't have to obey their parents without question, except in the strictest families but they are expected to be polite, saying *Please* and *Thank you* a lot. They may be expected to help at home and with younger brothers/sisters but may be paid for doing so. A lot of children get pocket money from an early age.

2-4 They listen to three children and complete the information in the chart in their book. They listen again and list the things these children are expected to do/not to do.

Tapescript

1

INTERVIEWER: Hello Tessa. How old are you?
TESSA: Nine years old.
INTERVIEWER: And where do you live?
TESSA: London.
INTERVIEWER: Whereabouts in London?
TESSA: North London.
INTERVIEWER: And, er, have you always lived in London?
TESSA: No, we lived three years in Spain.
INTERVIEWER: Really? Why was that?
TESSA: Because I was born in Spain and my, and my grandparents are from Spain.
INTERVIEWER: Your grandparents are, and what about your mum and dad?
TESSA: My mum's Spanish and my dad's English.
INTERVIEWER: Oh right, so do, you know, do you think you're English or Spanish?
TESSA: Half English, half Spanish.
INTERVIEWER: So, um when you're at home, is there anything you have to do?
TESSA: Um, go to bed at the right time.
INTERVIEWER: I see. What time?
TESSA: Half past nine.
INTERVIEWER: Uh huh. And how about helping around the house - do you have to do any housework?
TESSA: Not normally.
INTERVIEWER: Right. Now is there anything you mustn't do?
TESSA: Speak English to my mum.
INTERVIEWER: I see. So, er, you know, when you compare parents in England and parents in Spain, do you think, er, your parents are particularly strict?
TESSA: Not really.

2

INTERVIEWER: Hi, Manual. How old are you?
MANUAL: I am fifteen.

INTERVIEWER: And where do you come from?

MANUEL: I come from Peru.

INTERVIEWER: Whereabouts in Peru?

MANUEL: Lima.

INTERVIEWER: That's the capital city?

MANUEL: Yes.

INTERVIEWER: And, um, where do you live now?

MANUEL: Now I live in London.

INTERVIEWER: Why's that?

MANUEL: Well, my parents are both working here.

INTERVIEWER: They're both Peruvian, of course.

MANUEL: Yes.

INTERVIEWER: And, how do your parents compare with English parents? Are they, er, stricter, or less strict?

MANUEL: They're stricter.

INTERVIEWER: Now, why do you say that? In what way are they stricter?

MANUEL: Well, er, when I'm out, they're always asking who I'm going to be with, and where I'm going to be.

INTERVIEWER: Talking about your parents, and home, um, what do you have to do at home?

MANUEL: Er, tidy my room, keep it, er, clean, and do the dishes.

INTERVIEWER: You do that every day?

MANUEL: No, I take it in turns with my mother and father.

INTERVIEWER: Right. Um, do you have to do things like visiting your grandparents – go and see them back in Peru?

MANUEL: Er, No, but I like to.

INTERVIEWER: How often?

MANUEL: Every two years.

INTERVIEWER: And, um, is there anything you mustn't do?

MANUEL: Well, let the dog into the house.

INTERVIEWER: What kind of dog have you got?

MANUEL: It's an Alsatian.

INTERVIEWER: And you mustn't let it in the house at all?

MANUEL: No.

INTERVIEWER: Really. Where does it live?

MANUEL: It lives outside in the kennel.

3

INTERVIEWER: Hi, Sarah. How old are you?

SARAH: I'm sixteen.

INTERVIEWER: And where do you live?

SARAH: I live in Paris.

INTERVIEWER: Wow, that's very nice. Why are you in England then?

SARAH: Well, I come to England to see my dad.

INTERVIEWER: Uh huh. And who do you live with in Paris?

SARAH: I live with my mum in Paris.

INTERVIEWER: Right. Is she French?

SARAH: Yeah. My mum's French and my dad's English.

INTERVIEWER: Right. So how do you see yourself then – English, French, or what?

SARAH: I think I see myself as more English, really.

INTERVIEWER: Why is that?

SARAH: Um. I spent most of my younger life in England, and I feel that I can relate to English people more than French people.

INTERVIEWER: Mm. Is your mum very strict?

SARAH: Um. Yeah, I'd say she was fairly strict.

INTERVIEWER: How is she strict?

SARAH: Um. She's very strict about work, school work.

INTERVIEWER: Oh, I see. And, er, how does she compare with your dad?

SARAH: Well, I don't live with my dad so it's not the same, but I'd say she was more strict than my dad.

INTERVIEWER: Um. When you're in your mum's house, is there anything you have to do?

SARAH: I have to do my homework before I go out.

INTERVIEWER: Right. And anything you mustn't do?

SARAH: I mustn't go out late without phoning her first, tell her where I am.

INTERVIEWER: How about pocket money? Do you get pocket money in France?

SARAH: Yeah, I do.

INTERVIEWER: Do you have to buy everything with that?

SARAH: I have to pay for most things but I don't have to buy my own clothes, my mother buys them for me.

INTERVIEWER: I see. So, where would you rather be, in Paris or in England?

SARAH: I'd rather be in England I think.

INTERVIEWER: Why?

SARAH: Um. I think I like the lifestyle more in England, and I have a few more friends in England.

Answers

2

	Tessa	Manuel	Sarah
Their age	9	15	16
Where they live	North London	London	Paris, France
Their nationality	Half English, half Spanish	Peruvian	Half English, half French – feels English
How strict they think their parents are	Not very	Thinks his parents are stricter than British parents.	Thinks her mother is stricter than her father

117

3

a) Tessa has to go to bed at 9.30 pm.
b) She doesn't usually have to do any housework.
c) She mustn't speak English to her mother.

a) Manuel has to tidy his room, keep it clean, and do the dishes.
b) He doesn't have to visit his grandparents.
c) He mustn't let the dog into the house.

a) Sarah has to do her homework before she goes out.
b) She doesn't have to buy her own clothes.
c) She mustn't go out late without phoning her mother to tell her where she is.

Check that the students know the children's names so that they will recognise them when they hear them. Give them time to read and copy the chart so they know why they are listening.

Play the tape straight through and let them confer between listenings. If necessary, replay the tape in sections so that they complete the information for one child before going on to the next.

This exercise is made up of three separate recordings which together provide for extended listening practice, furthering the development of the listening skill. If you think your particular class is not yet ready for this, we suggest you limit their listening to one or two of the recordings only. In this case, draw an abridged version of the chart in the Students' Book on the board for them to copy and complete. Alternatively, treat the exercise as a 'jigsaw' activity (see page 16).

5 Students discuss a number of statements and compare their own attitudes to children.

Give students time to read the statements in their book and to clarify any problems of meaning before they discuss, in groups of four or five.

6 They write a paragraph about one of the subjects discussed, using conjunctions.

Establish their articles are for an international magazine for parents. There is an example of this type of magazine on page 91.

Encourage students to write their paragraph in pairs or small groups either working with someone from their own country or from a number of countries, giving a variety of views. They should begin by saying where they come from and how representative their ideas are of those in their country/countries.

Encourage them to use dictionaries to check meaning and/or spelling of words.

When they have finished the first draft, get them to show it to another student/group so that they can point out anything that isn't clear to the reader. The original writer/s can then rewrite their short article before handing it in. These articles could form the focus of another issue of their class magazine (see English in Action, Unit 1).

2 Language in context: corporal punishment

AIMS

- To develop the skills of reading for general and specific information.
- To introduce a set of vocabulary associated with children and punishment.
- To provide an opportunity for freer spoken practice.

1 Students read the quotes in the article and answer the questions in their book.

Answers

1 The first was said by a parent, the second by a child psychologist, the third by a child, the fourth by a government and the last by a teacher.
2 a belt, a cane, a slipper, a hand.

Introduce the topic with reference to the photograph in the article and establish that *smacking* and *naughty* are words usually used with reference to children.

Give students time to read the questions and deal with any new vocabulary. Use illustrations or the real thing to check/teach belt, slipper, etc.

Make sure the students know to limit their first reading to the five quotes in italics and that there is a quote (not on a blue background) to be included at the end of the article itself. Establish that speech marks show they are the exact words of the speaker.

Check their answers open-class.

2 Students read the complete article and do the tasks in their book.

Answers

1

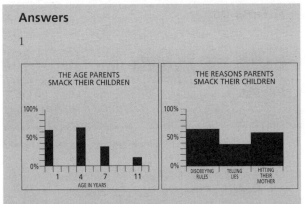

2 4-year-old children are smacked most often.
11-year-old children are smacked least often.
3 a) Britain, America, Australia, New Zealand.
b) Finland, Denmark, Norway, Sweden.

Students complete the graphs and questions, working together if they prefer to. As they finish, they can compare their answers with those of another student/s.

3 Students discuss childhood 'crimes' and possible punishments.

Ask students whether they think the article is generally for or against smacking children and what the legal situation is in their country.

Refer students to the list of children's misdemeanours in their book and deal with any vocabulary problems.

Put students in groups of four or five, mixing nationalities if possible, to say what they think about the misdemeanours. Suggest they put them in order from the most/least naughty before coming to a consensus about the appropriate punishment for each offence.

3 Thinking about learning: improving your memory

AIMS

- To provide a selection of fun activities to help improve students' memories.
- To revise language introduced in Units 11–14.

Students can either work their way through the activities on this double page at their own speed, asking for clarification from you if necessary. Or, you can guide them from exercise to exercise.

A Test your memory

Students test their ability to memorise numbers and associated nouns and then learn a method to help them memorise more effectively.

Give students two minutes to memorise the list then direct them to the test on page 124. Make sure they don't look at the unit page while they do this.

Ask students how many words they were able to remember.

Put them in pairs to follow the instructions on page 124 to improve their memory. They refer to the original list on page 92 again and then redo the test individually.

At feedback, find out how much better they did using the new system.

B Would you make a good witness?

Students revise the Past Continuous by answering questions about a picture of a bank robbery.

Answers

1 'I' was standing in a queue in the bank.
2 An old man was standing in front of me.
3 He was counting money.
4 One of the men was holding a bag and the other was holding a gun. One was short and fat; one was tall, slim and bald.
5 The child was sitting on a chair reading a book.
6 She was writing a cheque.
7 She was wearing a green skirt, top and sweater.

Tell students to look at the picture in their book and give them two minutes to remember as much detail as possible.

Refer them to page 125 and get them to write full answers to the questions.

They can check their answers with another student and ask you about any discrepancies.

At feedback, ask what other things they can remember from the picture.

C See connections and learn patterns by heart

Students put sentences in pairs, learn some of them by heart and then use them as the basis of a longer dialogue with their partner.

Answers

1b 2d 3a 4c

Teach students the expression *to learn by heart*. Find out what elements of language your students learn by heart; is it vocabulary, expressions, irregular verbs, etc?

After practising together, some students could act out their dialogues to the rest of the class.

D Learn rhymes by heart

Students read a traditional rhyme and try to solve its puzzle. They then learn to say the rhyme by heart.

Tapescript

As I was going to St. Ives
I met a man with seven wives
Each wife had seven sacks
Each sack had seven cats
Each cat had seven kits
Kits, cats, sacks, wives
How many were going to St. Ives?

Answer

One(!). The others were coming *from* St. Ives.

You may like to play the tape to the students as they read. Give them time to work out the mathematical sum implied by the rhyme, before telling them the answer and getting them to work out why.

Get them to predict contrastive sentence stress in this rhyme and then play the tape so that they can repeat and learn to say it themselves.

Puzzles to keep your mind active

Tell students than an active mind leads to a good memory.

A Time game

Students solve the puzzle.

Answer

Half past one

Give students time to work on the puzzle, explaining the solution to one another as they discover it. Invite a student to the board to draw the mirror version and the real clock.

B Word game

Students make as many words as possible of three or more letters from the word *PARLIAMENTARY*.

Write *PARLIAMENTARY* on the board and elicit one or two examples of three letter words that can be made from it (eg. ten, rat).

Set a time limit and treat it as a competition.

At feedback, get the student with the most words to read them out. Ask other students to tick off words on their list as they hear them. At the end they can contribute any words that have not been mentioned.

C Chain game

Students play a chain memory game.

Check students can remember how to say the alphabet. Refer them to the alphabet chart in Unit One if necessary.

Seat students in a circle or, if your class is large, form two or three circles.

Begin the chain by getting a student seated on your left to say *I went to market to get an apple*. You now say *I went to market to get an apple and a banana*. Indicate to the student on your right to repeat this and carry on, adding to the list alphabetically.

D Improve your general knowledge

Students answer the questions in the quiz, choosing their answers from the given possibilities.

Give students time to do this individually, then get them to check their answers with their partner by reading and asking them the questions so that they repeat the subject and object question forms.

Deal with discrepancies open-class.

E Think imaginatively

Students make up a story based on the photograph and questions in their book. They listen to other students' stories and decide which are the most imaginative.

Make sure students understand that there is no correct answer to the questions. They should use their imagination since research suggests that the more one pays attention to detail, the more active the mind and the better your memory becomes.

Students work in pairs. When they are satisfied with their story, each one in the pair tells a student from another pair their story.

Hear some of the stories open-class and get students to assess how imaginative they are.

F Feel relaxed – it helps you learn!

Students decide what makes them feel good and make five promises to themselves as rewards for learning.

Students work individually to decide which four things make them feel most relaxed. They add one other thing of their own choice.

Get them to write down their promises to themselves, based on the example using *will*, expressions of time and sequencers.

Check what you know 3

1 LISTENING

Tapescript

WOMAN: 50 years. Can you believe it? 50 years ago next week we got married.

MAN: Yes, we met at school you see. Knew each other for five years before that. We went to school together you see.

WOMAN: You're right. 55 years really. And we got married here in our hometown, didn't we Bert? Never been away. Lived here all our life.

MAN: Yep. Moved to our present house in 1950 when Joe was born.

WOMAN: Yes, Joe was born in 1950 and then Christine and Margaret. Three kids all born in the same house.

MAN: No need to move really. Had a good job at the butcher's. Started work there when I was 16, as soon as I left school.

WOMAN: Yes, a good job. We've been lucky really, except for my back, but then . . .

MAN: But your back was okay then. It's only been the last four years really.

WOMAN: Yes, only four years. No problems at all until four years ago. Then me back started . . .

1

1 How long have they known each other?
2 How long have they been married?
3 How long have they lived in the same house?
4 How long has he worked at the butcher's?
5 How long has she had problems with her health?

3

1 They have known each other for fifty five years.
2 They have been married for (nearly) fifty years.
3 They have lived in the same house since 1950.
4 He has worked at the butcher's since he was 16.
5 She has had problems with her health for the last four years.

2 PRONUNCIATION

1

/ɒ/	/ɔː/	/əʊ/
cot	caught	coat
clock	divorce	spoke
politics	war	ago
shop	forty	
watch	water	

3 GRAMMAR

1 for
2 gone
3 too
4 although
5 mustn't smoke

6 was having
7 reminded
8 hit
9 to
10 will phone

4 READING

1 mustn't
2 shouldn't
3 mustn't

4 don't have to
5 shouldn't
6 don't have to

5 VOCABULARY

1

Life changes	Shops	Political issues
birth	chemist's	education
marriage	newsagent's	taxation
death	baker's	unemployment

2

1 death 2 taxation 3 baker's 4 unemployment
5 newsagent's 6 education 7 birth 8 chemist's
9 Marriage

16 *How much is too much?*

LANGUAGE CONTENT

Productive language
• Names of animals
• Adjectives for describing people/animals
• *Want* + object + infinitive
• *When/as soon as/after/before*
• *Who* in relative clauses
• *A* vs *the* (introducing and repeating a subject)
• Infinitive of purpose

• Products and packages
• *Much/many/a lot of* + countable/uncountable nouns

Receptive language
• *(I know) someone who . . .*
• *Need/would like* + object + infinitive

1 Preparation

AIMS

• To revise/teach the names of common animals.
• To extend students' vocabulary for describing animals/people.
• To revise prepositions of place.

1 Students find and name animals hidden in the picture.

Answers

a fox, a bird (crow), a fly, a spider, a cat, a dog, a goat, a cow, a horse, a donkey

Ask students to brainstorm the names of animals they know open-class and write these on the board. Make sure the ten animals in the picture are included. Either use flashcards to check meaning or ask them to imitate animal sounds. (Useful and fun pronunciation work, particularly on open vowel sounds, can be done by getting students to compare the sounds animals make in their language with the English equivalents eg. *baa* /baː/; *moo* /muː/; etc.)

Refer students to the picture in their book and put them in pairs to find the hidden animals.

At feedback, revise simple prepositions of place, getting students to tell you where the animals are in the picture eg. *There's a cat, up the tree on the right of the picture.*

2 Students check the meaning and pronunciation of adjectives and decide which animals each adjective best describes.

Possible answers

In Britain foxes are typically considered to be sly, dogs faithful and affectionate, lions brave, pigs dirty, cats independent, peacocks vain, donkeys stupid

Students continue to work in pairs to do these exercises, comparing their decisions with another pair when they finish.

At feedback, highlight any differences in attitude between different nationalities.

2 Speaking

AIMS

• To provide speaking practice.
• To revise regular adverb formation

1-2 Students recreate the story of *The Fox and the Crow* orally from the pictures. They then answer the questions in their book.

Answers

1
A crow stole a large piece of cheese from a house and flew with it into a tall tree. A fox, who had seen this happen, said to himself, 'If I am clever, I will have cheese for supper tonight.' He thought for a moment, and then decided on his plan.
'Good afternoon, Miss Crow,' he said. 'What a beautiful bird you are! I'm sure you sing beautifully too!'
The crow, very pleased with the words of the fox, wanted to prove that she could sing. As soon as she opened her mouth to try, the cheese fell to the ground and the fox jumped on it.
As he ate the cheese he made things worse by telling the crow, 'I may have talked much about your beauty but I said nothing about your brains.'
2
1 The fox is sly, the crow is vain and stupid.
2 The moral of the story is 'Don't be fooled by flattery'.

Refer students to the pictures for the story and elicit that it was originally a Greek story by Aesop.

Put students in small groups to recreate the story, making sure that the students who know it are well distributed between groups. If nobody in your class has heard the story, elicit it open-class.

As students finish, refer them to the follow-up questions. Otherwise, deal with these at feedback, after hearing one or two versions of the story from different groups.

Refer the students to the speech bubble containing the fox's words in the picture. Get them to identify the adjective and adverb and to say how regular adverbs are formed. Refer them back to the adjectives in Exercise 1 Preparation for them to check the adverbs for these words in pairs.

3 Grammar: *want* + object + infinitive

AIMS

- To introduce the use of *want* + object + infinitive.

1 Students deduce the difference in meaning between *want* + infinitive and *want* + object + infinitive by studying example sentences and answering questions in their book.

Answers

1 a) the fox b) the crow
2 it

Put the example sentences on the board and ask the check questions open-class. Show how *it* can replace both the direct and indirect object by crossing the nouns out and inserting *it* in their place on the board.

2 Students use the prompts in their book to make sentences about the story.

Answers

1 The fox wants to eat the piece of cheese.
2 The fox wants the crow to sing a song.
3 The fox doesn't want the crow to swallow the piece of cheese.
4 The fox wants the crow to open its mouth.
5 The crow wants to eat the piece of cheese.
6 The crow wants to show off its beautiful voice.
7 The crow doesn't want the fox to eat the piece of cheese.
8 The crow wants the fox to flatter it more.

Use the example prompt in their book to show students that both example sentences already on the board could be made from the same prompts. Elicit that only sentence b) is true of the story.

Students make other sentences from the story based on the prompts in their book. The words *swallow* and *flatter* may be new; they are easily explained by showing how you swallow and using *vain* to say what type of people like to be flattered.

They check their answers with another student. Deal with any discrepancies open-class.

4 Writing

AIMS

- To provide practice in collaborative story writing.
- To revise the Past Continuous and Past Simple as narrative forms and the time expressions: *when, as soon as, after, before*.

1 Students write the story, using past narrative forms and time expressions.

Establish that the story should be written in the past. Refer students to the opening sentence for the story in their book and elicit that the Past Continuous is used to set the scene and *when* probably introduces an interruption. Get them to suggest ways of completing the sentence, highlighting the use of the Past Simple.

Point out that the time expressions do not necessarily refer to future time (as they did in Units 8 and 13).

Encourage them to add details to make their story as interesting as possible. Since each picture tells a distinctive part of the story, they may need to start a new paragraph for each picture.

2 Students read one another's stories and make suggestions for improvement. They then correct and rewrite their own story.

Encourage students to critically assess one another's work particularly for clarity of meaning. Get each pair of students to work with another pair, read their stories to one another and question them if something is unclear. They should also correct any mistakes they find.

Give students time to rewrite their story so that the version they give you has taken into account the comments made by their fellow-students.

5 Listening

AIMS

- To develop the skill of listening for specific information.
- To revise the use of the infinitive of purpose.
- To provide contextualised examples of the definite and indefinite articles and *who* in relative clauses.

1 Students listen and answer questions about the song they hear.

Tapescript

See the Students' Book page 136 for tapescript.

Answers

1 fly, spider, cat, dog, goat, cow, horse
2 She swallowed them.
3 By swallowing a horse.

Establish that *lady* is another word for *woman* and that the song tells a story involving a number of the animals hidden in the picture. Refer students to the questions in their book and the list of animals in their notebook, and then play the song.

If students can't agree on the answers then play the tape again. Get them to number the animals in the order they are first mentioned in the song.

2 Students practise using the infinitive of purpose, asking and answering about the animals in the song based on the example in their book.

Answers

- Why did she swallow the bird?
  To catch the spider.
- Why did she swallow the cat?
  To catch the bird.
- Why did she swallow the dog?
  To catch the cat.
- Why did she swallow the goat?
  To catch the dog.
- Why did she swallow the cow?
  To catch the goat.
- Why did she swallow the horse?
  To catch the cow.

NB Answers

1 a   2 the

Ask one of the students why the old lady swallowed the spider, and elicit the two-line example dialogue.

Refer students to the NB box *a vs the* to clarify why they use the definite article in this exercise. Ask the check questions open-class.

Put students in pairs to take it in turns to ask about all the animals mentioned.

6 Grammar: relative clauses

AIMS

- To introduce and practise the use of *who* in (identifying) relative clauses.
- To highlight the use of *someone* to talk about a non-identified person.

1 Students identify the use of *who* for making two sentences into one by studying examples and answering questions in their book.

Answers

1 *who* 2 *She*

Put the sentences in example a) on the board and elicit how to turn them into one sentence. Accept *and* as a possibility but elicit or supply *who* by asking who *she* refers to.

Ask the check questions open-class.

2-3 Students write sentences about interesting people they know and decide whose person is the most interesting.

Encourage students to check their sentences orally with their partner before they write them.

Put three or four pairs of students together to hear one another's sentences and decide which person is the most interesting.

Then get class feedback from each large group and vote on the chosen sentences to find the most interesting.

7 Vocabulary: products/packages

AIMS

- To revise/teach some basic foods and household products.
- To introduce a variety of packages these things come in.
- To highlight catenation and the weak forms of *a* /ə/ and *of* /əv/.

1-2 Check students' comprehension of the products and packages by getting them to answer the questions in their book and identify some of them in the photograph.

Answers

1
1 toothpaste, cigarettes, soap, matches
2
a piece of cheese, a can/tin of soup, a tube of tomato paste, a bar of chocolate, a packet of biscuits, a jar of jam, a box of matches, a bottle of milk.

Students work in pairs to do these two exercises. If possible, give them a picture dictionary to check any vocabulary they don't know. If you think a lot of this vocabulary is unknown to your students, show flashcards or the real thing.

Pronunciation

1-2 Students check their answers to the last exercise against the tape and answer questions focusing on their pronunciation. They then repeat the expressions.

Answers/Tapescript

a piece of cheese	a packet of biscuits
a can of soup	a jar of jam
a tube of tomato paste	a box of matches
a bar of chocolate	a bottle of milk

1
1 Main stress is generally on the food eg. a packet of <u>biscuits</u>.
2 *a* is pronounced /ə/, *of* is pronounced /əv/.

Play the tape for them to check their answers and ask the pronunciation questions open-class.

Write the example expression on the board, showing how the final consonant before *of* is linked to the /ə/ sound.

Play the tape again and get the students to repeat the expressions, making sure they link the sounds correctly.

3 Students decide which package each product can go in.

Begin this exercise open-class, referring students to the complete list of products in their book. Put students in small groups to continue. At feedback, accept any answers they can justify.

4+5 Students listen to a tape of British people doing the exercise and listen out for differences between these people's ideas and their own. They then think of one more product for each package.

Tapescript

The tapescript for this activity is on page 157. If you wish, you can photocopy and distribute it to students after the activity.

Possible answers

5
a piece of toast
a can of Coke
a tube of glue
a bar of gold
a packet of rice
a jar of sweets
a box of chocolates
a bottle of wine

Ask students to copy the list of products into their notebook. As they listen to the tape they write the name of the package mentioned next to the product.

At feedback get them to tell you what the British people thought and any different ideas they had.

Finally, put them back in their pairs to think of one more thing that can go in each package. Make a list of these on the board at feedback.

8 Grammar: *much/many/a lot*

AIMS

- To introduce and practise the use of *much/many/a lot* with countable/uncountable nouns.
- To revise the use of the Present Perfect for the recent past.

1 Students consider the use of *much/many/a lot* in example sentences and answer questions to deduce their own guidelines for use.

Answers

1 Cans, boxes and matches are countable. Soup is uncountable.
2 We ask *How many. . .?* with countable nouns and *How much. . .?* with uncountable nouns.
3 We generally use *much/many* in negative answers.
4 We generally use *a lot* in positive answers.

Refer students to the grammar box in their book and the photograph of the shopping to establish the difference in quantity between *not much/many* and *a lot*.

Ask the check questions open-class.

2+3 Students make questions, using *How much/many . . .?* and the Present Perfect, based on the prompts in their book. They then take it in turns to ask their partner their questions.

Answers

2 How much wine have you drunk?
  How many clothes have you bought?
  How much English homework have you done?
  How many times have you phoned your parents?
  How much television have you watched?
  How many books have you read?
  How much money have you spent?

NB Answers

Pounds, francs, yen and dinars are countable.

Give them time to work out their questions, referring them to the NB box *much/many and money*, as well as the prompts in their book.

They check that their questions are correctly formed with a student sitting next to them.

Put them in pairs with the student sitting on their other side to ask and answer the questions. Before they begin, nominate a student to ask you a question. Give a detailed answer like the example in their book to show that they should say as much as possible.

9 Reading

AIMS

- To develop the skill of reading for specific information.
- To develop the skills of listening for general and specific information.

1-3 Students discuss chocolate consumption as a lead-in to the text. They predict the answers to multiple-choice questions and then read the text to check their predictions.

NB Answers

lighter

Answers

1 4 A chocoholic is a person who is addicted to chocolate.
2
1 a   2 c   3 b   4 a   5 c

Use the photograph in the book to introduce the topic of the reading. Ask the questions in the first exercise open-class. When you discuss the third question, begin by talking about the number of bars but then ask how big the bars are, to introduce the concept of pounds and kilos. Refer students to the NB box *Weight in lbs and kgs* and ask the check question.

Students answer the multiple-choice sentences individually, making a note of their answers.

They then read the text and decide on the correct answer. They compare their answers with another student.

Listening

Tapescript

Yeah, it's true. I love chocolate. I suppose I am addicted to it. I always carry a couple of bars around with me. I hate to think I can't have some when I want some. I don't know how much I eat a week, but I know I spend about £150 on it a month. I know that because it's caused money problems at home and I've had to borrow money from my parents to pay some of the bills.

I usually have a black coffee and a Mars bar or two for breakfast. I can't eat anything else - the thought of cereal or toast makes me feel quite sick. I think I eat more chocolate when I feel depressed and also when I have a lot of work to do, it keeps me going. My husband doesn't like the way I eat so much - he says it's unhealthy but then he smokes and I don't like that, so he can't really say anything, can he? And anyway I never have any problems with my teeth and I don't get fat, so I don't see why I should stop.

Answers

1
1 No
2 To eat less chocolate
3 To stop smoking

2
1 For breakfast, when she feels depressed and when she has a lot of work to do.
2 It has caused money problems at home.
3 • She always carries a couple of bars around with her and hates to think she can't have some when she wants some.
   • She spends £150 on chocolate a month and this has resulted in money problems.
   • She has chocolate for breakfast and the thought of anything else makes her feel sick.
4 Apparently very little.

Make sure students read the first set of questions before they listen. They should check their answers with a partner and ask to hear the tape again if there are discrepancies.

At feedback, accept short answers initially. Then ask students to give you complete answers using *want/would like* +/- an object + infinitive (eg. *She doesn't want to stop eating chocolate*).

Students read the second set of questions, then listen to the tape again and check their answers together. Deal with any discrepancies open-class.

English in action

AIMS

• **To allow students to simulate a variety of activities in a British bank.**
• **To teach students to complete cheques in English.**
• **To introduce a set of banking vocabulary.**

Answers

100 French francs	= £11.96
300 German marks	= £121.46
2,000 Greek drachmas	= £6.62
200 American dollars	= £121.95

Ask students if they know the current rate of exchange for their national currency into sterling or dollars.

Use the chart in the book or a current chart from a newspaper as a basis for the mathematical exchanges. First check that students can say the numbers correctly.

If you want to continue this number practice, get students to ask one another about other sums of money in other currencies.

Answers

3
1 help 2 change 3 to 4 (depends on destination) 5 for 6 (depends on nominated currency) 7 large/small

Tell students to choose a destination from those listed in the chart but not to tell their partner.

They work individually to complete the gaps in the conversation in their book. Circulate as they work and prompt them to correct themselves if you notice mistakes.

They take it in turns to be the bank clerk, working out the sum for the exchange on the spot.

5 Students use prompts in their book to ask for various services in the bank.

Do this open-class, dealing with vocabulary difficulties as they arise and accepting all possible correct answers. If students suggest *Can I . . ., please?* ask if they know how to say this another way. If they suggest *I want to . . .*, ask them how to say this more politely to elicit *I would like to . . .*

6 Students listen to a tape of a customer in a bank to find out what she wants to do and what she actually achieves.

Tapescript

BANK CLERK: Hello. Good morning. What can I do for you?

WOMAN: Hello. I'd like to cash this cheque, please.

BANK CLERK: Fine. No problem. How would you like it, in 10s or 20s?

WOMAN: Oh, um, in tens, please. I'd also like to send some money to the States, if that's possible.

BANK CLERK: To America?

WOMAN: Yes, I've got the account number.

BANK CLERK: Ah, well, you need the overseas counter. That's not me, I'm afraid. You'll need that queue over there.

WOMAN: Oh. OK. Just one more thing.

BANK CLERK: Yes?

WOMAN: How do I apply for some sort of credit card. I haven't got one and I thought I . . .

BANK CLERK: Oh that's simple. Just fill in this form and send it in.

WOMAN: Oh, I can't get one immediately, then? Oh, I hoped. . .

BANK CLERK: I'm afraid not. It has to be sent in.

WOMAN: OK. I'll do that then. Thanks for your help.

BANK CLERK: Not at all. Goodbye.

WOMAN: Bye.

Answers

She wants to cash a cheque, arrange a transfer to the USA and to apply for a credit card.
She actually cashes her cheque. The other two things can't happen immediately.

At feedback first elicit short answers and then ask students to tell you what the customer wants/manages to do.

Highlight that *want* is fine when talking about a third person but that when you make a request yourself *would like* is more polite.

7-8 Students use the completed cheque in their book as a model for writing other cheques.

Refer students to the completed cheque in their book. Ask them where you write the date, the amount and the signature.

Give them time to copy the blank cheque into their notebook so that they can write a cheque for themselves and then their partner. They will probably ask you how to say a cheque bounces!!

Language review 16

a
1 Do you need to use the computer now?
2 I want you to finish this exercise for homework.
3 I would like to work for an international bank.
4 What do you want me to do?
5 Do you want to go out tonight?
6 Would you like me to lend you that book?
7 They need us to take them home.
8 Does he want me to help him?
b
She is a selfish person *who* always does what she wants.
He was a young man *who* liked to play football.
There were a lot of people *who* had the same idea.
She is a very friendly person *who* likes meeting people.
My teacher was the person you saw *who* had short, black hair.
c + d
1 I - There are not *many* animals that I don't like.
2 I - A lot *of* people like dogs but I don't.
3 I - Cats are *a lot of* work.
4 I - I haven't got *many* friends but my pets keep me company.
5 C
6 C
7 I - You haven't given the cat very *much* food.
8 I - There is *a lot of* work to do.
9 C
10 I - How *much* fruit did you buy?

17 *The man who died twice*

LANGUAGE CONTENT

Productive language
- Present Simple and Past Simple passives
- Passives + *by/with*
- *I think so/I don't think so* (giving opinions)
- *So* vs *such* (emphasis)

- Causes of death

Receptive language
- Selected vocabulary from a newspaper article
- The names of punctuation marks

1 Preparation

AIMS

- To introduce the use of the Present Simple passive for talking about where products are made/produced.
- To contrast the Present Simple passive and active forms, highlighting the change in subject focus.

1+2 Students focus on the Present Simple passive form and then say where listed products are made/produced.

Answers

1
Tartan scarves are made in Scotland.
Mulberry bags are made in England.
Pasta is produced in Italy.
Duc d'O chocolates are made in Belgium.

2
Seiko watches are made in Japan.
Gucci bags are made in Italy.
Scotch whisky is produced in Scotland.
Lindt chocolate is made/produced in Switzerland.
Audi cars are made in Germany.
Persian rugs are made in Iran (formerly Persia).

NB Answer

1 the Japanese
2 the watches

Focus on the products and their labels in the photograph. Elicit where they are made/produced. (*made* = constructed, *produced* = natural products.)

Refer students to the NB box *make vs are made* and ask the check questions.

Put students in pairs to decide where the things listed in the second exercise are made/produced.

At feedback, check that students use the singular and plural forms correctly.

2 Reading

AIMS

- To develop the skill of reading for specific information.
- To motivate students to write their own questions.

1-4 Students write questions, prompted by a newspaper headline. They read the article to find answers to their questions.

Before students work on the newspaper article, check that they understand the difference between *a cliff* and *a mountain*, so that these words will be recognised in the article to come. Draw a mountain on the board to elicit the word. Then refer students to the illustration of the cliff on page 101 and establish the difference.

Ask students to close their books. Write the headline of the article on the board. Ask them what makes them want to read the article.

Put students in groups of three to write questions prompted by the headline. What information would they like to find out when they read the article? Check their questions open-class and write them on the board.

Ask students to read the article to find the answers to the questions. They check these with their group. Make sure they realise that some of the questions may not be answered.

At feedback, rub off the answered questions as students tell you the answers. Leave any unanswered questions on the board as these may get answered by the end of the lesson.

3 Speaking

AIMS

- To provide a chance for freer speaking practice.
- To introduce and give practice of *I think so/ don't think so* for expressing opinions.

130

Introduce *I think so/I don't think so* by writing the two expressions at the top of two columns on the board. Ask individual students if they believe Clive Reed and Clive Greenwood are the same man and write their name in the appropriate column. As you ask more students the same question, they should begin to offer *I think so* or *I don't think so* of their own accord. Tell them they may be able to use these expressions in the next activity.

Ask students to imagine the story behind the newspaper article. Make sure they realise they only have to imagine, there is no correct answer.

Refer them to the questions in their book and put students in groups of four or five to speculate about possible answers. Circulate as they do this and inject further questions/ideas if they begin to dry up.

As they finish, put two groups together to tell one another about their story and to create further discussion.

Elicit the ideas of a particular group at feedback and encourage other students to disagree or add further suggestions.

Answers

1
1 He went to Scotland because he was in trouble with the police/to make a new life.
2 At work in Scotland.
3 They were colleagues/friends, and lived in the same lodgings.
4 She fell 500 ft. in the Scottish mountains.
5 He died of the cold, trying to get help.

Explain that the second, more detailed article comes from a later edition of another newspaper. While reading it to see how it compares to their imagined story, students should see if they can find answers to the remaining questions on the board.

Give them time to compare their findings with another student. Then, get individuals to summarise the story for you so the whole class can be sure to have understood the main points.

Answers

1 to save   2 to fail   3 to identify   4 to drown
5 former   6 to disappear   7 valuable   8 anxious

Students work in pairs to do this, one of them has their book open at the article on page 126, the other reads out the definitions on page 101.

Check their answers open-class. Although these words are mainly for passive recognition, some students may want to activate them so check they are pronounced and used correctly. Do this by asking students to put the words into complete sentences.

4 Grammar: the passive

AIMS

- To highlight the form and use of passive statements.
- To introduce a selection of past participles.
- To provide written practice of the Past Simple passive.

Answers

1 Clive found Hilary's body. We don't know who found Clive's body.
2 Sentence a).
3 Because who found the body is not important or not known.
4 a) *am/is/are found.*
    b) *was/were found.*

Elicit the example sentences to the blackboard and ask the check questions open-class.

When you have established that the verb *to be* and the past participle are used together to make the passive form, direct students to the verb chart in their book. Get them to complete the chart individually and to compare their answers with a partner.

When you check their answers open-class, elicit that the Past Simple form and the past participle are often the same but that they are different for the verb *go*. Remind them of the difference between *been/gone* by asking the check questions from the NB box *been vs gone* on page 66 again.

Students work in pairs to do the exercise, saying the sentences aloud as they work.

At feedback, reinforce the concept of the forms chosen after each sentence by asking eg. *Who found Clive's clothes?* In an active sentence this should elicit someone's name. In a passive sentence this should elicit either *We don't know* or passive + *by* + the name of the agent.

5 Speaking

AIMS

- To provide spoken practice of the Past Simple passive form.
- To introduce a set of vocabulary which explains how people die.

Elicit that in the newspaper story Clive died of the cold and Hilary died of her injuries. Refer students to the questions in their book and clarify the other causes of death they mention. What do we say when someone dies of old-age/kills themselves, etc? Elicit that the verbs in question 3 are in the passive form because we are focusing on the person who died, not the person who killed them.

Refer students to the names of the famous people in the exercise. How many have they heard of? Ask them where they came from? (Mao Tse Tung – China; President Kennedy, Martin Luther King, Marilyn Monroe – The USA; Julius Caesar – Rome; Indira Gandhi – India; John Lennon – Britain; Emperor Hirohito – Japan; Napoleon – France).

Put students in groups of three or four to complete the sentences with passive or active Past Simple forms of the verbs supplied. Discussion should ensue as they pool their general knowledge about the famous people.

As they finish, get them to ask another group about people they remain unsure about.

Finally check their answers as a class. Encourage as much discussion and information-giving as possible.

6 Listening

AIMS

- To develop the skill of listening for specific information.
- To introduce and practise the difference between *so* and *such* as 'emphasisers'.
- To highlight the intonation and stress commonly used with *so/such*.

1 Students listen to the tape and complete the chart in their book.

Tapescript

1
My heroine is Indira Gandhi. She was really strong. India was a big and divided country. She kept it together - united. She travelled a lot and she was cosmopolitan in attitude, open to other countries. She understood other nationalities and represented India well to the rest of the world. She valued the traditions of her country too so she didn't make too many changes too quickly. Some people say she was cruel but I think she was strong. She was a woman in a man's world. People respected her - she was such a respected person. That's such an important thing for a politician.

2
I think Martin Luther King is the person I admire most. He dreamed of a better, less racist world. Although he faced violence throughout his life he didn't change his ideas. He didn't use violence but he did fight the system. He was such a gentle, non-violent man. He led a quarter of a million people in Washington demanding that black people be given the vote. Thanks to him black people were given the vote in 1962. He was so sure he was right. I would love to be that certain of things.

3
My favourite person is Marilyn Monroe. I know she isn't really a historical person but she represents something important to me. She was such an ordinary person with such big dreams. I think everyone needs dreams. She had such an unhappy life but, even so, she tried hard to enjoy it. She was so beautiful and successful on one level but so frightened and alone on another. That's why I like her I think. Her life was a disaster although she was in such a lot of successful films. She represents success and disaster - a good warning for life!

Answers

	Favourite person	Reasons
Person 1	Indira Gandhi	strong, united India; travelled, was cosmopolitan; represented India well; valued traditions, didn't make changes too quickly; well respected.
Person 2	Martin Luther King	Dreamed of a better, less racist world; faced violence but didn't change ideas; fought the system but non-violent; won the vote for black people; convinced he was right
Person 3	Marilyn Monroe	Ordinary person with big dreams; unhappy life but tried hard to enjoy it; beautiful and successful but also frightened and alone

Make sure students realise that the people referred to on tape are included in the list of famous people in Exercise 5 Speaking.

Copy the outline of the chart from the book onto the board and get students to do the same in their notebook.

Tell the students why you admire one of the other people on the list, getting them to write down her/his name in the chart. Say something like this: *The person I like best is John Lennon because he wrote brilliant and innovative pop music. He was a rebel but showed that you don't have to conform to become successful.*

Tell them to listen to you again for the important information words which explain why you like him. Write these on the board under *Reasons* in the chart to show that they should write notes and not complete sentences as answers eg. *brilliant, innovative pop music; successful rebel.*

Now play the tape right through, getting them to compare answers between listenings. If necessary, play the tape in sections in subsequent listenings, getting students to note and check each speaker's opinion, before moving on to the next.

Grammar: *so* and *such*

1 Students deduce the difference in form and use between *so* and *such* by answering questions about the example sentences.

Answers

1 so   2 such   3 stronger

133

Elicit the first sentence in the grammar box onto the board by writing it up with a gap instead of *so*. Get students to complete the sentence, based on what they heard about Marilyn Monroe. Now do the same thing with the second sentence, leaving out *such*.

2+3 Students complete a written exercise, inserting *so* or *such* as appropriate. They then listen to check their answers against the tape, and repeat the sentences copying the intonation.

Tapescript/Answers

1 Indira Gandhi was *such* a respected person.
2 That's *such* an important thing for a politician.
3 Martin Luther King was *such* a gentle, non-violent man.
4 He was *so* sure he was right.
5 Marilyn Monroe was *such* an ordinary person with *such* big dreams.
6 She had *such* an unhappy life.
7 She was *so* beautiful and successful, but *so* frightened and alone.
8 Her life was a disaster although she was in *such* a lot of successful films.

Put students in pairs to do the exercise in their book. As they finish, get them to compare their answers with another pair. Then play the tape so students can correct their answers.

Play the tape again, getting students to repeat the sentences. Nominate individuals to repeat after the tape. Encourage them to use a wide voice range to reflect the emphasis of their words. Then get the other students to mumble drill themselves with equal feeling. (For advice on drilling, see page 15.)

4 Students talk about people they admire, using *so* and *such*.

Give students a few minutes to prepare what they are going to say. Suggest they note the important things at the end of their listening chart so that they work from notes and not complete sentences. Make sure they realise that they can choose anyone, dead or alive, to talk about.

As they listen to their partner, they should note the main information in their chart. You can then hear one or two examples back as some students recode what they heard to the class.

7 Pronunciation: /s/, /z/, /ʃ/

AIMS

- To highlight a selection of sounds made by the letter *s*.

1+2 Students listen and repeat the sentence, then isolate the three sounds and categorise other words by sound.

Tapescript

He was so sure he was right.

Answers

/s/: sometimes, bus, sea, sell, writes, sock, strong
/z/: nose, sometimes, use, lose, easy, choose
/ʃ/: sugar, shoe, should

Elicit the example sentence onto the board and play it on tape.

Ask an individual student to read the words and write the phonemic symbol above them.

Nominate a student to say the isolated sounds when you point at each phonemic symbol in turn.

Students work in pairs to say and categorise the words listed in their book.

3-4 They write sentences using words with the target sounds in them. Finally, they read these and other students' sentences aloud.

Students continue to work in pairs to write a sentence with as many *s*'s as possible in it. Make sure they realise they can add new words.

They change pairs, reading first their own and then their new partner's sentence aloud.

They count the number of *s*'s in each sentence and tell you who has the most. Get the student with the most to read it out to you.

5-6 Students read the tongue-twister and answer the question at the end of it. They then learn the tongue-twister by heart.

Answer

There are no *s*'s in *that* - T.H.A.T.

Establish that this is a traditional tongue-twister and the aim is to say the sentence as quickly and correctly as possible. Check that they know what a *(sea) shell* is by reference to the photograph. Elicit that the *seashore* is another word for *beach* (see picture on page 101).

Say the tongue-twister to them as they read it and try to solve the puzzle.

Get them to read the rhyme to their partner three times as quickly as possible. They then try to say it by heart.

8 Writing

AIMS

- To revise/teach the names of punctuation marks.
- To revise and practise rules of punctuation and capitalisation.

1-2 Students revise when to use capitalisation and check their answers against the text.

Answers

Names of people, months of the year, nationalities, countries, days of the week, languages.

Students do these exercises in pairs.

At feedback, brainstorm the vocabulary areas listed in Exercise 1, quickly eliciting as many words as possible.

3 Students match punctuation marks to their names and discuss their use in the text they have just read on capitalisation.

Answers

a comma = , (used in lists, before closing speech marks, etc.)
an apostrophe = ' (used in contracted forms, possessives)
a question mark = ? (used at the end of a question)
a full stop = . (used at the end of a sentence)
an exclamation mark = ! (used to show surprise or indignation)
speech marks = " " (used to show the exact words spoken)

Students continue to work in pairs.

At feedback, in a monolingual class, highlight any differences between the English use of punctuation and that of the students' own language. In a multilingual class, ask students to tell you about differences they perceive. After each contribution, ask students of other nationalities to say whether their language is more like English or the other language.

4-5 Students punctuate a text about Rasputin and then read it to answer questions.

Answers

4

The evil Russian monk, Rasputin, was seen as a bad influence on the Russian royal family. Prince Felix Yussupov with three friends decided to kill him. They invited him to a wild party in a cellar and fed the monk cakes and wine, poisoned with cyanide. Unfortunately, the victim was immune to cyanide. To the horror of the murderers he continued eating and drinking happily. Finally, the prince tried to shoot him but was stopped by the hypnotic eye of Rasputin. Yussupov ran away. Rasputin tried to follow him but was shot, stabbed and hit repeatedly. His hands and feet were tied and finally he fell into the icy River Neva. It was afterwards discovered that his death was by drowning, not poison or gunshot wounds.

5
1 Rasputin drowned.
2 Prince Yussupov and three friends tried to kill him. They shot, poisoned, stabbed and hit him because he was seen as a bad influence on the Russian royal family.

NB Answers

1 The prince   2 A gun

Refer students to the photograph of Rasputin in their book and ask what they know about him. How do they imagine his character from the picture? Elicit or supply this basic information. *He was a Russian monk who strongly influenced the Russian royal family at the beginning of the twentieth century. Some people considered him evil.*

Give students a few minutes to work on punctuating the text alone, then let them work together to pool what they can.

When they finish, refer them to the follow-up question and the NB box in their book.

If possible, give each pair a copy of the corrected text above to compare with their own. Deal with any queries open-class.

English in action

AIMS

- To encourage students to research and use English outside the classroom.
- To provide a context for freer practice of language from this and earlier units.

1-2 Students choose an area of local interest to study and arrange how they will do so.

Use the photographs on the page to arouse interest in the past. Where do they think the photos were taken and what activities do they depict?

Ask what they know about the area they study in. If students are studying in a foreign environment, you could stimulate curiosity by providing a reading about some of the places/people/events of local interest.

Give students time to decide what they would like to find out and to formulate some questions of their own.

Write suggested topic areas on the board and for each one get a keen student to expand on what they would like to research. When there are enough ideas, ask students to change places so that they can sit and work in groups with people who are interested in the same subject area.

Get them to brainstorm how they will collect their information in their groups.

You need to organise and inform students about the timing of this work. You may set it for weekend homework or make it the basis of a longer project, lasting over a number of lessons. Students will probably need to collect at least some of their information out of class time. If possible, provide some resource materials to start them off. You could also consider organising a class visit to a local museum or library. Make sure students understand the time span involved and to which lesson they should bring the information they have collected. Don't worry if research has to take place in the students' own language, their task is to communicate what they find out in English.

3-4 Students pool their information and make a poster to show other students.

They either make one or a number of posters per group depending on the amount of information they have to share.

If possible, provide time and materials for this to happen in class; encourage students to communicate naturally in English as they work.

If possible, display their posters so that they all see what the other students have found out. If this is not possible, you could make their work the basis of another class magazine (see English in Action, Unit One).

Language review 17

a
1 I was met at the airport by a friend last night.
2 My bags were checked by Customs Officers at the airport.
3 Wine is produced in the south of England.
4 The children were told a story before they went to bed.
5 All the food at the party was eaten before nine o' clock.
6 A large new hospital was opened by the Queen last weekend.
7 £100,000 was stolen from a bank in Birmingham this morning.
8 The post is collected at 9 am and 1 pm every day.
9 A bell is rung at the end of school each day.
10 The policeman was hit with a bottle by angry teenagers yesterday evening.

b
Actual answers
Mercury is the smallest of the planets and the nearest to the Sun.
1 No, the Angel Falls in Venezuela is the highest waterfall in the world.
2 No, there are 50.
3 Yes.
4 Yes.
5 Yes.
6 Yes.
7 No, it was a gift from France to America.
8 Yes.

c
Possible answers
1 He was so intelligent. He had such a good sense of humour.
2 It was so expensive. It was such a long way from the centre of town.
3 The weather was so beautiful. The people were so friendly. The hotel was so near the beach.
4 It's so big. It's got such a lot of character.
5 I had such a good time. The people were so interesting.

Murder

AIMS

- To provide a fun activity whereby students revise some of the language taught so far, particularly the Past Simple passive.

Students read the rules of the game and play it in groups.

Before you begin, you might like to familiarise the students with the board for the game by getting them to focus on the furniture in the different rooms of the house. Do this as follows: either put the name of each room on the classroom board and get students in groups to brainstorm the furniture they expect to find in each one. Or, show them the picture in their book for a few minutes and then use it as the basis of a memory game, like the one on page 72. Finally, they should check their answers against the picture in their book.

Set the scene by explaining that someone has been murdered in the house pictured in their book. Their job is to find out who did it, in which room and with which weapon. The possible weapons are illustrated on the page. Check that students know which is the knife, the poison, the rope and the gun.

Put students in groups of four to six players with one book open between them. Each group needs a dice and each player needs a different coloured counter which is placed initially on the square of its own marked 'start'. They also need three sets of cards. Photocopy the cards on the next page and give each group a set of weapon cards, room cards and as many blank suspect cards as there are players in their game. Each student writes their own name on one of these blank cards as they are the suspects.

Ask students to read the rules in their book to find out how to play the game and to note any unknown vocabulary to ask you about.

When you have clarified any problems, ask students to make a list of all the possible weapons, all the possible rooms and all the possible murderers. They can check these against their sets of cards.

Tell one student in each group to shuffle the three packs of cards separately and, without looking, to select one from each pack. These three cards are the solution to the murder and should be kept face down to one side.

The other cards are dealt out between the players in each group in strict rotation. Students

look at their own cards and tick them off their list of possible weapons, rooms and murderers. These cards cannot be in the 'murder pile'.

Demonstrate how to play the game by drawing a few squares leading to a room on the board at the front of the class. Throw the dice and move that number of squares towards the room. Throw the dice again and go into the room and make an accusation which includes that room like this: 'The murder was committed in *the kitchen* by *Graziella* with *the gun.*'

The easiest way to get the rest of the rules across is probably to play/watch a game. We suggest one group plays with your supervision and the others watch until they understand what to do. A player begins by throwing the dice, and moves towards the room of her/his choice. Students may move in any direction but <u>not</u> diagonally. They play in clockwise order until someone throws a number at least as large as that required to enter a room.

When a player gets into a room they must make an accusation mentioning the room they are in, a possible weapon and a possible murderer*. If the player on the accuser's left has any of the cards mentioned they show *one* of these to the accuser but not to the other players. The accuser ticks this card off her/his list. If the player on the accuser's left has no cards mentioned then the next player on the left shows one of his/her cards if possible and so on. <u>One</u> card only is shown each turn and the accuser's turn finishes as soon as <u>one</u> card has been shown.

After playing like this for some time, a player will be sure she/he has the solution to the murder since all the other cards have all been ticked off her/his list. At this point, at the end of her/his turn, she/he can write down her/his full accusation and check the three cards which were put to one side at the beginning of the game. If the cards match her/his accusation, she/he has won the game. If the cards don't all match, she/he can no longer move or make accusations her/himself but she/he must continue to show her/his cards in the normal way when they are mentioned by other players.

*The counter of an accused player is moved to the room the accusation is made in. They must use their next turn to move from that room or make an accusation there themselves. A player may stay in a particular room for any number of turn as long as she/he makes an accusation including that room each turn.

Murder game cards

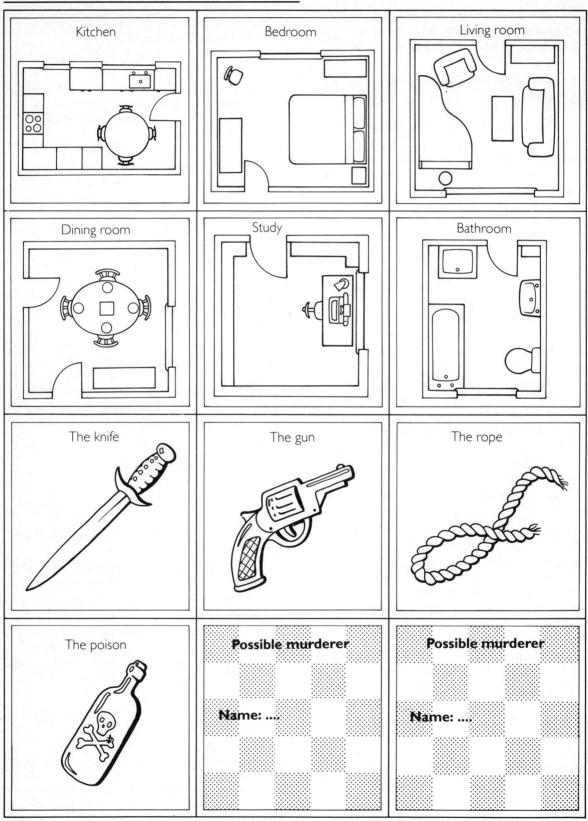

Kitchen

Bedroom

Living room

Dining room

Study

Bathroom

The knife

The gun

The rope

The poison

Possible murderer

Name: ....

Possible murderer

Name: ....

18 *What would you give up?*

1 Preparation

AIMS

- To revise/teach vocabulary of household equipment and rooms of the house.
- To preview *would* for speculation.

1 Students identify some of the equipment listed in the photograph and allocate the rest of the vocabulary to appropriate rooms.

Answers

1 a telephone, a radio, an electric kettle, a dishwasher, a cooker, a microwave, a toaster, a cooker, a fridge.

2 living room – a video, a CD player, an answerphone, a television, a stereo
study – a computer
bathroom – a hairdryer, a washing-machine/dryer
kitchen – a freezer

Put students in pairs and refer them to the photograph and exercise in their book. If you know that certain words are unknown or unrecognisable from their own language, then use pictures or a picture dictionary.

If necessary, refer them to the picture of rooms on the previous page to prompt them into completing the second part of the exercise.

2 Students discuss which of the household equipment they own and which they would/ wouldn't be prepared to give up.

Mention something on the list that you own and love; something you definitely *wouldn't give up*. Then mention something you are fairly indifferent about and *would give up*. Treat this as idiomatic language at this stage; work on the structure will be done in the next part of the lesson.

Put students back in their pairs to do this activity.

Hear a few examples of what individual students would/wouldn't give up open-class.

2 Grammar: *would* (speculation)

AIMS

- To introduce/practise *would/could* to express speculation.

1 Students answer questions about the use and form of *would* after considering examples in the grammar box.

Answers

1 No
2 This person is imagining the action.
3 *'d* stands for *would*.
4 Invert *would* and the subject eg. *Would you give up the video?* Possible short answers are: *Yes, I would* and *No, I wouldn't*.

Elicit the examples to the board and ask the check questions open-class.

2 Students complete the dialogue in their book with different forms of *would*.

Answers

A: What *would* you do with £2,000?
B: I *'d* buy a motorbike. *Would* you do something different?
A: Yes, I *would*. I *'d* put it in the bank.
B: Oh, I *wouldn't*. That's boring! I *'d* spend it immediately. It *wouldn't* do anything in the bank.
A: Yes, it *would*. It *'d* make lots of interest. Then I *'d* buy a bigger, better motorbike.

Give students time to do this individually and then to compare their answers with another student.

At feedback, deal with any discrepancies open-class then get students to practise the dialogue in pairs, taking it in turns to begin.

3 Students discuss what eight possessions they would choose to buy if they had limited funds.

NB Answers

1 a   2 b

Put students in groups of three and set the situation as explained in their book.

Before they begin discussing, refer them to the NB Box *could vs would* and ask the check questions open-class.

As they discuss what they would buy, circulate in the class, and note down typical mistakes they make. Use these as the basis for a correction spot at the end of the activity or lesson.

3 Reading

AIMS

- To develop the skills of reading for general and specific information and inferred meaning.
- To encourage students to select words for dictionary study.
- To revise the use of the Present Perfect for indefinite time and *used to* for past habit.

1-2 Students read the articles to answer the questions.

Answers

1

1 Rachel was forced to give up her phone.
  Rob gave up his TV.
2 In both cases they feel it has had a positive effect on their lives.

2

1 When Rachel's boyfriend left her, he took the phone with him.
  For Rob it was a New Year's resolution to give up his TV.
2 Rachel wasn't able to call her mother or friends. Her office couldn't contact her and she couldn't get food delivered any more.

The most difficult thing for Rob was the reaction of his friends who thought he must either be mad, an intellectual or a snob.

3 For Rachel:
  - no ringing bells on Sunday mornings or in the middle of the night
  - no more wrong numbers or salesmen selling insurance
  - no more enormous phone bills
  - she has started writing and receiving letters again
  - her health has improved because she is cooking decent meals for herself
  For Rob:
  - he and his wife have started talking more
  - they have both started doing old hobbies ie. playing the piano and painting
  - they see their friends more often

4 Possible answers include:
  – Rachel used to get woken up by the phone. She used to get enormous phone bills etc.
  – Rob and his wife used to watch a lot of TV. They forgot how to communicate and didn't use to have hobbies, etc.

Give students time to read the questions before they read and to compare answers afterwards.

At feedback, encourage students to speculate as much as possible about the past lives of Rachel and Rob.

This exercise provides extended reading practice. If you think your class is not yet ready for this we suggest you treat it as a 'jigsaw' acivity (see page 16).

3-4 Students choose five words from the article to look up in a dictionary and then tell one another their meaning, pronunciation and how to use them.

Provide a class set of dictionaries if possible or get students to bring an English-English dictionary to class (such as the *Longman Active Study Dictionary*).

Give them time to select their five new words and then to complete the task in their book.

As students finish, they tell another student about their words and write down example sentences for any other new words their partner tells them. They then change partners and talk to another student.

Finally, elicit the new words to the board.

4 Speaking

AIMS

- To provide an opportunity for freer speaking.
- To introduce and practise ways of expressing agreement/disagreement.

1-2 Students use expressions of agreement/ disagreement to discuss what they think of television, based on ideas in their book. They report their opinions back to the class.

Introduce the expressions of agreement/ disagreement by writing something contentious on the board and asking a student if they agree. eg. *To give up life's luxuries is to give up living.* Rephrase what the student says back into one of the expressions in their book. Drill it and write it with plus or minus signs on the board. eg.

–	I don't really agree.
+	I agree.
++	I couldn't agree more.

Ask if anyone disagrees with the last student and elicit how they feel about the original statement on the board. Rephrase their words into another of the expressions in the student's book and proceed as above.

When all three expressions are on the board, get students to locate the stressed last word in each expression as you say it to the class. Highlight the British preference for tentative disagreement as opposed to the more aggressive and direct *I don't agree.*

Write the following statements on the board.

- Young people are more violent than they used to be.
- Rich countries should be more responsible for poor countries.
- Unemployment is too high a price to pay for low taxation.
- All places of work should provide free childcare facilities.
- All young people should spend some time in the army.
- Smoking should be made illegal.
- Education should be free for everyone.

Put students in pairs to practise responding to these statements, using the expressions of agreement and disagreement.

At feedback, invite students to express their views on one or two of the subjects they feel strongly about.

Change the subject to television for the next activity by asking students how much television they watch and whether they would stop or limit their children's viewing.

Put students in groups of four or five and refer them to the statements about television in their book. Make sure that they realise these are the basis for discussion and that they are only expected to use the expressions of agreement/ disagreement if they are appropriate, not every time they speak.

At feedback, their job will be to tell the rest of the class the main opinions held in their group and how many statements they could all agree on.

5 Writing

AIMS

- To highlight the differences between formal and informal letters.
- To provide practice in writing a formal letter.

1 Students read a variety of advertisements and answer questions in their book.

Answers

1 New Dawn Recordings (eating/smoking/drinking too much)
2 Multi activity holidays and corrective eye surgery

Give students time to read the advertisements and to discuss answers to the questions in pairs.

2 Students separate the jumbled letters in their book and answer questions highlighting some differences between formal and informal letter-writing.

Answers

Informal letter: e, g, d, l, n, b, i
Formal letter: h, a, m, j, f, k, c

Give students a few minutes to unjumble the letters individually and then get them to continue in pairs if they prefer to.

At feedback, elicit the two letters to the board. Ask the questions about layout open-class. Elicit that in a formal letter the address of the company goes below the sender's address and the date, but on the left-hand side of the letter.

3 Students write a letter to the advertisement of their choice.

If possible, provide students with a piece of writing paper on which to write their final version. To get maximum motivation, encourage them to really send their letter to the address in the advertisement.

6 Listening

AIMS

- To develop the skill of listening for specific information.
- To provide contextualised practice of *would* for speculation.

1 Students listen to the beginning of the interview with Anthony Hopkins and answer the questions in their book.

Tapescript

INTERVIEWER: This week our castaway is the actor Anthony Hopkins. Tony I know that music means a great deal in your life, you play the piano?

ANTHONY: Yes.

INTERVIEWER: Were you put to it or did you take to it?

ANTHONY: I took to it quite early, I started at about the age of six.

INTERVIEWER: Did you ever consider taking it up professionally?

ANTHONY: Yes, I did for a while, er, for about ten years I think and then I discovered I didn't have the technique or the talent really to play as a concert pianist. That's what I wanted to be, was a concert pianist so I more or less gave up, or it gave me up.

INTERVIEWER: Yes, the top or nothing.

ANTHONY: Top or nothing, that's been it all my life, yes.

INTERVIEWER: Do you play discs a lot?

ANTHONY: Yes, I play music a lot when I'm working on plays, you know, I choose something that will help me get in the mood when I'm reading.

INTERVIEWER: Well you have just eight for what may be a long time. How did you set about

choosing them? Are you choosing nostalgically?

ANTHONY: They're nostalgically, yes I've chosen a few that, um, made an impression on me when I was a child.

Answers

1 The piano
2 The dream of being a concert pianist.
3 Music that made an impression on him as a child – nostalgic music

Introduce the subject of the interview by referring students to the photo of Anthony Hopkins and eliciting anything they know about him or his films. Ask if anyone saw the film *The Silence of the Lambs* for which he got an Oscar.

Put the name 'Desert Island Discs' on the board and say it is a popular BBC radio programme. Elicit/tell them that each week a famous person chooses eight pieces of music to take to an imagined desert island. They are going to hear a section of an interview with Anthony Hopkins.

Get students to read the questions before they listen for the first time. Play the tape again if they can't agree on the answers.

2 Students listen to the end of the interview and complete Anthony Hopkins' choices.

Tapescript

INTERVIEWER: Did you pick up enough local knowledge to put up a hut, do you think, some sort of shelter?

ANTHONY: No, I can't even knock a nail in a wall.

INTERVIEWER: Well you wouldn't have any nails.

ANTHONY: No I wouldn't have any nails. All I would want to take is a piano. Of course I can't take a piano with me.

INTERVIEWER: Yes you can, that's your luxury.

ANTHONY: A piano tuner?

INTERVIEWER: Not a tuner, no.

ANTHONY: Well I'll take a piano and tune it myself.

INTERVIEWER: Right. What about food. Any idea? Can you fish?

ANTHONY: An everlasting supply of, er, English sausages and cheese.

INTERVIEWER: You have had your luxury.

ANTHONY: I've had my luxury.

INTERVIEWER: You have to make your own cheese from turtle milk or something. How long do you think you could endure it?

ANTHONY: How long could I survive on a desert island? Well, knowing my fortitude and my resilience, I'll probably give myself about two weeks.

INTERVIEWER: If you could take only one disc of the eight you have chosen which would it be?

ANTHONY: I think I would take Myfanwy – Triorchy Male Voice Choir.

INTERVIEWER: And you've told us your luxury - that's going to be a piano.

ANTHONY: Yes.

INTERVIEWER: One book. You have The Bible and the complete works of Shakespeare already for you on the island.

ANTHONY: I'd take *The Great Gatsby*.

INTERVIEWER: *The Great Gatsby?*

ANTHONY: Yes, I've read it a few times and I find it a haunting book.

INTERVIEWER: Who's it by?

ANTHONY: F Scott Fitzgerald.

INTERVIEWER: Right. *The Great Gatsby* by F Scott Fitzgerald. And thank you, Anthony Hopkins, for letting us hear your desert island discs.

ANTHONY: Thank you.

Answers

Luxury: a piano
Food: English sausages (and cheese)
The one piece of music he would most like to take:
Myfanwy – sung by the Triorchy Male Voice Choir
Book: *The Great Gatsby* (by F Scott Fitzgerald)

Check that students understand the concept of *a luxury* and also that they need to listen for the one piece of music, of those listed, which he would most like to take.

Play the tape and get students to compare their answers. Play the tape again if there are any discrepancies.

3 Students interview a partner to find out what she/he would take to a desert island.

Give students a few minutes to note what they would take based on the questions in their book.

They work in pairs to interview each other.

At feedback, ask students to tell you about anything particularly interesting that their partner would take.

7 Grammar: *If* + past + *would*

AIMS

- To provide written practice of *would* in full second conditional sentences.

- To highlight and practise the use of *If* + Past Simple to talk about 'unreal' or impossible present /future situations.

1 Students deduce the form and use of second conditional sentences by answering questions about the example sentence in their book.

Answers

1 imagined
2 future
3 a past form

Elicit the example sentence to the blackboard by asking students what luxury Anthony Hopkins said he would take and what it depended on.

Ask the check questions open-class.

Elicit that your voice goes up in the middle of the sentence and down when it is finished at the end.

2 Students practise the *If* + Past Simple form by deciding under what conditions they would/ wouldn't do certain things.

Elicit the question with *would* by writing *steal a loaf of bread?* on the board and getting a student to ask you the question. Answer using one of the example answers from the book. Drill this and then elicit the other possible answer. Drill this answer too.

Put students in pairs to ask and answer the other questions.

3 Students write complete second conditional sentences.

Get students to do this individually, paying attention to the form of the sentences. They check their completed sentences together.

At feedback, get individual students to read out their complete sentences once again checking intonation as they do so.

8 Vocabulary: types of music

AIMS

- To revise a selection of adjectives and to highlight the pronunciation of their *-ed* ending.
- To introduce a lexical set of different types of music.
- To introduce *It makes me feel* + adjective.

1 Students listen to the adjectives ending in *-ed* and decide if it is pronounced /t/, /d/, or /ɪd/.

Tapescript/Answers

depressed /t/   frightened /d/   annoyed /d/
excited /ɪd/   relaxed /t/   worried /ɪd/

Put the phonemic symbols for the three pronunciations of *-ed* on the board and ask students to read them back to you. Then play the tape, getting them to write the correct phonemic symbol above each adjective in their notebook.

2 Students hear examples of different types of music and number the types accordingly in their book.

Answers

1 reggae   2 classical music   3 jazz
4 pop music   5 blues   6 folk music

Tell students that they are going to listen to six pieces of music chosen by someone to take to the desert island. Refer them to the names of the different types of music in their book. As they listen they number the names in the order they hear them.

3-4 They listen to the music again and choose an adjective to say how the music makes them feel. They tell their partner, using the pattern: *It makes me feel . . .*

Before they talk to their partner, give an example yourself saying how the music makes you feel. Elicit that *the* is used before the music because we already know what music we are talking about (see NB box *a vs the* on page 95) and there will be contrastive stress on the word before *music* each time you say it (see the Students' Book page 35).

Students tell their partner about each piece of music they heard in turn.

5 Students conduct a class survey to find out what type of music is preferred by the class as a whole.

If possible, give each student a name list of the students in the class. By their own name they write the type of music they like best.

They then mill around the class asking each student what type of music she/he likes best and writing her/his answer next to her/his name.

Finally, they tell you the result of the survey.

If your class is very large, divide it into groups alphabetically or by seating arrangements and make each group responsible for part of the survey. Finally, combine the information open-class.

English in action

AIMS

- To develop the skill of reading for specific information.
- To provide practice of *would* for speculation.
- To provide a chance for freer spoken practice.

1 Students decide which three concerts in the advertisement they (or a relative) would most like to go to.

Set the scene for the activity by referring the class to the advertisement and reiterating the introductory rubric in their book (that they want to go on a musical tour of Europe). Make sure students have heard of the singers*, whose first names are written down the side of each advert and that they know that the cities are in France (Paris and Lyon), Germany (Cologne and Dusseldorf), Belgium (Antwerp, Brussels). If possible, use pictures and a map to arouse interest.

Give students time individually to choose three concerts.

*If one or two of the students in your class are not interested in any of the singers mentioned, persuade them to go on the tour just for the travel (they get free flight and bed and breakfast as well as the concert). Or, they could give the prize to another member of their family eg. a child or nephew/niece and should plan the tour with them in mind.

However, if all your students are unfamiliar with these singers, you may prefer to use advertisements of concerts taking place more locally and to proceed as suggested.

2 Students tell their partner their choices and then come to a compromise so that they can attend the same three concerts. They answer the questions in their book.

Put students in pairs. Make sure that they understand the situation. They have entered the competition together so they can only go to the same three concerts. They need to persuade their partner that their choices are best but they also need to compromise.

When they have decided where to go, they should answer the questions in their book.

At feedback, find out where people wanted to go and where they would go together if they won the competition. Highlight the imagined, 'unreal' possibility of the students having to pay by asking questions, like this:

T: Are you going to buy the tickets yourself?
S: No.
T: Why not? Do you have to pay?
S: No.
T: But imagine you had to buy them.
S: Then, *I'd have to pay £ . . .*

This should reinforce the concept of speculation using the second conditional.

3-4 Students listen to the music agent's side of a telephone conversation to see if there are places available for the concerts they want. They then listen again and take down the music agent's words as dictation.

Tapescript

MA: Hello. Live in Europe. Can I help you?
YOU: . . .
MA: I see. What concerts would you like to go to?
YOU: . . .
MA: That's fine. What countries are they in?
YOU: . . .
MA: Now, what dates do you want?
YOU: . . .
MA: OK. No problem. First let me check the details. You'd like to see...

Answers

3 Yes.

Before feedback of the dictation, write the layout for the dialogue on the board like this:

Music Agent :

You:

MA:

You:

Invite students to come to the board in turn and to write the music agent's words in the appropriate places; other students tell them what to write and how to spell problem words. They leave the *You* spaces blank.

5-6 Students practise the dialogue first with a partner and then in response to the tape.

Put students, back to back, in pairs with a new partner to have the dialogue as if on the phone. They take it in turns to be the music agent and gradually stop having to read that part from the board.

Wipe the board clean and play the tape again a few times, getting individual students to reply to the voice on the tape.

Language review 18

a
Possible answers
1 I'd call the police.
2 I'd open all the windows.
3 I'd ask them to go to the back of the queue.
4 I'd tell my friend.
5 I'd phone a friend to come and rescue me!
6 I'd increase everyone's salary!
c
1 If she had a lot of money, she would buy a house.
2 What would you say if you met the president?
3 They wouldn't live abroad if they had the choice.
4 If I had a car, I would give you a lift.
5 Would you marry him if he asked you?
6 We wouldn't ask you if we didn't want you to come.

19 *Do the right thing*

1 Preparation

AIMS

- To introduce the theme of the unit.
- To provide practice in a variety of verb forms for talking about the past.

1-2 Students tell one another three things about their past, one of which is a lie. They guess each other's lie.

Demonstrate what they have to do by telling the class three things about your past life and getting them to guess the one deliberate lie.

Give them time to think, then put them in groups of four or five to give their information and detect the lies.

2 Vocabulary: *say* vs *tell*

AIMS

- To highlight words that collocate with *say* or *tell*.
- To check/teach that *tell* takes an indirect object.
- To introduce reported speech idiomatically.
- To provide personalised speaking practice.

1-2 Students put words into the *say* or *tell* column in their book. They check them against their use in the questionnaire and add another word/phrase to each column.

Answers

Say	Tell
three things	a lie
goodbye	the time
something	a secret
nothing	someone
yes	a story
No, thank you	the truth

Put two columns headed *say* and *tell* on the board. Get students to copy them into their notebooks.

Elicit *three things* into the *say* column and *a lie* into the *tell* column by getting students to tell you what they had to do in the last exercise.

Put them in pairs to do the exercise, referring them to the questionnaire as they finish to check their answers and find one more example to put in each column.

Speaking

1-3 Students complete the questionnaire themselves and then interview their partner to find out how they would act in each situation. They report what their partner said.

NB Answer

b)

Give students time to read the questionnaire and to ask you about any problems of vocabulary.

They read the questionnaire and note their answers, a), b) or c). Then put them back in their pairs to ask the various questions, using the same structure as the example in their book. They note their partner's answers, a), b) or c).

Elicit an example of reported speech from an individual student by asking her/him to tell you what their partner said. It is not intended that you highlight the form of reported speech at this point but refer students to the NB Box *say vs tell* to clarify that *tell*, not *say*, takes the indirect object and to show that *that* is optional in these sentences.

Put students in a group of four or five which does not include their partner, to tell the others what their partner said.

3 Reading

AIM:

- To give students practice in reading for specific information.

1 Students discuss ideas for punishments for people who steal £3 million.

Elicit their ideas open-class.

2 Students read the article quickly to answer the questions.

Answers

1 'Lady' Cecilia Farrington stole the money from the children's charity where she worked.
2 She got a sentence of four years in jail, but she will probably be in prison for only ten months.
3 She doesn't seem to be sorry for her crime because she is likely to make a great deal of money from the film rights and a book of the story.

Students check their answers together as they finish.

At feedback, encourage them to discuss how fair they think the situation is open-class.

4 Grammar: reported statements

AIMS

- To enable students to work out some basic 'rules' for the formation of reported statements.
- To give students controlled practice in using reported statements.

1 Students scan the article again to identify who said the lines.

Answers

a) the judge   b) Ms Farrington   c) her lawyer
d) her fiancé   e) her lawyer

Put students in pairs to do this exercise so that they repeat the direct speech together, then check their answers open-class.

2 Students compare the direct speech in the above exercise with the reported speech used in the article and work out the 'rules' for changing one to the other.

Answers

The verbs change tense by going back one step eg. Present Simple changes to Past Simple, *will* changes to *would*, etc.
I becomes *she* or *he*, and *we* becomes *they*.

Check answers to these questions open-class, giving students time to note the 'rules' for future reference.

3 Students work together to make the direct speech into reported speech.

Answers

1 She said (that) Edward was wonderful.
2 She said (that) she was going to buy a Caribbean island for her 30th birthday.
3 He said (that) she thought of herself as overweight and unattractive.
4 He said (that) they would all welcome her when she came out.
5 He said (that) the serious part of this matter was the large amount of money involved.

Get students to write the sentences in reported speech as they decide on them.

Writing

1+2 Students rewrite the article to include the information from the last exercise. They decide which sentences to put in direct and which to put in reported speech.

Answer

They are inside speech marks.

Check students understand how to use speech marks and the position of the comma before or after *he/she said*.

Put them in pairs to decide where and how to write the new information.

Discuss some of their ideas open-class and get them to write their article for homework.

5 Vocabulary: large numbers

AIMS

- To teach/practise the conventions for saying large numbers.

1-3 Students listen and write the sum they hear in figures. They answer questions about the conventions involved and then practise saying numbers in pairs

Answers

1 £2,458,837
2 1 the words *million* and *thousand*
2 after *hundred*

If necessary, play the tape more than once for them to write the number. Elicit the answer in words and let a correct student (or the tape) act as the model when they do the next exercise.

Make sure they know to take one line each when saying the new numbers so they each try to say numbers of different lengths. Hear some examples open-class.

4 Students ask questions to complete gaps in the two charts. (Student B's chart is on page 125).

Drill the question in the example.

Put students in pairs and check who is Student A and who is Student B. Tell Student B to turn to page 125 and Student A to ask the first question. They work in closed pairs.

When they have finished, get them to check their answers against their partner's chart.

5 Students use the categories on their chart to make questions to ask their partner about their own spending habits.

Refer students to the speech bubbles in their book and elicit that these express imprecise answers. Get students to practise them by doing a mumble drill (see page 15).

Then ask an individual student how much she/he spends on one of the categories in the chart, eg. wine, as an example of what to do. Point out that we usually treat wine as an uncountable noun and omit the 's'.

Put students back in pairs to ask their questions and note each other's answers. Finally,

ask for some details of their partner's spending habits open-class.

6 Listening

AIMS

- To develop the skill of listening for general and specific information.
- To provide a context for practice of reported speech, *would* for speculation and *should* for giving advice.

1-3 Students listen to a radio phone-in to find out what the caller's problem is and what he lied about.

Tapescript

COUNSELLOR:	Hi. Rick from Hackney in London. Are you on the line?
RICK:	Yes. Hi.
COUNSELLOR:	How can I help you?
RICK:	Well, I'm in a bit of a mess.
COUNSELLOR:	That's what I'm here for. Do you want to tell me about it? Take your time.
RICK:	Well, you see I met this girl on holiday in Tenerife and I really like her.
COUNSELLOR:	Well that sounds OK. What's the problem?
RICK:	Well. It's stupid really. But I thought she wouldn't be interested in me so I said I was French.
COUNSELLOR:	To make yourself more interesting?
RICK:	Yes, and you know I did a bit of French at school and I can't say much but I can do 'a good French accent.'
COUNSELLOR:	Yeah. Not bad at all.
RICK:	Well, she believed me and it just sort of went on like that and I didn't think much about it. I told her my name was Pierre and I lived in Marseilles in the south of France. It was a bit of a laugh really.
COUNSELLOR:	Yeah.
RICK:	Well, we got on really well, had a great holiday and then we went back to England. Except I said I was going back to France.
COUNSELLOR:	Uh huh.
RICK:	She lives up north near Manchester and I live. . . .
COUNSELLOR:	In Hackney, London.
RICK:	Yeah right. Well, we wanted to keep contact, so I said I'd phone her.
COUNSELLOR:	Right.
RICK:	Anyway, I said she couldn't phone me. I

told her I had a new flat and I didn't
have a phone and. . .

COUNSELLOR: Got it.

RICK: Well, I wanted to see her again so I
phoned and said I was coming to
England, for my job you know, and she
invited me to meet her family.

COUNSELLOR: In Manchester?

RICK: Yeah.

COUNSELLOR: And they realised the truth?

RICK: No. No. They liked me.

COUNSELLOR: Still with your French accent?

RICK: Yes.

COUNSELLOR: Uh huh.

RICK: In fact, they took me really seriously.
They asked my advice about the wine
and everything.

COUNSELLOR: I see. You are in a bit of a fix aren't you.

RICK: Yeah. Well that's just it. What do I do
now? I really like her. I really like them. I
think they like me. What should I do?

Answers

1

1 A radio phone-in is a radio programme where
listeners are encouraged to contribute by phoning
the broadcaster.

2

1 A counsellor

2 The caller's main problem is that he met a girl
while on holiday and pretended he was French.
He has continued to see her and keep up the
pretence, including a French accent! Now he
doesn't know what to do.

3 He lied about: his nationality, his name, his
address, his flat, his phone, his job.

Ask the lead-in questions open-class and check
that students know the difference between a
doctor, a counsellor and a lawyer.

Make sure they know why they are listening
each time they do so.

**4-6 Students compare their answers to the
listening exercise using reported speech. They
then decide which advice to give the caller.
They listen and compare this to the
counsellor's advice at the end of the phone-in.**

Tapescript

COUNSELLOR: I see. You are in a bit of a fix aren't you.

RICK: Yeah. Well that's just it. What do I do
now? I really like her. I really like them. I
think they like me. What should I do?

COUNSELLOR: Well Rick. I think you know what to do,
don't you?

RICK: Run! Run as far away as possible!

COUNSELLOR: I don't think you really want to, do you?
Or you wouldn't have rung me.

RICK: I suppose not.

COUNSELLOR: Well, if I were you, I'd buy a big bunch
of flowers and tell her the truth. I
certainly wouldn't tell any more lies. She
can only tell you...

Answers

4

He told his girlfriend his name was Pierre.
He told his girlfriend he was French.
He told his girlfriend he lived in Marseilles.
He told his girlfriend he had a new flat.
He told his girlfriend he didn't have a phone.
He told his girlfriend he was coming to England for
his job.

6

The counsellor advises Rick to buy her a big bunch
of flowers and tell her the truth.

Encourage students to discuss the pros and cons
of each bit of advice suggested in their book in
order to arrive at the best advice to give Rick.

Ask various students what they think before
they listen to the end of the tape and check what
advice he was actually given. Encourage students
to disagree with this if they wish to.

7 Grammar: *If I were you*

AIMS

- To introduce and practise *If I were you + would*
for giving advice.
- To highlight the effect on pronunciation of the
intrusive /w/ between *you* and *I*.

**1-3 Students focus on the form of *If I were you*,
used to give advice, based on examples from
the listening.**

Answer/Tapescript

1 If I *were* you, I*'d* buy a big bunch of flowers.

2

1 If I were you, I'd tell her the truth.

2 If I were you, I wouldn't tell her any more lies.

3 The counsellor is giving Rick advice.

NB Answer

We generally use *were* to give advice.

Elicit the counsellor's words to the board and

play the tape for students to check or complete the sentence.

Elicit the other examples of the form to the board, based on the prompts in their book.

Ask question 3 open-class.

Finally, refer them to the NB Box *If I were/was* and check their answer to the question.

Pronunciation

1-2 Students repeat the example sentences, paying particular attention to the intrusive /w/. They then practise the form, giving each other advice based on the illustrations in their book.

Answers

1 1 unstressed, pronounced /wə/.
   2 *would*.
1
Suggested answers
1 If I were you, I'd take an aspirin.
2 If I were you, I'd get a new job.
3 If I were you, I'd take it back to the shop.
4 If I were you, I'd call a mechanic.
5 If I were you, I'd stop waiting for the phone to ring.

Nominate a student to repeat after the tape. Write the /w/ between the words *you* and *I* in the example sentence on the board. Get students to mumble drill the sentence and then ask individual students to say it to the class. (For advice on drilling, see page 15.)

Demonstrate what they need to do in the next activity by holding your head and saying *I've got a terrible headache*. This should elicit an *If I were you* response. Then refer students to the example in their book and the illustrations. Put them in pairs to take it in turns to express their problem and offer advice.

8 Vocabulary: shopping rights

AIMS

• To provide students with expressions to talk about faulty goods.

1 Students match new expressions to their definitions.

Answers

1 d   2 e   3 b   4 a   5 f   6 c

Students do this in pairs.

At feedback, elicit the expressions in complete sentences, like this:

T: *What do they do if they give you your money back?*

S: *They give you a refund.*

Check that main sentence stress falls in the expressions as follows: 'refund, re'pair, a'pologise, ig'nore, 'credit and re'place.

2-4 Students say what they think would happen in Britain in various situations and then check their answers against information on page 126. Finally, they say what would happen in their country.

Answers

3 a) give a refund
   b) nothing because you are not the buyer (but they'd probably refund, exchange or repair it)
   c) give a refund
   d) nothing (but they would probably give a refund)

Put students in groups of three to do this, mixing nationalities if possible.

At feedback, encourage discussion of the situation in the students' own country or countries they know well.

English in action

AIMS

• To develop the skill of reading for specific information.
• To practise reported speech in a complaints situation.
• To provide controlled and freer speaking practice.

1 Students read a text about how to complain successfully in Britain and compare it with the procedure in their country.

Ask students to read the questions before they read the text. Then get feedback open-class.

2 Each student learns a different sentence by heart and then finds another student who has learned the sentence which goes with theirs.

Answers

1 That'll be £80 for the room and £12.50 for breakfast.
   But they told me breakfast was included.
2 The parts for the Renault come to £95, plus £50 labour.
   But they told me labour was included.
3 Can I ask you for £10 airport tax please?
   But they told me airport tax was included.
4 That'll be £30 for two set menus plus 10% for service.
   But they said service was included.
5 That's £350 for the bed and £35 extra for delivery.
   But they said delivery was included.

Divide the class into two groups. Each student in group A learns one of the sentences on this page and each student in group B learns one sentence from page 126. If necessary, individual sentences can be learned by more than one student as long as its matching sentence in the other group is also being learned by more than one student. Or, you may like to create extra matching sentences in the same style.

When students have learned their sentence, get them to mill around the classroom saying it until they hear the sentence which goes with theirs. They sit next to the student with the complementary sentence.

If it is not possible for students to mill around, divide students into groups by seating arrangements eg. five students in one row could learn the group A sentences and five students in the row behind them could learn the group B

sentences. Group A students then turn round to speak to the Group B students behind them. When they find their partners, they change places within this group so that they can sit opposite their partner.

4-5 Students make up a complete complaints conversation incorporating their two sentences. They listen to other students' conversations to see how each pair solves their problem.

Elicit that the pair of sentences probably come in the middle of a longer conversation. Get students to read the instructions in their book for making the complete conversation and ask one student to recode them so that everyone knows what they are doing.

When students have finished their conversation, get some of them to role-play their situation to the class. Other students listen in order to answer the questions in their book. Elicit answers to these open-class at the end of each roleplay.

Language review 19

a
1 said   2 told   3 tell   4 say   5 tell   6 told
7 Say   8 said

b
1 She said/told me her husband was too tired to go out.
2 She/He said/told me he couldn't take me home because she/he couldn't drive.
3 She/He said/told me she/he would help me if she/he could.
4 They said/told me they often went to the theatre.
5 She/he said/told me they didn't know my address.
6 They said/told me they were spending the weekend in France.
7 She/he said/told me he wouldn't come to the party.
8 She/He said/told me she/he had sugar in tea but not in coffee.
9 She/He said/told me he could come if he liked.

c
Possible answers
1 If I were you, I'd see the doctor.
2 If I were you, I'd tell her to come home earlier.
3 If I were you, I'd go camping.
4 If I were you, I'd start looking for a new job.
5 If I were you, I'd come by train next time.

20 *Consolidation*

Language revised
- Large numbers and percentages
- Everyday actions
- Expressions for talking about the cinema
- Selected vocabulary groups
- *How much/many. . .?*
- *I (don't) think so*

- *Who* in relative clauses
- Present and Past Simple passives
- *Would* (speculation)
- *If* + past + *would* (second conditional)
- *-ing* activities
- *Going to* (future)
- *Need*

1 Across cultures: marriage

AIMS

- To revise *How much/many*; *I think so/I don't think so*; *who* in relative clauses, Present and Past Simple passives.
- To practise saying large numbers.
- To develop the skill of reading for specific information.

1-3 Students insert *How much* or *How many* in the questions in their book. They select one of the possible answers to each question and then check their answers in the article at the bottom of the page.

Answers

1
1 How many 2 How many 3 How many 4 How many 5 How much 6 How many 7 How many 8 How much

3
1 about 350,000 2 70% 3 a quarter 4 37% 5 more than £1.4 billion 6 more than 30% 7 70% 8 more than £570,000

Students work individually to complete the sentences then compare what they write with another student.

Deal with any discrepancies open-class.

They work with their partner, saying the numbers out loud and guessing the correct answer to each question.

As they finish, refer them to the article to check their answers.

At feedback, make sure the large numbers are said accurately.

4 They say whether they think the situation reported in the article is similar or very different in their country.

Put students in groups of three or four, mixing nationalities if possible, to discuss the points raised in the article.

5-6 Students match names of people at a wedding to their definitions and then write sentences using *who* to say what role each person has.

Answers

5
The bride - She marries the bridegroom.
The bridegroom - He marries the bride.
The bridesmaids - They help the bride.
The best man - He helps the bridegroom.
Wedding guests - They are invited to the wedding.

6
The bridegroom is the man *who* marries the bride.
The bridesmaids are the girls/women *who* help the bride.
The best man is the man *who* helps the bridegroom.
The wedding guests are the people *who* are invited to the wedding.

Students do the matching exercise in pairs and then check their answers with those of another pair.

At feedback, elicit the example sentence using *who*.

Based on this, students write their sentences individually and check their answers with their partner.

7-8 Students number the events at a traditional British wedding in the order they happen. They compare this wedding to a wedding they've been to in their country.

Answers

7
1 The bride is taken to the wedding by car.
2 Wedding rings are exchanged.
3 Confetti is thrown and photographs are taken.

4 Guests are driven to the reception for a meal.
5 Telegrams are read and toasts are made.
6 The wedding cake is cut and eaten.
7 Music is played so people can dance.
8 The married couple's car is decorated.
9 The couple are driven away on honeymoon.
10 The guests are left to enjoy themselves.

If the students' own culture is extremely different and they have no idea what happens, then do this exercise open-class. Otherwise, put students in groups of three. Circulate and clarify vocabulary if necessary.

At feedback, get students to read each sentence out loud as they say where it goes in the sequence.

In a multilingual class, put students in groups of three or four, mixing nationalities, for them to tell their group about the wedding customs in their country. In a monolingual class, elicit this open-class.

Encourage individual students to tell the class about their own wedding or the last wedding they went to. Try to make this less formal by encouraging other students to ask questions.

2 Language in context: love

AIMS

- To revise a variety of structures: *want* +/- object + infinitive; *would* for speculation; ways of agreeing/disagreeing; and *If* + past + *would*.
- To heighten awareness of links between sounds and spelling.
- To develop the skill of listening for specific information.

1 Students speculate about their perfect relationship, deciding which things listed they would want to do and which they would want their partner to do.

Introduce the idea of the perfect relationship open-class, by asking students what is most important for them. Would they want total agreement of ideas, total fidelity, total acceptance of their friends and family?

Then refer them to the list of activities in their book. Give them time to read the questions and think about their answers before you put them in small groups.

At feedback ask individual students to tell you

what they think. Encourage other students to agree/disagree and say how they think differently.

2-6 Students put the words of the song in the correct order. They listen to the song to check their order and then listen again to see what changes are made when the song is sung by someone of the opposite sex. Finally they sing along.

Tapescript/Answers

3
If you were the only girl in the world
(Verse 1)
If I were the only boy in the world
And you were the only girl
Nothing else would matter in the world today
We would go on loving in the same old way
A garden of Eden just made for two
With nothing to mar our joy
I could say such wonderful things to you
There would be such wonderful things to do
If you were the only girl in the world
And I were the only boy.

(Verse 2)
If you were the only boy in the world
And I were the only girl
Nothing else would matter in the world today
We would go on loving in the same old way
A garden of Eden just made for two
With nothing to mar our joy
I could say such wonderful things to you
There would be such wonderful things to do
If you were the only boy in the world
And I were the only girl.

(Verse 3)
If you were the only girl in the world
And you were the only boy
Nothing else would matter in the world today
We would go on loving in the same old way
A garden of Eden just made for two
With nothing to mar our joy
I could say such wonderful things to you
There would be such wonderful things to do
If you were the only girl in the world
And you were the only boy.

Introduce the song referring to the photograph, eliciting the era (1930s) and type of song (a love song).

Refer students to the words in their book, saying they are in the wrong order except the first line. Get them to read the words silently

153

to themselves, using the glossary to clarify the difficult words. If any other words need clarification, encourage them to explain to one another.

Put students in pairs to organise the lines. Remind them to think about sounds and rhymes as well as meaning.

As they finish, they compare their order with that of another pair. When most of them have finished play the song for them to check their order.

Elicit the changes they expect a woman to sing open-class. Play the second verse and confirm their suggestions.

Now play the final verse and encourage students to follow in their book or sing along.

If your class want to hear the song again, play it from the beginning. Some students will be happy to join in the verses, others will prefer just to listen.

3 Thinking about Learning: outside the classroom

AIMS

- To equip students with ideas for learning English outside the classroom.
- To revise a variety of vocabulary and structures from earlier units.
- To give students practice in extended listening.
- To provide a fun and motivating end to the book!

Students listen to the radio broadcast in sections and complete the tasks. They then listen again from beginning to end.

Tapescript

The tapescript for this activity is on page 158. If you wish, you can photocopy and distribute it to students.

Answers

1
Person 1: Trying to meet English people (in the pub, at the bus stop).
Person 2: Going to the cinema, watching films and watching English TV
Person 3: Listening to songs in English on her Walkman and reading the lyrics. Exchanging letters and cassettes with her penfriend in America

2
1 time
2 a 15 minute tape
3 a cassette recorder with a microphone
4 a quiet room
5 to be relaxed

3
Caller 1: Marcia Silva, Brazilian, sports (tennis, swimming), 29
Caller 2: Lutz, German, reading and going to the theatre, 40

4
Miguel talks about his family, his work, the weather, his studies, the radio

5
1 Checking the news in newspapers in your language.
2 Looking at the headlines in British newspapers.

6 Britain, America, Germany, France, Japan, Brazil

7
1 France, England, Germany, Japan
2 They are all about trains/the railway.

9
For each country, elicit two or three of the films on in English, the name of the cinema and the times they are showing.
English titles include:
1 Driving Miss Daisy
2 Dead Poet's Society
3 The Return of Flash Gordon

10
1 Scudder, Lord Harkness, Porton, Karolides, Appleton
2 A man walks down some steps and counts to 39. Scudder tries to explain his fears about the possibility of war in Europe.
Lord Harkness is murdered.
Porton is shot.
Appleton disappears.

Set the scene; students are going to listen to a radio programme about learning languages. Also, give students time to look at the radio magazine pages in their book so they are prepared for what is coming.

Explain that you will stop the programme so that they can do each task but they will have a chance to hear it all in one go at the end.

At each stage, get students to read the task and check any difficulties with you before they listen. They should listen out for the main instruction words in their book as these are also on the cassette.

Music introduces each new activity so stop the tape as soon as you hear it and give students a chance to complete the preceding task.

By letting them compare their answers after each listening you will see whether they need to listen to the tape again. Check their answers as a class before going on to the next task.

When all the tasks, except their own plans for learning outside the classroom, have been completed, tell students to relax and listen to the complete programme from beginning to end. You may prefer to do this on aother day. This should be a motivating experience as they will be able to understand most of what is said, despite the length.

Finally, get them to decide if/how they can continue to learn outside the classroom.

Check what you know 4

Tapescript

FATHER:	OK, you win. I am going to buy you a pet for your birthday.
DAUGHTER:	Great!
FATHER:	But I'm not sure what you'd prefer. Do you want a cat or a dog?
DAUGHTER:	A dog. They are much more interesting than cats and more friendly.
FATHER:	And more expensive. I really can't afford an expensive dog, you know. It'll be an ordinary dog.
DAUGHTER:	I know. I don't mind what it is. I just want a dog.
FATHER:	They are a lot of work you know.
DAUGHTER:	I know but I promise I'll take it for walks and remember to feed it.
FATHER:	Good then that's settled. You can meet me at the pet shop after work tomorrow and choose the one you want.

1
1 A pet
2 A dog because they are more interesting and friendly than cats.
3 They are more expensive and more work than cats.
4 To take it for walks and feed it.
5 Meet at the pet shop to choose one.

2

Her father told her he *was going* to buy her a *pet*. He asked her what sort she wanted and she said she *would prefer* a *dog*, because it *would be* more *interesting and friendly* than a *cat*. He said he *could not* afford an expensive one and she said she *didn't mind*. He reminded her that animals *were* a lot of work. She said she *knew* and that she *would* take hers for *walks* and remember to *feed* it. Her father said she *could* meet him and choose her present the next day after work.

2 PRONUNCIATION

Tapescript

1 What will you do when you get here?
2 Can you get me a packet of aspirins from the chemist's?
3 If I were you, I'd phone him.
4 She was so shocked she sat down.
5 His birthday is on Tuesday, the third of February.

3 GRAMMAR

1 I want you to give my brother this book tomorrow.
2 He has got a lot of money but not much time.
3 If I were you I would have a holiday.
4 It is such a nice day that I will go swimming.
5 What would you do if you did not have to work?
6 He told me he wanted to go to the cinema.
7 These TVs are made in Japan and are sold all over the world.
8 He likes people who are interested in art.

4 READING

One teabag per person is put into a warm teapot.(1)
When the tea is ready, it is poured into the tea-cups. (5)
During this time, a little milk is put into each tea-cup. (4)
Boiling water is poured into the teapot. (2)
Sugar is added at the end, if necessary. (6)
The pot of tea is left to stand for about five minutes. (3)

6 VOCABULARY

Across: 1 dirty; 2 fridge; 3 soap; 4 matches;
5 wine; 6 packet; 7 stop; 8 washing; 9 piece;
10 refund
Down: dishwasher

Additional tapescripts

Images

Let's begin by looking at the picture of the sky at night. Look at all the stars shining in the sky. Look at the hundreds of stars. It's a very clear, cold night. Imagine looking up at the stars and beginning to count them. Now look at the full moon. The light from the moon is shining over the countryside below. And now the first light of morning begins to spread across the sky, to go over the sky. And the sky starts to turn red, to go red and orange and all the many colours of morning. You see beautiful birds flying across the sky. Look at the birds: imagine how they feel as they fly. They are flying towards the mountains, high, high mountains. Look at the snow on the mountain tops. The sky continues to change colour. What does the snow look like when the sky changes colour?

Imagine the cold, cold snow. It comes slowly down the mountainside, slowly changing to water as it comes down the side of the mountain. Watch as the water falls into the clear, cool river at the bottom of the mountain. And now imagine going into the picture. You walk into the picture, into the scene, and go up to the river. Bend down and touch the icy cold water. How does it feel on your hands? Stand up and walk by the river. The day is becoming a warm summer day. Feel the sun on your face. Walk along the river and look at the sheep, the trees, the flowers and the grass around you. What do they look like? What do they smell like?

You are coming up to a wall, a tall, red brick wall and in the wall there is a door. An old door. Can you see the door? Very slowly you are going to open the door and very slowly you are going to go through the door.

Close your eyes, close your eyes and imagine opening the door. Put your hand on the door handle and slowly open the door. The door begins to open. It makes a strange noise as it opens. What does it sound like? Keep your eyes shut and imagine the garden behind the door. Look at the flowers, so many beautiful colours. What colours are they? Take a deep breath; what do the flowers smell like? Bend down and touch the petal of a flower, touch the flower. How does it feel? Touch its soft green leaves. What do they feel like. The flowers are under a tall, tall tree. Look up at the tree. What does it look like against the sky? Go up to the tree and touch it. What does the tree feel like? Look past the tree, and you can see water. It's a small pond of water. You can hear water splashing into the pond from the fountain. There's a fountain in the middle of the pond. Around the pond you can see a low brick wall. Sit on the wall and put your fingers into the water. What does the water feel like? Now put your hands into the water and take a long drink. What does the water taste like? Look into the water and see the fish swimming in the pond. What colour are they? What do they look like as they swim? The grass on the other side of the pond looks soft, comfortable and inviting. Lie down in the grass with your face in the sun. The sun feels warm on your face. You feel comfortable and relaxed. You hear the birds singing. Listen to the birds. Listen to the song of one particular bird. Continue lying in the garden with the sun on your face and the sound of the birds singing above you.

Now it is time to leave the garden and return to the classroom. Relax and let the garden slowly disappear. Breathe deeply and continue to enjoy the relaxed feeling. In a moment you will hear me count from 1 to 5. When I say the number 5, wake up, open your eyes, feel refreshed, and wide awake back in the classroom. I am starting to count now. One, two. You are slowly leaving the garden. Three. You are beginning to feel awake. Four and five. Open your eyes, take a deep breath and stretch. Now look around the room. Feel refreshed, wide awake and ready to speak English again.

Unit 16 Exercise 7: 4

MAN 1: Right, let's think of toothpaste. What sort of package does toothpaste go in?

WOMAN: I buy it in a tube but, when I was at school, we, there was a fashion for buying it in tins, little round tins.

MAN 2: Oh yes, yes, I remember.

MAN 1: Yes, you can get it in tins, certain toothpastes.

MAN 2: But certainly tins or tubes.

MAN 1: But usually a tube.

WOMAN: Yes.

MAN 1: What about mayonnaise?

WOMAN: A jar, I think. Even if I make my own I store it in a jar.

MAN 1: Do you?

MAN 2: But you can also have it in little, I remember in the factory canteen, er. . .

WOMAN: Oh those little plastic packets?

MAN 2: Mayonnaise in little plastic packets, mm.

MAN 1: Packets. What about chocolate?

MAN 2: Chocolate? Well,

WOMAN: I like boxes, personally.

MAN 1: A box of chocolates, yes. Um. A packet of chocolates.

MAN 2: A tube of chocolates? Can you have a tube of chocolates? No.

WOMAN: Well not really. Not just plain chocolate.

MAN 1: Well, biscuits then. You can certainly have a packet of biscuits.

WOMAN: Oh yes.

MAN 1: Or a box of biscuits.

MAN 2: Yes.

WOMAN: Or a tin.

MAN 1: Yes, a tin or a box of biscuits, er.

WOMAN: Yes, a big tin of biscuits.

MAN 1: More easily opened than a packet of biscuits. And coffee?

WOMAN: Well, I buy beans in a plastic, plastic bag, plastic packet.

MAN 1: Yes, but if it's instant coffee, then a jar.

MAN 2: It'll come in a jar, wouldn't it?

WOMAN: Yes. And of course it used to come in bottles. That liquid 'gluggy' coffee.

MAN 2: Ah yes, very true. I'd forgotten that. That was liquid coffee.

WOMAN: Yes. And soup. I don't know about soup.

MAN 1: Well, a can obviously.

WOMAN: Oh yes. And packets of course.

MAN 2: And bottles. You can get soup in bottles too, sometimes.

MAN 1: Really.

WOMAN: Can you?

MAN 2: Yes. Fish soup.

WOMAN: Oh yes. And cardboard boxes of soup. Of course. They're very nice.

MAN 1: So, soup comes in everything. Now, what about water?

WOMAN: Well, I buy plastic bottles of water.

MAN 2: A bottle of water. Yes, so do I. Let's see, I can't think of any other oh, a jar of water, of course. . .

WOMAN: Well

MAN 2: . . . if you're going fishing.

WOMAN: Yes, some people, it's usually either glass or plastic bottles though, isn't it?

MAN 2: Yes, I think plastic bottles.

WOMAN: They don't do boxes of water. Why not?

Radio Magazine

1

LISA TAYLOR: Hello and welcome to Radio Magazine. This is Lisa Taylor.

WINSTON GEORGE: And Winston George.

LT: With this week's edition of Radio Magazine, on the subject of 'learning languages'. Many of you have told us that you go to language classes and we have decided to find out just how people learn English outside the classroom, without a teacher.

WG: First, we went to the West End of London. Listen to the people we interviewed in the street. We asked just one question. 'What do you do to improve your English outside the classroom?'

PERSON 1: Me? Oh, um, I try to meet English people. I go to the pub and I always talk to someone new, or when I am waiting at the bus stop, I talk about the weather or how late the bus is!

PERSON 2: I go to the cinema. I watch lots of films in English. I also watch English TV. It really helps me learn.

PERSON 3: Well, um, I listen to English songs on my Walkman and, er, I try to sing along in my head. I look at the words too if they are written on the cassette. My penfriend, in the States, sends me American cassettes, and I write a lot to her. Writing letters helps me a lot.

LT: Many of you say you have, or you would like to have, penfriends. So we have an idea for you: why not try corresponding by cassette! If you have a cassette recorder and don't really like writing letters, speak onto a cassette. You can have a penfriend and improve your speaking in English too! If you are interested, phone in with your address and details. We can pass them on and you can start recording straight after the programme. Our lines are open now. Phone in on London, that's 071, 633 9788. But first, listen. Winston is going to tell you how to make a penfriend cassette.

2

WG: OK, so to make your penfriend cassette, well, first you need time – lots of it but it's time well spent. Then you need a 15 minute tape. Fifteen minutes is a lot of speaking! You need a cassette recorder with a microphone. Make sure you are in a quiet room. Finally you need to relax! Remember, you can stop and start again if you want to. You're in control! Just like with writing you'll probably need more than one try. The more you record yourself and the more you practise, the more confident you will become!

3

LT: Thank you, Winston. Now let's listen to our callers. Our first caller is on the line. It's Marcia from Brazil. Hello Marcia. Can you tell us something about yourself?

MARCIA: Hello. Yes. My name is Marcia Silva. I am Brazilian, as you said, and I would like a penfriend.

LT: And have you got any particular interests, Marcia?

MARCIA: Well, yes, I like sports. I play tennis and I swim a lot in the summer. I would like to correspond with someone who also likes sports.

LT: Fine. And how old are you Marcia?

MARCIA: Twenty-nine.

LT: Thank you, Marcia. We've got your address, so if anyone would like to send penfriend cassettes to Marcia, please phone us for her address.

WG: Now, we have Lutz from Germany on the line. Hello Lutz. Are you sporty too?

LUTZ: Oh no, not at all! I like reading and going to the theatre. I hate sport.

WG: And how old are you Lutz?

LUTZ: Forty, but age is not important to me. I am happy to speak to anyone from any country - as long as we speak English.

WG: Great! Well, goodbye Lutz.

LUTZ: Goodbye.

WG: Phone in now if you'd like Lutz's address in Germany.

LT: And we'll have more calls for you next time.

4

WG: We thought you'd like to hear an example of a completed cassette. Listen to Miguel Gonzales, from Madrid in Spain. He has sent his cassette for you to hear. Which different things does he talk about?

MIGUEL: Hello, Yoshi, this is Miguel, your new Spanish cassette-friend. I live in Madrid with my parents and three sisters. I work in a bank in the centre of Madrid. I like my job – it's interesting and I meet a lot of people. I speak a lot of English there too because we have a lot of tourists, especially in the summer. They come to change their traveller's cheques, and to complain about the weather! They find it very hot and uncomfortable because we're not near the sea. In fact, if they came at other times of the year, the climate is very pleasant.
I am studying English at the university in the evenings. My teacher and the other students are very nice but I need to speak much more English if I want to pass my university exams. They are very difficult. I try to listen to English on the radio every day. So, what about you? Do you live in the centre of . . .

5

LT: Thank you Miguel for sending us that cassette. We're pleased to hear that you listen to English on the radio. You can listen to English radio programmes almost anywhere in the world – if you listen every day you'll be surprised how much you begin to understand.
The BBC is famous for its news programmes. Why not listen to the news in English! First find out the subject of the important stories by listening to or reading the news in your own language or try looking at the headlines in English newspapers, if you can.

7

WG: Now, listen to the news.
This is the nine o'clock news. Plans for a new high-speed train service between France and England may now be seriously delayed due to lack of investment. So far only half of the necessary finance has been found and the British government has said that it is not prepared to increase its present funding for the project.
Once again, most parts of Germany have been affected by strikes by railway workers. Train services have been severely restricted and it looks as if the strike could spread to other industries by the end of the week. The government is currently holding negotiations with the unions.
We're getting reports of a train crash in Japan. Apparently two passenger trains collided near Sapporo in the north of the country but there are no reports yet of any serious injuries.
That is the end of the news from the BBC. Our next news broadcast is at ten o'clock.

8

WG: Listening to the news is one way of hearing English. But don't forget TV, videos and the cinema. If you can see films in English the pictures will help you understand more. At the cinema in your country you can read the sub-titles in your language but you will hear English. Check local newspapers and entertainment guides. Find out the names, places and times of English films. Find out what's on in English, where it's on and when it's on.

9

LT: As well as films there are lots of books in really easy English. Begin with graded readers, books specially written for foreign students. You can buy them in bookshops all over the world. Many graded readers have got cassettes so you can listen while you read. To finish the programme, you can listen to the beginning of *The Thirty-nine Steps*. Relax and enjoy it. Learning English is fun. It takes time but it's fun. So, it's goodbye from me. Lisa.

WG: And from me, Winston.

LT: . . . and everyone who has taken part in this special edition of Radio Magazine on 'learning English'! Oh, and good luck with your English! Now here is *The Thirty-nine Steps* by John Buchan.

10

A man is walking down some steps. Ten, eleven, twelve. He walks down the steps, and he is counting. He is counting the steps. Thirty-six, thirty-seven, thirty-eight. The man stops. He has a small black notebook in his hand. He writes in the notebook: *thirty-nine steps*.

The next day, Scudder is talking to two men. They are Lord Harkness and Porton. 'Lord Harkness,' Scudder says. 'There are spies in London. The spies want a war – a war in Europe! We must stop them!'

'A war?' Lord Harkness says. 'Oh, no, Scudder.'

'Please listen to me,' Scudder says. 'You are Members of Parliament. You can help. These men have a plan. I know the plan – I have it in my notebook here. They want a war in Europe.'

'What is this plan?' Porton asks. 'And who are these men?'

'Well, I don't know their names – their English names. But they aren't English. They are spies.'

The three men are talking, and they can't see another man. But there is another man, too. He is watching them – watching and listening.

'You must believe me!' Scudder is saying now. 'We are in danger. Europe is in danger!' Scudder is shouting.

'And these spies – what are they going to do?' Lord Harkness asks. He looks at Porton and he smiles. 'You see spies everywhere, Scudder.' 'Listen. On the fifteenth, Karolides is coming to London,' Scudder says. 'He's going to speak in Parliament.'

'The Greek Prime Minister?' Porton asks. He is listening now.

'Yes,' Scudder says. 'Karolides can stop the war. They know that. And they want the war. On the fifteenth, they are going to kill him!'

Lord Harkness gets up. 'I'm sorry, Scudder,' he says. 'But I don't believe you.'

The next day, Scudder is walking along the street. He sees a newspaper. LORD HARKNESS MURDERED the newspaper says.

'Murdered?' Scudder thinks. 'Dead? Oh, no! Where is Porton? I'm going to find Porton!'

Porton is coming out of his club. He is coming down the steps, and Appleton is beside him. Appleton is another Member of Parliament. Porton and Appleton stop in front of the club. They are talking. Scudder sees them, and he runs towards them. 'Porton!' he shouts. 'Porton, be careful! Lord Harkness is dead – murdered! Be careful!' Then there is a noise from a high window above them.

Porton looks up. Then another noise. A shot! It's the noise of a gun. And another shot. Porton falls to the ground – dead! Scudder runs to him. People are screaming, running. 'Stop! Stop!' a policeman shouts. 'Appleton!' Scudder shouts. He looks round. But – where is Appleton? He isn't there.

Workbook Key

Unit 0

1 1 a3; b4; c5; d1; e2
  2 1 Excuse me?
     Yes?
     How do you spell *headache?*
     Sorry, I don't know.
   2 (1) exercises; (2) practise; (3) vocabulary; (4)
     students' book.

   3
I/you we/they	do	
he/she/(it)	does	the exercises regularly.

   4 listen to the cassette
     watch the video
     do the exercises
     read the text
     check your answers
   5 1 What does *match* mean?
     2 How do you spell *cassette?*
     3 I speak English very well.
     4 I don't understand.

2 1 to finish (or to end)
  2 ate
  3 interested in
  4 She hasn't got a computer.
  5 like
  6 's (is)
  7 (car)'s
  8 those ones
  9 one: the first *do*
  10 worse
  11 fall
  12 were
  13 people
  14 how much
  15 to
  16 to start (or to begin)

3

Across		Down	
1	lock	2	cereal
3	smile	4	mouth
8	astronaut	5	ear
11	plane	6	map
12	hotel	7	knee
13	museum	9	stamp
15	card	10	clean
17	pen	11	potato
18	radio	14	skirt
19	nose	16	dress
22	suitcase	20	ham
23	eyes	21	leg

Unit 1

1 1 1 are; 2 do; 3 Have; 4 Is; 5 Does; 6 does; 7 Are; 8 Do;
     9 Has; 10 have
   2 a6; b7; c5; d2; e4; f1; g8; h3

2 2 What does she do?/What's her job?
  3 When did she (first) arrive in London?
  4 Where is she from?/Where does she come from?
  5 What did she study?
  6 What does she like doing at the weekend?
  7 When did she start studying Italian?
  8 Where does her best friend come from?
  9 Does she speak Italian?

3 Name: Raul Ribeiro
  Nationality: Brazilian
  Marital status: Married
  Occupation: Cameraman
  Address: 28 Grove Rd, West Clapham
  Telephone number: 071 318 0122

5 write/writer
  act/acting
  designing/designer
  nurse/nursing
  directing/director
  report/reporter
  studying/student

7 1a; 2b; 3a; 4b; 5a.

8 good news: terrific; fantastic; wonderful; fabulous;
     tremendous
  bad news: awful; horrific; disastrous; terrible
  good or bad news: incredible; unbelievable; amazing

9 1 travelling; 2 packing; 3 making; 4 standing; 5 hearing;
  6 arriving; 7 changing; 8 arguing; 9 finding; 10 visiting;
  11 ordering; 12 worrying; 13 getting

10 1 When did you start studying English?
   2 Do you enjoy reading English books?
   3 Do you speak English with your friends?
   4 Do you watch films in English?
   5 Are you going to study English next year?
   6 Have you got an English dictionary?

Unit 2

1 2 finger; 3 feet; 4 belt; 5 wrist; 6 neck; 7 earrings; 8 hat

2 2 Mt Whitney isn't as high as Mt McKinley.
  3 The Amazon is longer than the Mississippi.
  4 Albuquerque isn't as interesting as Santa Fe.
  5 Vermont is more beautiful than Virginia.
  6 Minneapolis isn't as industrial as St Paul.
  7 Minneapolis is larger than St Paul.

3 3 They used to have the same friends, but now they
     don't.
  4 They still laugh at the same jokes.
  5 They used to go to the same parties, but now they
     don't.
  6 They still like the same kinds of music.
  7 They used to watch the same TV shows, but now they

don't.

8 They still go to the same movies.

4 1 and 2 are twins.

5 2 I'm not as old as Ann. /ə/ /ə/

3 She isn't as nice as her sister. /ə/ /ə/ /ə/ /ə/

4 We used to live together. /ə/ /ə/ /ə/

5 The weather used to be warmer. /ə/ /ə/ /ə/ /ə/

6 Life used to be better than now. /ə/ /ə/ /ə/

7 Things aren't what they used to be. /ə/

7 2 My sister looks like me.
3 What is the weather like?
4 Who do you look like?
5 He doesn't look like his brother.

8 1 Three years.
2 Goupil and Co.
3 1873.
4 Because of the unfriendly way he treated the clients.
5 In Holland.
6 27.

9 b

Unit 3

1 2 go; 3 missed; 4 got on; 5 got off; 6 take; 7 got in; 8 got out

2 1 sunglasses; toothpaste; postcard; backpack; suitcase; handtowel; facecloth; hairbrush.
2 the stress is on the first syllable of each word.

3 **Across**: 3 cheques; 5 map; 6 clock; 8 shoes; 9 lotion; 10 tickets
Down: 1 phrasebook; 2 sunglasses; 4 passport; 7 camera

4 1 a Tlemcen; b Constantine; c Tamanrasset

3 1 the largest; the best
2 the best
3 the most outstanding; the most gentle

5 Accommodation   5
Travel companions   2
Transport   6
Places   4
Activities   3
Time   1

6 1 Accommodation – undecided
Travel companions – decided
Transport – undecided
Places – decided
Activities – undecided
Time – decided
2 3 He's going to go on his own.
4 He's going to go to the south.
5 He hasn't decided. Maybe he'll rent a car.
6 He hasn't decided. Maybe he'll go camel trekking; maybe he'll go to the beach.

8 **Suggested answer**
Dear Sir/Madam,
   I am planning a trip to Tamanrasset and I would be grateful if you could provide me with the following information.
   First of all, are there any hotels in Tamanrasset, and do they have swimming pools?
   I would also like to know if there are any tours from Tamanrasset. If so, where do they go, how long do they take and how much do they cost?
   Finally, could you tell me if there are any return flights to Tamanrasset from Algiers?
   Thanking you for your co-operation,
      Yours faithfully,

Unit 4

1 lifeguard 6; priest 2; plumber 5; lawyer 7; coach 1; architect 4; newsreader 3

2 2 has to; 3 have to; 4 have to; 5 have to; 6 have to; 7 has to; 8 has to; 9 have to; 10 don't have to

3 2 You should plan ahead.
3 You shouldn't arrive late.
4 You should make a reservation.
5 You shouldn't smoke.
6 You should take an umbrella.
7 You should arrive early.

5 1 8; 2 8; 3 6; 4 7; 5 7; 6 8

6 1 lifeguard.
2 newsreader

2

Constantine	tiled patios; mosques; Roman monuments	handicrafts; handwoven textiles	spring
Tamanrasset	camel expeditions; walking tours; solitude, beauty of landscape	handicrafts, jewellery	winter
Tlemcen	Great Mosque; beaches; festival	ceramics	spring; summer

7 1 a5; b6; c4; d2; e1; f3

2 a pw; b eves; c pa; d wpm; e ph; f comm

8 advertisement; accountant; experience; assistant; business; correspondence; responsible; confident; disappointed; references

9 2 They're his.
3 It's theirs.
4 They're yours.
5 It's mine.
6 They're theirs.
7 It's ours.
8 It's his.
9 They're mine.

10 1 2 ambition; 3 organisation; 4 punctuality; 5 creativity; 6 patience; 7 intelligence; 8 honesty; 9 assertiveness.
2 2 creativity; 3 ambitious; 4 patience; 5 assertive; 6 honesty

11 2 invite; 3 buy; 4 go; 5 see; 6 make; 7 watch

Unit 5

1 Greece; Finnish; Swiss; Turkey; Sweden; Portuguese; Irish; Wales; Danish

2 1 a3; b7; c1; d5; e2; f6; g4
2 ac; bb; ca; dg; ee; fd; gf

3 1 Tricycle; 2 Odette's; 3 Tricycle; 4 Odette's; 5 Mustoe Bistro; 6 Odette's; 7 Mustoe Bistro; 8 Odette's

5 Beef spring rolls; chicken spring rolls; sweet and sour; curried prawns; two teas

6 1g; 2i; 3b; 4c; 5h; 6e; 7j; 8d; 9f; 10a

Unit 6

1

Football	Horseracing	Tennis	Baseball	Golf
match	jockey	racket	bat	green
goalkeeper	saddle	court	base	club
ground	track	net	pitcher	hole

2 1 jogging, squash, golf, badminton, cycling, windsurfing, tennis
2 a How old is Janet?
b What does Richard do?/What's Richard's job?
c Where do they live?
d How many miles does he jog a day/daily?
e What sports does he play?
f How many children do they have/have they got?

3 2 Faiza often takes the bus. (Faiza takes the bus often.)
3 I occasionally watch the news. (I watch the news occasionally).
4 They always work on Sundays.
5 She sometimes buys a newspaper. (Sometimes she buys a newspaper; She buys a newspaper sometimes).
6 We never go to the opera.
7 He always smokes cigars.
8 Norma quite often drives to work. (Quite often Norma drives to work; Norma drives to work quite often).

4 1
A: Would you like some coffee?
B: I prefer tea, if you have it.

A: Do you always drink tea?
B: I drink tea in the evening.
A: I prefer coffee in the evening.
B: Coffee keeps me awake.
A: Nothing keeps me awake!

5

	Main worry	Frequency
Charlotte	two cats	quite often
Rosa	her daughter	constantly
Paul	his health	every day
Matt	money	every month
Julia	passing exams	once a week

6 1 don't mind; 2 don't like; 3 don't mind; 4 don't like; 5 don't like; 6 don't mind; 7 don't like; 8 don't mind

7 1 2 On Monday mornings
3 teaches the advanced class.
4 On Monday / teaches the beginners class.
5 On Monday / Martha
6 On Monday afternoons / teaches
2 2 This morning Greta is teaching the intermediate class.
3 This morning nobody is teaching the advanced class.
4 The advanced class is watching a video.
3 1 is teaching; 2 teaches; 3 is teaching; 4 teaches; 5 teaches; 6 is teaching; 7 teaches; 8 is teaching; 9 are watching

Unit 7

1 (Night Sun) beautiful; mysterious; surreal; fine; fascinating; glorious
(L.A.Story) hilarious; funniest; affectionate; enjoyable; crazy; good; witty; glorious; funny.

3 a5; b2; c7; d4; e1; f6; g3

4 1 2 has, act; 2 1 began; 3 2 man, Italian; 4 2 sang, Japan; 5 1 banned; 6 1 ran; 7 3 Jack, Batman

5 2 watched a video; 3 go to the theatre? 4 had a pizza; 5 going for a walk? 6 go and see Sam; 7 played chess

6

Film	Setting	Type of film	Critic's opinion
Romauld & Juliette	a yoghurt factory	romance	positive
Ay! Carmela	Spanish Civil War	tragicomedy	negative
Ju Dou	a workshop in rural China	tragedy	positive

7 2 went; 3 did you do; 4 eaten; 5 visited; 6 gone; 7 Did you watch; 8 have just heard; 9 rained

8 1 Franco; 2 a young girl; 3 child; 4 Romauld and Juliette; 5 Romauld; 6 Juliette; 7 Serrrau

9 1 his; 2 his; 3 his; 4 He; 5 their; 6 him; 7 He; 8 his; 9 his; 10 her; 11 he; 12 he; 13 its; 14 its (or her)

10

Jenny	Mediterranean	positive
Charlotte	Thelma and Louise	positive
John	My Own Private Idaho	negative
Matt	A State of Grace	positive

Unit 8

1 2 It was very expensive so I didn't buy it.
3 We went to the beach because it was very hot.
4 I had a cold so I stayed at home.
5 I didn't read the book because it was very boring.
6 She likes reading so I gave her a book.
7 We went to the cinema because it was raining.
8 He went to bed because he was tired.
9 We didn't have any food in the house so we went to a restaurant.

2 1 2 fees; 3 title; 4 student; 5 graduate; 6 hotel

3 b

4 Name: Margarida Soares.
Date of birth: May 16th, 1953
University: Liverpool
Course applied for: Dentistry
Nationality: Portuguese
Status: Home

5 I would like to apply to study in a British University. I am a US citizen. But I have been resident in Germany for the last three years. I would like to know, therefore, if I qualify as a 'home' student or as an 'overseas' student? Could you also tell me if I am eligible for a student grant?

6 2 will you; 3 finish; 4 won't; 5 are; 6 go; will you; 7 will; don't

8 2 do; 3 I'll live; 4 want; 5 don't; 6 will, 7 I'll leave

9 listen; take; look; teach; ask; lead

10 1 1 universities; 2 institutions; 3 academic; 4 graduate; 5 degree; 6 education
2 b

Unit 9

1 2c; 3e; 4f; 5d; 6b; 7a

2 c

3 2 Kate and Antonio
3 Louis
4 Kate
5 Antonio
6 Louis
7 Antonio
8 Sayuri
9 Kate and Antonio
10 Sayuri and Louis

4
Across
3 single; 5 fan; 8 disc; 10 CD; 11 one; 12 record;
13 drummer; 14 tour
Down
1 hit; 2 band; 4 guitar; 6 actor; 7 singer; 9 concert; 13 DJ

5 2 They've already recorded the B-side.
3 They've already taken the publicity photos.
4 They haven't written the sleeve notes yet.
5 They haven't designed the album cover yet.
6 They haven't filmed the video clip for the A-side yet.
7 They've already filmed the video clip for the B-side.
8 They've already planned the promotional tour.

Unit 10

1 1 shopping; 2 buy; 3 spend money; 4 shopping; 5 pay;
6 afford; 7 costs; 8 price

2 1 two packs of blank cassettes; one floppy disk
2 £8.89

3 2d; 3a; 4b; 5e

4 1 Li Yuen Streets East and West
2 Central and Causeway Bay
3 Queen's Road East
4 New Territories
5 Stanley
6 Li Yuen Streets East and West

5 2 buy; 3 do you spend; 4 shouldn't; 5 am just looking; 6 I am going to buy; 7 did you buy; 8 I'll get; 9 don't have to

6 **Suggested answer**
Dear Belinda,
I have a problem. I am a compulsive shopper. For example, I never go into a department store without buying something. What's more, I often buy things that I don't need or can't afford. I even dream about shopping! My family and friends are beginning to worry about me. Can you tell me if this is a form of addiction? Can it be cured?
Yours, R. J.

7 2 on; 3 window; 4 help; 5 colour; 6 these; 7 take;
8 credit

Unit 11

1 2 death; 3 birth; 4 health; 5 marriage; 6 employment;
7 dying

2 3 confidence; 4 consultancy; 5 separate

3 1 1 F; 2 F; 3 T; 4 T; 5 T; 6 F; 7 T; 8 T; 9 T; 10 T
2 2 finished; 3 unfinished; 4 unfinished; 5 unfinished;
6 unfinished; 7 finished; 8 finished; 9 unfinished; 10 unfinished

4 2 He has been retired for a year.
3 They have lived in Woking for six months.
4 Geraldine has know Peter for three years.
5 She has been abroad for one month.
6 They have lived together for ten years.
7 I have had this ring for a long time.

5 2 last Tuesday; 3 three months; 4 we got married; 5 1975;
6 a year; 7 birth

6 1 a3; b1; c4; d2
2 1 Peter and I have a very good relationship because there's a lot of love and mutual respect between us.
2 My family was very disapproving when I first started going out with Peter.
3 Also, since marrying, I've lost touch with a lot of my friends.
4 My life has changed so much since meeting Peter.

7 2 I read it to them.
3 Did you give it to him?
4 Send them to him.
5 We gave it to them.
6 Alan sent it to them.
7 Can you give them to her?

9 2 March; 3 to; 4 them; 5 for ages; 6 two; 7 four; 8 a long time

10 a4; b6; c2; d7; e3; f1; g8; h5

Unit 12

1 1 recognised; 2 remember; 3 forgotten; 4 memory; 5 remember; 6 remind

2 B

3 1 d, b
   2 b

4 1 was walking; 2 saw; 3 was getting; 4 noticed; 5 recognised; 6 said; 7 met; 8 were staying; 9 visited; 10 were having; 11 were watching; 12 said; 13 said; 14 was passing; 15 stopped; 16 got

6 Remember, remember
The fifth of November:
Gunpowder, treason and plot.

I remember, I remember
The house where I was born.
I remember, I remember
The roses, red and white.

Do you remember
That night in December
That wonderful night when we met?
Do you remember that night in December
You said you would never forget?

7 a6, b3, c7, d2, e1, f5, g4.

8 2 He was watching TV when the phone rang.
   3 She was eating when the policeman arrived.
   4 He was climbing the mountain when it started snowing.
   5 She was changing money when the robbers came in.

Unit 13

1 2 educated; 3 unemployed; 4 defend; 5 taxes; 6 environmental; 7 healthy

2 2 same; 3 different; 4 different; 5 same; 6 different; 7 same; 8 different

3 1 T; 2 T; 3 T; 4 F; 5 F; 6 T; 7 T

4 2 Who pardoned Nixon?
   3 When did Reagan defeat Carter?
   4 Who shot Reagan in 1981?
   5 Who did George Bush defeat in 1988?
   6 When did Reagan meet Gorbachev?

5 b5; c7; d1; e6; f4; g2

7 2 she's meeting the Turkish PM.
   3 she's visiting an arms factory.
   4 she's giving a TV interview.
   5 she's holding a press conference.

6 she's opening a children's hospital.
7 she's not doing anything.
8 she's flying to Paris.
9 she's giving a speech in Strasbourg.
10 she's watching the tennis semi-finals.

8 This information should change on the diary:
Tuesday 18:   am   Give TV interview
              pm   Prepare for press conference
Thursday 20: am   Fly to Paris
Friday 21:   pm   —

9 1 Good idea; 2 How about you? 3 I'm afraid; 4 That's fine; 5 See you then

10 2 "I'll do the shopping if I have time."
   3 "We'll write as soon as we can."
   4 "I'll lend you the book when I have read it."
   5 "I'll look after the children if you die."
   6 "We'll fix the car as soon as we can."

11 1 on; 2 at; 3 in; 4 (–); 5 on; 6 (–); 7 in; 8 (–); 9 at; 10 in

Unit 14

1 2 get; 3 keeps; 4 stay; 5 keeps; 6 get; 7 stay; 8 getting; 9 get, keep; 10 stay

2

Vicki	39	natural and fresh	good food and exercise
Pete	37	little sugar, fat; lots of vegetables	don't smoke or drink too much; healthy food and exercise.
Belinda	31	no meat	not worrying

3

Georgia	yoghurt	herbal medicines; family life; happiness
Bama	wild grasses, snakes, lizards, special wine	–
Japan	mostly vegetables	hard physical work

4 1 b5; c1; d3; e2
   2 2 You shouldn't make a change.
     3 You should take it easy.
     4 I don't have to settle down.
     5 I have to go away.
     6 You should listen to me.
     7 You mustn't turn away.
     8 You don't have to go away.
     9 You mustn't go away.

6 2 I'm not old enough to drive.
   3 This flat is not big enough.
   4 You're too short to be a policeman.
   5 This shirt is too dirty to wear.
   6 This room is not quiet enough to work in.
   7 These shoes are not big enough.
   8 She's not old enough to be your mother.
   9 I'm not old enough to leave home.
   10 You're not confident enough to be a singer.

7 2 positive; 3 negative; 4 positive; 5 negative; 6 positive; 7 negative; 8 positive; 9 positive

9 1 T; 2 F 3 T

Unit 15

1 1 a; 2 b; 3 b; 4 28 days; 5 2; 6 No; 7 No; 8 No; 9 Yes

2 HARRISON
ANTHONY FRANCIS
277 HORNSEY ROAD, LONDON
SW6 5FA
081 435 2389
14 09 76
18
M

3 2 was driving; 3 had; 4 ran; 5 was waiting; 6 got;
7 recognised; 8 have been; 9 knew; 10 was wearing;
11 did; 12 said; 13 corrected; 14 did; 15 recognised

4 2 However; 3 So; 4 However; 5 So; 6 although; 7 So;
8 although; 9 so

5 1 ninety; 2 have two; 3 beer; 4 shouldn't do; 5 working;
6 they're; 7 must improve; 8 March

Unit 16

1 a4; b5; c6; d1; e3; f2

2 1 1d; 2e; 3f; 4c; 5a; 6b
2 The Duty of the Host.

3 a can of tomatoes a; a packet of biscuits d; a glass of
juice f; a bar of chocolate e; a teaspoon of sugar i; a loaf
of bread h; a cup of coffee g; a bottle of oil c; a jar of jam
j; a piece of cheese b

4 Half a pound of tuppeny rice

And half a pound of treacle:

That's the way the money goes.

Pop goes the weasel!

5 1 How much; 2 How many; 3 How many; 4 How much;
5 How many; 6 How much; 7 How many; 8 How much;
9 How many

6 1b; 2c; 3a

8 2 There was a woman who had seven sons.
3 A long time ago there was a king who had a beautiful
daughter.
4 Once upon a time there were three bears who lived in
a house in the forest.
5 There was an old man who lived under a bridge.

9 1 any; 2 some; 3 many; 4 an, the; 5 a; 6 a, the; 7 much;
8 any

Unit 17

1 1 discovered; 2 begun; 3 built; 4 invented; 5 started;
6 found; 7 formed; 8 fought; 9 written

2 1 2 The Sagrada Familia was begun in 1882.
3 Penicillin was discovered in 1928.
4 The steam engine was invented in 1769.
5 The UN was formed in 1945.
6 The Declaration of the Rights of Man was written in
1789.
7 The Spanish-American War was fought in 1898.
2 2 When was the Spanish-American War fought?

3 When was the steam engine invented?
4 When was penicillin discovered?
5 When was the Eiffel Tower built?

3 1 a3; b2; c1; d4
2 1 poisoned; 2 shot; 3 stabbed; 4 ran over
3 2 Lincoln was shot in a theatre.
3 Caesar was stabbed in the senate house.
4 Gaudí was run over by a tram in Barcelona.
4 2 Where was Lincoln shot?
3 When was Caesar stabbed?
4 Where was Gaudí run over?

4 2 Two tourists were poisoned yesterday.
3 The Prime Minister was shot yesterday.
4 A lost child was found yesterday.
5 A teacher was jailed yesterday.
6 A policeman was arrested yesterday.
7 Three students were killed yesterday.
8 A dog was run over yesterday.

5 1 a4; b3; c1; d2
2 was sent; was knocked down; was found; was last
seen; was attacked

6 1 3
2 1 was arrested; 2 was robbed; 3 was tested; 4 was
closed

8 2 It's such an old building.
3 It's such a long film.
4 It was such a dirty restaurant.
5 He was so funny.
6 It's so hot.
7 It's such an interesting book.
8 This is such a difficult exercise.

9 Dr Crippen, the poisoner, was hanged at Pentonville
Prison in November 1910. Crippen, a U.S. citizen and his
wife, a singer, lived in London. She was last seen alive on
January 31, 1910. Crippen and his girlfriend, Ethel, were
on a ship in the Atlantic Ocean when his wife's body was
found under the floor of Crippen's house. Crippen was
arrested at sea. This was the first time that radio had been
used in a criminal investigation.

10 1 It's so lonely on your own.
2 Why don't you phone home?
3 Do you think it will snow?
4 No, I don't think so.
5 Who wrote 'Showboat'?
6 I don't know. Was it Jerome Kern?
7 How low can you go?

Unit 18

1 2 hair dryer; 3 plays records; 4 rice cooker; 5 opens tins;
6 water heater; 7 food mixer; 8 processes words; 9 dries
clothes

2 a4; b8; c6; d7; e1; f3; g5; h2

3 2 did; 3 would; 4 would; 5 did; 6 Did; 7 would; 8 would

4 2 would go; 3 would study; 4 had; 5 would do; 6 did; 7
would look; 8 was/were; 9 would go: 10 would start; 11
would do

5 1 I'd; 2 I'll; 3 did; 4 wouldn't; 5 have; 6 he'd; 7 you'd like

6

Catie	running shoes	black bear	television producer
Jenny	passport	tortoise	designer
John	a painting	hare	writer

8 2 Sport makes me feel tired.
3 Your letter made me feel worried.
4 The news made him feel excited.
5 The photograph made her feel sad.
6 The lesson made them feel bored.
7 Does this medicine make you feel depressed?
8 Exercise will make you feel relaxed.

10 1 1f; 2h; 3c; 4e; 5j; 6d; 7b; 8i; 9g; 10a
2 1 steel-string guitar; electric guitar; violin; harp; double bass
2 saxophone; trumpet
3 oboe; flute
4 drum

Unit 19

1 2 I said I'd have the chicken.
3 I told the waiter (that) the chicken was not properly cooked.
4 He said he was very sorry.
5 He said he would get me another one.
6 She told me she ate there often.
7 I told her I would never eat there again.

2 a3; b2; c5; d1; e6; f4

3 Waiter: You should try the fish.
Customer: Waiter! This fish is not cooked!
Waiter: I'm terribly sorry. I'll get you another one.
Customer: I'm not hungry. Can I have the bill, please?

4 2 say; 3 tell; 4 Tell; 5 tell; 6 said; 7 tell; 8 say; 9 say; 10 tell

5 2 b the customer (probably)
c the restaurant
d the customer

6 c

7 Suggested answer
I ordered the chicken. It wasn't properly cooked. I told the waiter it was underdone. He asked me what I meant. I said it wasn't cooked. He said that it was. I said that it wasn't. He said that that was how they always served it. I told him that I didn't want it and that I wouldn't pay. He said that I would pay, whether I ate it or not. I asked to see the manager. He told me he was the manager.

8 1 a
2 1 10.05; 2 10.00; 3 5; 4 Walton; 5 the restaurant

10 1 1 unfinished; 2 finished; 3 finished; 4 unfinished; 5 unfinished; 6 finished 7 finished; 8 unfinished; 9 finished
2 1,345,618; 2 1,345,000; 3 6,900,009; 4 85,000; 5 85,212

11 1 the gentleman; 2 the mouse, 3 the other customers; 4 a mouse

Unit 20

1 2 out; 3 get; 4 wedding; 5 spent; 6 marriage; 7 love; 8 been

2 4

4

Person 1	house of a friend	12½ years
Person 2	Barcelona; dinner party	2½ years
Person 3	a bus stop	5 years
Person 4	in a school corridor	3 years

5 1 2 was studying; 3 was; 4 asked; 5 was making; 6 gave; 7 waited, waited; 8 rang
2 1 started; 2 got; 3 have been; 4 like; 5 have; 6 have worked; 7 am working

6 1 1 Goupil & Company; 2 Ophelia; 3 one; 4 Dukakis; 5 Bama; 6 yes; 7 Ethel
2 GOODBYE!

Test
1b; 2a; 3b; 4c; 5b; 6a; 7d; 8c; 9a; 10b; 11a; 12c; 13c; 14d; 15a; 16b; 17c; 18a

Irregular verbs

Infinitive	Past Simple	Past Participle
be /biː/	was /wəz, wɒz/	been /bɪn, biːn/
become /bɪˈkʌm/	became /bɪˈkeɪm/	become /bɪˈkʌm/
begin /bɪˈgɪn/	began /bɪˈgæn/	begun /bɪˈgʌn/
break /breɪk/	broke /brəʊk/	broken /ˈbrəʊkən/
bring /brɪŋ/	brought /brɔːt/	brought /brɔːt/
buy /baɪ/	bought /bɔːt/	bought /bɔːt/
can /kən, kæn/	could /kʊd/	been able /bɪn ˈeɪbl/
catch /kætʃ/	caught /kɔːt/	caught /kɔːt/
choose /tʃuːz/	chose /tʃəʊz/	chosen /ˈtʃəʊzn/
come /kʌm/	came /keɪm/	come /kʌm/
cost /kɒst/	cost /kɒst/	cost /cɒst/
cut /kʌt/	cut /kʌt/	cut /kʌt/
do /dʊ, də, duː/	did /dɪd/	done /dʌn/
draw /drɔː/	drew /druː/	drawn /drɔːn/
drink /drɪŋk/	drank /dræŋk/	drunk /drʌŋk/
drive /draɪv/	drove /drəʊv/	driven /ˈdrɪvn/
eat /iːt/	ate /et/	eaten /ˈiːtn/
fall /fɔːl/	fell /fel/	fallen /fɔːln/
find /faɪnd/	found /faʊnd/	found /faʊnd/
fly /flaɪ/	flew /fluː/	flown /fləʊn/
forget /fəˈget/	forgot /fəˈgɒt/	forgotten /fəˈgɒtᵊn/
get /get/	got /gɒt/	got /gɒt/
give /gɪv/	gave /geɪv/	given /ˈgɪvn/
go /gəʊ/	went /went/	gone /gɒn/ been /bɪn, biːn/
grow /grəʊ/	grew /gruː/	grown /grəʊn/
have /həv, hæv/	had /(h)əd, hæd/	had /hæd/
hear /hɪə/	heard /hɜːd/	heard /hɜːd/
know /nəʊ/	knew /njuː/	known /nəʊn/
lose /luːz/	lost /lɒst/	lost /lɒst/
learn /lɜːn/	learnt /lɜːnt/	learnt /lɜːnt/
leave /liːv/	left /left/	left /left/
lend /lend/	lent /lent/	lent /lent/
make /meɪk/	made /meɪd/	made /meɪd/
mean /miːn/	meant /ment/	meant /ment/
meet /miːt/	met /met/	met /met/
pay /peɪ/	paid /peɪd/	paid /peɪd/
put /pʊt/	put /pʊt/	put /pʊt/
read /riːd/	read /red/	read /red/
ride /raɪd/	rode /rəʊd/	ridden /ˈrɪdn/
run /rʌn/	ran /ræn/	run /rʌn/
say /seɪ/	said /sed/	said /sed/
see /siː/	saw /sɔː/	seen /siːn/
sell /sel/	sold /səʊld/	sold /səʊld/
send /send/	sent /sent/	sent /sent/
show /ʃəʊ/	showed /ʃəʊd/	shown /ʃəʊn/
shut /ʃʌt/	shut /ʃʌt/	shut /ʃʌt/
sing /sɪŋ/	sang /sæŋ/	sung /sʌŋ/
sit /sɪt/	sat /sæt/	sat /sæt/
sleep /sliːp/	slept /slept/	slept /slept/
speak /spiːk/	spoke /spəʊk/	spoken /ˈspəʊkn/
spend /spend/	spent /spent/	spent /spent/
stand /stænd/	stood /stʊd/	stood /stʊd/
swim /swɪm/	swam /swæm/	swum /swʌm/
take /teɪk/	took /tʊk/	taken /ˈteɪkn/
teach /tiːʃ/	taught /tɔːt/	taught /tɔːt/
tell /tel/	told /təʊld/	told /təʊld/
think /θɪŋk/	thought /θɔːt/	thought /θɔːt/
understand /ʌndəˈstænd/	understood /ʌndəˈstʊd/	understood /ʌndəˈstʊd/
wear /weəʳ/	wore /wɔːʳ/	worn /wɔːn/
win /wɪn/	won /wʌn/	won /wʌn/
write /raɪt/	wrote /rəʊt/	written /ˈrɪtn/